SETTLERS OF MARYLAND
1679–1700

SETTLERS OF MARYLAND

1679–1700

Peter Wilson Coldham

CLEARFIELD

Published by Genealogical Publishing Co., Inc.
Baltimore, Maryland
1995, 1996

Library of Congress Catalogue Card Number 95-75723

Reprinted for Clearfield Company by
Genealogical Publishing Company
Baltimore, Maryland
2011

ISBN 978-0-8063-1477-8

Made in the United States of America

INTRODUCTION

The decision to abstract and index the records of Maryland land grants between 1679 and 1700 came about almost by accident. Several years ago I set out to compare some of the more unusual names of emigrants listed in my *Complete Book of Emigrants, 1661–1699*[1] with immigrant names catalogued in Gust Skordas's superlative work *The Early Settlers of Maryland*[2]. This led to a number of intriguing revelations, including some quite unexpected evidence that many felons listed in English Patent Rolls as having been reprieved for transportation to Barbados and the West Indies were, in fact, frequently landed in Maryland before 1680. An examination of sample pages from Maryland Patent Books also indicated that the earlier volumes contain a number of ships' passenger lists—a fact not immediately evident from Skordas's work.

These considerations led to a determination to extend the invaluable work already carried out by Skordas, and as far as possible upon the pattern he developed, by setting out in print the names and properties of those emigrants to Maryland who settled there in the last quarter of the seventeenth century. The close examination of the calendars of Maryland Land Registers which has been necessary in order to prepare this volume strongly suggests that records of land grants for the Province are virtually complete from its earliest years, and that enormous care was taken to ensure that such records remained accessible to successive generations. Evidence for this comes from the painstaking word-for-word transcriptions made in 1725–1727, 1770 and 1835 of several of the earlier registers which had clearly suffered deterioration over a century or more of storage and use.

The following table describes the content of each of the fifteen Land Office "Libers" examined in order to obtain data for the compilation of this index.

Volume	Content	Dates	Microfilm	Remarks
Liber 24 (WC3 & WC5)	Certificates 555 pages	1679–1683	WK26-1	1726 copy
Liber 25 (SDA & SDB)	Certificates 445 pages	1682–1688	WK26-2	1726 copy
Liber 26 (A 23 & B 2)	Patents 281 pages	1694–1695	WK27-28-1	1726 copy
Liber 27	Patents	1694–1695	WK27-28-2	1835 copy of Liber 26
Liber 28 (CB 2)	Patents 544 pages	1680–1681	WK27-28-3	
Liber 29 (CB3)	Patents 528 pages	1681–1684	WK28-29-1	
Liber 30 (IB & IL C)	Patents 404 pages	1684–1700	WK28-29-2	
Liber 31 (SDA)	Patents 539 pages	1683–1684	WK28-29-3	
Liber 32 (NSB)	Patents 717 pages	1684–1689	WK29-30-1	
Liber 33 (NS2)	Patents 738 pages	1685–1688	WK29-30-2	
Liber 34 (WD)	Patents 535 pages	1689–1706	WK31-1	Only part abstracted
Liber 37 (BB-3B)	Patents & Certificates	1694–1699	WK32-33-1	
Liber 38 (CC4)	Patents & Certificates	1695–1700	WK32-33-2	
Liber 39 (CD4)	Patents & Certificates 319 pages	1695–1707	WK32-33-3	1727 copy Only part abstracted
Liber 40 (C 3)	Patents & Certificates	1695–1696	WK35-36-1	1770 copy

An excellent survey of these records, their development and history, is contained in *Land Office and Prerogative Court Records of Colonial Maryland* by Elizabeth Hartsook and Gust Skordas[3], and there is no reason to go over the same ground again. However, it may be useful to emphasize the fact that, because of the preservation of so much original material and the contemporary practice of duplicating information, it has proved possible to retrieve some notice of almost all Maryland land grants made between 1679 and 1700.

Until 1680 substantial numbers of grants were ceded on a "headright" basis, i.e. an allowance of fifty acres of land for each new settler transported into the Province to reside. There was consequently a brisk commercial trade in the disposal and sale of such rights conducted alongside an often bewildering succession of negotiations in land assignments whereby newly surveyed plantations changed hands until they came into the possession of the highest bidder—a practice not dissimilar from that adopted by property developers in our own times. In 1680 the headright system was done away with and land could normally be acquired only by purchase, although services rendered to the proprietary government, such as a successful military expedition, could be rewarded by the Proprietor, who also retained his prerogative of awarding lands without payment to relatives and favorites. Patents issued before 1689 customarily described the Proprietor as "Absolute Lord and Proprietory of the Province of Maryland and Avalon, Lord Baron of Baltemore."

The Land Registry set up in St. Mary's City in 1680 appears to have continued to operate between 1689 and 1715 while the proprietary form of government was suspended for Maryland to become a royal colony, and in 1695 the Registry moved to the new capital Annapolis.

The Records

As might be assumed, the compilation and maintenance of detailed land records over a period of over two centuries required the employment of a multiplicity of clerks with mixed educational backgrounds and a level of calligraphy of varying legibility. Some lapses and omissions undoubtedly occurred during the tedious processes of enrolling and copying details of grants and transcribing names between one volume and another. Nevertheless, a high standard of accuracy appears to have been demanded and maintained.

Three separate documentary processes were required to authenticate grants of land—Warrants, Certificates of Survey and Patents:

Warrants

These normally took the form of an instruction to a Deputy Surveyor in one of the counties to lay out a specified number of acres for a named person but were otherwise uninformative.

Certificates of Survey

Upon the completion of instructions given in the *Warrant,* the Deputy Surveyor would issue a *Certificate,* placing a copy in Land Office records, stating the exact location and boundaries of the newly granted land.

Patents

These highly formalised documents, also recorded in Land Office Registers, sometimes after an interval of months or even years, marked the final stage in the bureaucratic process. They again rehearsed the details contained in the *Warrants* and *Certificates* but now clothed in legal jargon and reciting the conditions of the grant including the rent payable.

The following is a fairly typical example of a matching *Certificate* and *Patent.*

> Co. Talbot 7th July 1680. Laid out for James Harrison of Talbott County, planter, part of a wart. for eleven hundred and fifty acres bearing date the nineteenth of March one thousand six hundred seventy nine granted unto Wm. Sharp of this County and by him assigned to the above said James Harrison, a parcell of land called Dover Marsh lying in Talbott County afd. and on the West side of Great Choptank River beginning at a marked black oak standing at the beginning of the North East line of a parcell of land now in the occupation of Thomas Loggins and running South East sixty four perches [etc., etc.] containing & now laid out for seventy and four acres more or less to be held of the Mannor of Baltemore. Per Richd. Peacocke, Depy. Surveyor. (Liber 24/172: Certificate).

> Charles etc. To all persons to whome these presents shall come, Greetings in Our Lord God Everlasting. Know yee that for and in consideration that James Harrison of Talbott County hath due unto him seventy four acres of land within this our said Province of Maryland, part of one hundred and fifty acres assigned him by William Sharpe, part of a warrant for eleven hundred and fifty acres granted the said Sharpe the nineteenth day of March Anno Domini One Thousand Six Hundred and Seventy Nyne as appears upon Record and upon such conditions and termes as are expressed in the Conditions of plantation of our late ffather Caecilius etc. of noble memory according to his declaration bearing date the two & twentieth day of September Anno Domini one thousand six hundred fifty eight, with such alterations as is made by his Instructions to us bearing date the eight & twentieth day of July Anno Domini one thousand six hundred fifty nyne and the one & twentieth day of March then next following . . . Wee doe hereby grant unto him, the said James Harrison, all that tract or parcell of land called Dover Marsh lyeing in Talbott County [there follows the description given in the Certificate] together with all rights, proffitts, benefitts & priviledges thereunto belonging, Royal Mines Excepted, to have and to hold the same unto him . . ., his heirs and assigns for ever. To be holden of us & our heirs of our Mannor of Baltemore in free common socage by fealty only for all manner of service, yeilding and paying therefore yearly unto us & our heirs att our Receipt att our Citty of St. Maryes att the two most usuall feasts in the yeare, vizt. the feasts of the Anuntiation of the blessed Virgin Mary and St. Michaell the Archangell by even & equall portions, the Rent of two shillings and eleven pence three farthings starling in silver or gold. And for a ffine upon every alienation . . . one whole year's rent in silver or gold or the full value thereof in such Commodities . . . as shall be appointed by us . . . Given att our said Citty of St. Maryes under the Great Seale of our said Province of Maryland this fourth day of July in the sixth yeare of our Dominion & Annoq. Domini One Thousand Six Hundred Eighty One. Witnesse our selfe. (Liber 27/458: Patent).

In attempting to reduce such a mass of documentation into assimilable form while uncovering the essential genealogical and geographical content, it has proved necessary to impose upon it some uniformity of structure. This will not please every reader since certain accompanying information (such as detailed descriptions of locations and the names of tenants of bordering plantations) have been suppressed in the interest of achieving timely publication of a work which has already taken over a year to bring to completion. But no self-respecting historian or genealogist would wish to crib information from a printed work without referring back to the original sources quoted!

Entries in this book are arranged by family name, county, name of tract granted, acreage, date, and reference to original source(s). Some clarifications may be helpful.

Names. Variations in spelling, even within the same document, have made it necessary to use phonetic principles in grouping surnames together, but the principal variations have been noted in parentheses.

County. It should be noted that the county shown denotes the area in which each tract of land was sited: where a different county of residence was shown for the grantee this fact has been included. County names have been abbreviated as follows:

AA = Anne Arundel	Bal = Baltimore
Cal = Calvert	Cec = Cecil
Cha = Charles	Dor = Dorchester
Knt = Kent	New = Newcastle
PG = Prince George's	Som = Somerset
StM = St. Mary's	Tal = Talbot

Name of Tract. Tract names assume great genealogical significance given the large proportion which were evidently based on nostalgic memories of streets, villages, towns and cities in the old country. Some ingenuity may be required to interpret correctly a few of the tortured renderings of familiar English place names such as Devices for Devizes, Dullidge for Dulwich, Ingerstone for Ingatestone, Bastable for Barnstaple, or Mamsbury for Malmesbury. Other names chosen often reflect the humor, circumstances or disposition of the buyer—Rogue Keep Off, Would Have Had More, Fried Bacon, Roundhead Proprietor, Little Worth, Poor Man's Portion—and what seems to be a disproportionately large number named for or after cuckolds. An index of tract names appears at the end of the book but omits such frequently recurring and genealogically unhelpful names as Addition or Adventure.

Acreage. A note of the acreage of each tract has been included as a rough guide to the status or affluence of the purchaser.

Date. The date shown in this column is either that of the Certificate of Survey or of the final Patent. Where neither has been found in the original text, the date of survey or a calculated year is shown in square brackets. There has unavoidably been some overlap in dates with Skordas's abstracts since he concluded his index with Liber 23, which has a notional terminal date of 1680, whereas this book begins with Liber 24, which includes many grants dating back to 1679. In order to keep to a terminal date of 1700 for grants included in this book, only the relevant earlier portions of Libers 34 and 39 have been abstracted.

Reference(s). In all cases these are to numbered folios in the Land Office Registers listed on p. ii.

It remains only to thank the staff of the Maryland State Archives in Annapolis for the unfailing courtesy and helpfulness which they have extended to me during the course of this project, and indeed for many years before that.

Peter Wilson Coldham
Purley, Surrey, England

AMDG
Lent 1995

[1] Baltimore: Genealogical Publishing Co., 1990.

[2] Genealogical Publishing Co., 1968.

[3] Genealogical Publishing Co., 1968.

SETTLERS OF MARYLAND
1679–1700

County	Name of Tract	Acreage	Date	Reference(s)
Abbot, George of Calvert Co., planter:				
Bal	Abbott's Forest	1,000	10 Jun 1684	25/34;30/58
Abbott, Samuel:				
Tal	Barren Ridge	100	10 Nov 1695	37/387
Tal	Mill Garden	35	10 Nov 1695	38/81
Tal	Walnut Garden	50	10 Nov 1695	38/84
Abbott, Thomas:				
Dor	Abbott's Addition	32	20 Jun 1681	24/341;31/381
Dor	Abbott's Chance	50	9 Nov 1680	24/278;28/471
Abington, Andrew, innholder, Deputy Surveyor for part of St. Mary's Co. from Nov. 1680:				24/207
Tal	Abington	500	5 Dec 1684	25/171;32/71,155
Tal	Abington's Square	300	1 May 1684	25/96
StM	Netherbury	200	30 Nov 1676	24/252;28/113
Tal	Vineyard	700	18 Feb 1685	25/171;32/165
Abbington, Joan:				
Transported by John Abington of Calvert Co. bef. Aug 1680				28/34
Abraham, Jacob, planter:				
Tal	Jacob & John's Pasture	340	15 Jly 1687	25/300;32/477
Abraham, John:				
Som	transported by Thomas Dent bef. Apr 1681			28/174
Ackworth, Henry:				
Som	Friends Discovery	300	15 Mar 1689	32/657
Acton, John:				
Cal	Acton's Chance	156	-- -- 1688	32/519
Adams, Philip:				
Som	Adam's Garden	100	26 Nov 1680	24/11
Som	Adams' Green	150	26 Nov 1679	24/62
Som	Adams' Purchase	100	1 Dec 1697	38/78
Adams, Summer:				
Som	Adams' Chance	180	1 Sep 1688	26/129
Addis, John:				
Cal	Island	2	15 Feb 1695	26/260
Addison, John of St. Mary's Co., Colonel by 1695:				
Cha	Addison's Folly	173	10 Nov 1695	39/33
Cha	Arran	300	17 Mar 1688	25/398
Cha	Ashen Swamp	180	4 Aug 1686	25/239;33/264
Cha	Boat Sail	60	18 Dec 1680	24/269;28/438
Cha	Carlyle	148	10 Nov 1695	37/170
Cha	Chesterton	480	23 Sep 1680	28/43
Cha	Friendship	856	10 Nov 1695	40/97
Cha	Friendship	1,571	10 Nov 1695	40/100
Cha	Glenings	340	10 Feb 1696	38/140
StM	Long Neck	100	10 Jun 1681	24/281;28/435
Cha	Long Point	253	1 Oct 1695	26/343
Cha	Mount Nibo	371	23 Jun 1685	25/273

County	Name of Tract	Acreage	Date	Reference(s)
Cha	Pasture	522	2 Dec 1686	25/272
Cha	Prevention	336	10 Nov 1695	40/110
PG	St. Elizabeth	1,430	25 Jly 1699	34/147
StM	Small Hope	56	5 Mar 1688	25/381;32/559
Cha	Strife	1,302	10 Nov 1695	40/98
StM	Swans' Harbour	345	1 Jun 1687	25/381;32/561
Addison, John of Calvert Co:				
Cha	Whitehaven	737	10 Apr 1696	37/164
Addison, Thomas:				
Deputy Surveyor for Prince George's Co. by 1698.				38/150
Adelett, Benjamin Jr. & John				
Som	[unnamed]	600	4 Oct 1698	38/105
Aderton, William of Somerset Co:				
Transported himself before Oct 1678				29/479
Agg, James:				
Dor	Agg's Range	50	11 Nov 1680	24/293;31/85
Dor	Angle	50	[6 Oct 1681]	24/421;30/92
Aisquith—See Asquith.				
Akee, George:				
Cal	Knighthood	50	7 Mar 1682	24/397;31/522
Alcock, Thomas:				
Tal	Alcock's Chance	100	3 Aug 1682	24/476;29/302
Tal	Allcock's Parsalia	300	10 Nov 1695	37/343
Tal	Strawbridge	263	17 Jun 1686	25/247;30/319
Alderen, William:				
Tal	Alderen Island	40	21 May 1696	37/515
Aldred [Alderid], Henry:				
Dor	Aye	17	10 Nov 1680	24/203;28/327
Dor	Beelow	50	10 Aug 1679	24/202;28/291
Dor	Brintree	50	10 Aug 1679	24/202;28/326
Dor	Dess	17	11 Nov 1680	24/204;28/349
Dor	Stone	16	9 Nov 1680	24/204;28/339
Dor	Tadecorne	50	12 --- 1680	24/203;28/321
Aldridge, Nicholas:				
AA	Aldridge's Beginning	300	20 Aug 1680	24/176;28/256
Alexander, Elizabeth, wife of Capt. Henry:				
Tal	Yowell	50	16 Feb 1685	25/172
Alexander, Capt. Henry:				
Tal	Alexander's Chance	250	16 Feb 1685	25/168;32/226
Alexander, Thomas:				
Tal, assigns land in Jun 1679				24/217
Alexander, William:				
Som	Hog Quarter	100	10 Nov 1695	40/284
Som	Rapho	200	10 Nov 1695	40/150

County	Name of Tract	Acreage	Date	Reference(s)
Alford, John, gent:				
Dor	Foxhill	166	17 Jan 1682	24/391
Dor	Gore	230	12 Nov 1679	24/194;29/98
Allat, Elizabeth:				
Cec	transported by Thomas Browning bef.1680			24/105
Allen, Philip:				
StM	Old Branford	350	27 Jan 1687	25/324
Allen, William:				
Tal	Allen's Neck	200	18 Jun 1685	25/222;32/326
Allome, Susan—See under Lowe, Susan.				
Ambrose, James:				
Som	transported Robert Jones bef. Apr 1681			28/129
Anderson, Andrew:				
Bal	Anderson's Addition	66	10 Oct 1698	38/128
Bal	Anderson's Camp	34	[1697]	39/35
Bal	Dundee	174	1 May 1696	38/83
Anderson, Cornelius, planter:				
Som	Anderson's Invention	200	3 Sep 1682	24/515
Som	Bilboe	200	29 Sep 1682	24/516;32/133
Som	Come by Chance	100	3 Sep 1682	24/516;31/522
Som	Hunting Quarter	100	28 May 1681	24/326;28/523
Som	Poor Quarter	150	10 Mar 1696	37/93
Anderson, John:				
Bal	Anderson's Lot	400	15 Oct 1685	25/288
Dor	Anderson's Lot	400	1 Oct 1698	39/48
Som	Hardship	200	13 May 1689	26/84
Som	Hog Quarter	1,350	12 Jun 1679	24/167;28/358
Anderson, Robert:				
Cal	Cattaile Meadows	500	15 Oct 1685	25/194;32/369
Anderson, Thomas:				
Tal	Addition	50	3 Jly 1679	24/218;28/590
Tal	Boninton	50	19 Jun 1679	24/215;28/430
Anderton, Francis:				
Dor	Anderton's Point	108	15 May 1696	40/582
Anderton, John:				
Tal	Lostock's Addition	50	3 Jan 1682	24/389;29/382
Andrews, George:				
Som	New Recovery	288	30 Nov 1682	24/519;33/179
Andrews, John:				
Dor	Hopewell	200	10 Nov 1695	40/577
Angel, Richard of England, mariner:				
Cec	Adventure	510	21 Jun 1683	24/525
Cec	Angel's Lot	1,200	21 Jun 1683	24/525;30/70

County	*Name of Tract*	*Acreage*	*Date*	*Reference(s)*
Anktell, Francis, deceased:				
Cha	Anktell's	500	[22 Aug 1659]	24/360
Anktell, Mr. Francis:				
Cha	Anktell's	500	[23 May 1679]	24/360
Anndepost, Thomas:				
Bal	Thomas's Desire	107	5 Nov 1697	38/133
Archer, Peter:				
Assignor of lands in Calvert Co. in 1679.				24/165
Cal	Archer's Meadow	150	11 May 1681	24/359;31/12
Cal	Archer's Pasture	350	7 May 1681	24/359
Arden [Arding], John, planter, partner of Edward Smith of Baltimore Co. who died without heirs in about 1677:				
Bal	Arden's Adventure	100	4 Apr 1682	29/103
Bal	Arding's Marsh	28	19 Jan 1687	25/289;32/490
Bal	Ardington	50	4 Apr 1682	29/141
Bal	Bachelor's Delight	260	1 Jun 1685	32/178
Bal	Harley Stone	45	21 Jun 1688	25/438;34/52
Bal	Walton's Neck Addn.	100	11 Aug 1683	25/38
Bal	Waterford	200	10 Sep 1679	24/73
Arenton, Cornelius:				
Dor	Rotterdam	50	15 Mar 1696	40/597
Armstrong, Edward:				
Cal	Rich Neck	121	22 Jan 1684	25/79
Arnold, Thomas:				
Cal	[unnamed]	480	21 Apr 1683	24/521
Arriss, Ambrose:				
Cec	Hills and Dales	115	2 Nov 1694	26/164
Arthey, George:				
Cha	Little Hall	75	23 Mar 1688	25/379;32/575
Cha	Stony Hill	88	20 Mar 1688	25/379;32/556
Arundell, William:				
Dor	Ridge	37	13 Nov 1680	25/243
Arundell, William Jr:				
Dor	Isle of Wight	50	27 Apr 1682	24/425;29/353
Ascue [Asque], Michael:				
Cal	Shippa?	16	21 Jly 1699	30/400
Ascue, Philip, planter:				
Som	Anne's Choice	150	25 Aug 1681	28/245
Som	Ascue's Choice	150	20 Nov 1679	24/291
Som	Tamaroone's Ridge	250	25 Jly 1679	24/290;28/265
Ashbury, Francis:				
Knt	Pascoe's Adventure	150	27 Feb 1682	28/375
Knt	Sparke Point	50	27 Feb 1682	28/375

County	*Name of Tract*	*Acreage*	*Date*	*Reference(s)*
Ashcombe, Ann:				
Dor	transported by her husband Nathaniel 1680.			24/68
Ashcombe, Mr. John:				
Cal	Ashcome's Marsh	32	14 Aug 1682	24/477;31/16
Ashcombe, Nathaniel:				
Dor	Ashcombe's Inclosure	150	10 Jan 1680	24/68
Dor	Ashcombe's Outlet	150	10 Jan 1680	24/68
Cal	Desart	1,048	25 Oct 1682	24/517
Ashcombe, Samuel				
Cal	Desart	1,048	25 Oct 1682	24/517
Ashcome, Nicholas:				
Cal	Ashcome's Marsh	32	14 Aug 1682	24/477
Ashford, Capt. Michael:				
Cha	Tatsall	60	27 May 1681	24/303;29/163
Cha	600 acres formerly of Geo. Goodrick		22 Mar 1681	25/100
Ashman, George, cordwainer:				
Bal	Ashman's Hope	512	10 Nov 1695	38/112
Bal	George's Fancy	100	2 Jan 1686	25/244;30/307
Ashman, Richard:				
Cha	Ashman's Purchase	60	19 May 1681	24/279;29/254
Asken, Philip:				
Som	Turkey Hall	116	20 Apr 1695	37/50
Som	What You Please	150	10 Mar 1695	37/52
Askin(s), William:				
StM	Askins' Choice	53	7 Jly 1686	25/243;33/344
Bal	Askin's Hope	100	15 May 1695	40/466
Aspinall, Capt. Henry:				
Cha	Aspinall's Chance	210	10 Nov 1680	24/258;29/137
Cha	Aspinall's Hope	150	16 Mar 1682	29/136
Asquith [Aisquith], William, gent:				
StM	Asquith's Folly	100	13 Jan 1682	24/357
StM	Beaver Dam	118	5 May 1698	39/5
StM	Birch Spring	125	23 Apr 1683	24/529;30/116
StM	Hickory Hills	100	7 Apr 1682	24/453,483;29/349
StM	Stainemore	100	20 Feb 1682	24/392;29/482
Asterly, Isaac:				
Transported by John Abington of Calvert Co. bef. Aug 1680				28/34
Athea, George—See Aythey				
Atkinson, James:				
Som	Kecoughtan's Choice	150	24 Apr 1689	26/47
Som	Poor Hall	350	22 Apr 1689	26/46
Atky, John:				
Cal	[unnamed]	150	4 Apr 1681	24/346

County	Name of Tract	Acreage	Date	Reference(s)
Atwood, John of Calvert Co:				
Cha	Atwood's Purchase	400	4 Apr 1685	25/165;32/182
Austin, John:				
Cal	Austin's Choice	156	10 Dec 1687	25/344
Austin, Thomas:				
Tal	Austin	200	4 Nov 1679	24/225;29/264
Averey, Robert:				
Som	Teague's Content	160	2 May 1687	25/355
Som	Unpleasant	240	30 May 1687	25/337
Aylward, William of St. Mary's Co., gent:				
Som	Aylward's Addition	100	4 Sep 1688	26/114
Tal	Aylward's Town	500	19 Nov 1686	25/259
Bal	Concord	500	20 Jan 1687	25/302
Aylward, William:				
Som	Aylward's First Lot	425	10 Nov 1695	37/380
Aythey [Athea], George:				
Cha	Hopewell	80	27 Sep 1680	28/44
Cha	Leads	100	23 Jun 1685	25/258
Cha	St. John's	220	10 Nov 1695	37/368
Bacock, John:				
Transported 10 persons [unnamed] bef. Sep 1680.				28/88
Baggs, Thomas:				
Tal	Baggs' Marsh	50	30 Oct 1681	24/356,446;31/342
Bailey—See Bayley				
Bainton, James:				
Tal	Thief Keep Out	72	10 Mar 1697	38/47
Baitson, Christopher, cooper:				
Tal	Beaver Dam	100	12 Dec 1682	24/495;32/58
Tal	Bradford	50	12 Dec 1682	24/494;32/56
Tal	Chance	200	17 Sep 1683	25/48;31/528
Tal	Prospect	125	27 Sep 1683	25/45;30/150; 32/69
Tal	Timber Neck	300	27 Sep 1683	25/48;33/74
Tal	Wilderness	75	27 Sep 1683	25/46;33/75
Baker, Andrew:				
Cha	Harrison's Gift	250	8 Feb 1688	25/378;32/569
Baker, Isaac:				
Som	Baker's Folly	150	10 Jun 1689	27/131
Baker, John of St. Mary's City, innholder:				
Assignor of land in Talbot Co. in 1680				24/194
Tal	Baker's Plain	600	6 Aug 1680	24/255;29/110
Cec	Cheapside	500	28 Jun 1684	25/107;33/3
StM	Governor's Friendship	1	12 Jun 1681	28/189
Dor	Shadwell	500	2 Dec 1684	25/145;33/5
Dor	Sheele's	510	7 Nov 1683	25/16;30/128

County	Name of Tract	Acreage	Date	Reference(s)
Baker, John:				
Som	Baker's Chance	500	28 Oct 1684	25/146;33/7
Dor	Burford's Hope	500	10 Mar 1685	25/130;33/4
Dor	Grove	500	29 Oct 1684	25/146;33/8
Baker, Morris:				
AA	Baker's Addition	263	19 Jun 1688	25/405;32/624
AA	Baker's Chance	330	16 Jly 1685	25/251;30/317
AA	Charles's Forest	295	18 Jun 1688	25/405;32/625
Baker, Samuel:				
Bal	Spring Garden	12	14 Oct 1697	38/9
Baker, Thomas:				
Cha	Harrison's Gift	250	8 Feb 1688	25/378;32/569
Baldwin, John:				
AA	Baldwin's Chance	415	16 Oct 1694	27/336
AA	Lydia's Rest	210	8 Jly 1681	24/287;28/148
Lands escheated for want of heirs to Elizabeth Coplyn, daughter of Henry Coplyn deceased, who married Thomas Watkins deceased, former husband of Lydia, now wife of Edmund Beetenson, who purchased the said lands in her widowhood.				
Ball, Benjamin:				
Cal	Addition	33	20 Jly 1696	37/469
Cal	Ball's Chance	100	2 Nov 1694	27/142
Ball, Michael:				
Cal	Ball's Good Luck	100	26 Feb 1682	24/394;31/15
Ballard, Charles:				
Som	Friends' Assistance	200	29 Jun 1688	25/394;32/638
Ballen, Elizabeth:				
transported by John Viner before Sep 1680				28/66
Baltimore, Charles, Lord:				
		1,000	8 Aug 1684	25/159
StM		2,400	30 Apr 1675	25/158
Cha	Baltimore	1,100	8 Feb 1685	25/168
Bal	Lord Baltimore's Manor	7,031	11 Jly 1683	25/112
Tal	Lord Propr.'s Manor	6,000	27 Jun 1681	24/339
Bampton, James:				
Tal	Partnership	36	10 Nov 1695	37/315
Banister, James, planter:				
Bal	Good Hope	200	9 Oct 1683	25/92
Banks, Nicholas, planter:				
Tal	Banks's Fork	200	20 Mar 1696	37/438
Tal	Haddon	400	3 Feb 1687	25/298;33/549
Banks, Thomas:				
Cal	Ripe	872	[14 Apr 1683]	24/520;29/273
Barber, James:				
Assignor of lands in Talbot Co. in June 1679.				24/214
Tal	Summerly	300	19 Jun 1679	24/215;29/245

County	*Name of Tract*	*Acreage*	*Date*	*Reference(s)*
Barber, John:				
Assignor of lands in Somerset Co. in Oct 1688.				27/136
Barber, Newman:				
Cal	Barnee	90	28 Nov 1685	25/212;30/210
Barbier, Luke, son & heir of Dr. Luke Barbier who died on 12 Nov 1665:				
StM	Westham	1,200	4 Feb 1680	24/80
Barefoot, Mary:				
Transported by John Erickson of Kent Co.				28/434
Barefoot [Bearfoot], Thomas, planter:				
Cha	Habberdeventure	150	16 Mar 1683	24/505
Barnaby, James: granted lands in Somerset Co. in 1679.				24/27
Barnett, Peter & Ann—See under Burroughs, William.				
Barracliffe, Edward:				
Tal	Herne Island	75	20 Sep 1685	25/227;32/367
Barret, Elizabeth:				
Transported by John Abington of Calvert Co. bef. Aug 1680.				28/34
Barry, Garratt:				
Transported by Job Chandler, gent, before 1651.				29/149
Barry, John & Margaret:				
Transported by William Jones of Bristol bef. Aug 1680.				28/31
Barton, William of Calvert Co:				
Transported by Christopher Rousby of Calvert Co.				24/22
Cal	Addition	100	27 Oct 1694	27/262
Cal	Barton's Hope	313	14 Aug 1694	27/234
Cal	Hazard	130	8 Feb 1695	27/236
Cal	Ruden	270	10 Aug 1694	27/170
Barwell, John:				
AA	Barwell's Inlargement	50	6 Apr 1682	29/139
AA	Barwell's Purchase	115	[26 Mar 1678]	24/167;28/151
Bassell, Ralph, planter:				
AA	Gray's Adventure	184	16 Aug 1686	25/250;30/331
Bastin, Henry:				
Tal	Harmonton	250	22 Nov 1684	25/170;33/159
Bate, Thomas:				
Transported by Robt. Menteship of Talbot Co. bef. 1680.				28/111
Bateman, Mary:				
Dor	Maiden Forest	500	29 Oct 1684	25/146;33/11
Bateman, William:				
Dor	Bateman's Content	500	29 Oct 1684	25/147;33/9
Batison, Thomas:				
StM	Poplar Point	100	29 Nov 1680	24/252;28/459

County	*Name of Tract*	*Acreage*	*Date*	*Reference(s)*
Battson, Edward, Deputy Surveyor for Calvert Co:				
Bal	Battson's Fellowship	150	1 Jun 1700	34/200;38/153
Cal	Batson's Fortune	50	1 Jly 1701	34/319
Cal	Yarmouth	70	12 Jun 1688	33/737
Battee, Ferdinando:				
AA	Suffolk	52	18 Jun 1683	31/412
Batts, Jonathan:				
Dor		50	[20 Jun 1680]	24/194
Dor	Crab Island	50	30 Jan 1680	24/150;28/184
Bayley, Henry:				
Tal	Betty's Chance	100	10 Nov 1697	38/28
Bayley [Bailey], John:				
StM	Bayley's Rest	350	24 Aug 1694	27/204
StM	Bottom	100	15 Aug 1685	25/173;32/460
Bayley, John, planter:				
Cha	Bayley's Rest	187	17 Aug 1680	28/27
Bayley, John:				
Tal	Bayley's Forest	135	10 Apr 1684	25/98;32/185
Bailey, Richard of Talbot Co:				
Dor		200	28 Jun 1683	25/130;32/192
Bayley, Richard:				
AA	Bayley's Content	24	24 Apr 1685	25/251;33/345
AA	Betty's Point	90	7 Apr 1684	25/105;32/217
AA	Piney Plain	70	8 Apr 1684	25/105;33/215
Baynam, George, cooper:				
Som	Baynam's Purchase	100	1 Oct 1687	27/108
Som	Locke	250	20 May 1682	24/444;29/446
Bayne, John:				
Cha	Irving	150	10 Sep 1695	37/191
Baynes, Christopher of Calvert Co., planter:				
Bal	Christopher's Camp	1,000	5 Jly 1684	25/106;33/57
Bazley, Walter:				
Bal	Bazley's Expectation	100	10 Nov 1697	39/30
Beadle, Edward:				
Bal	Beadle's ---?---	100	2 Feb 1683	30/41
Bedwart, Richard:				
AA	Thornbury's Addition	16	5 Aug 1682	24/461;31/421
Beale, Adam:				
Cal	Paradise	200	10 Nov 1695	40/95
Beale, Charles of Calvert Co:				
Cha	Turkey Thicket	548	13 Apr 1686	25/239
Beale, John of Calvert Co:				
Cha	Barrans	472	18 Apr 1686	25/239;33/361

County	*Name of Tract*	*Acreage*	*Date*	*Reference(s)*
Beale, Capt. (later Maj. & Col.) Ninian, Deputy Surveyor for Calvert Co:				
PG	Anglia	31	10 Nov 1696	38/10
Cha	Bachelor's Hope	440	19 Aug 1687	25/319;32/545
Bal	Beale's Camp	1,000	22 Sep 1683	25/84
Cal	Beale's Croft	43	14 Sep 1694	27/273
PG	Beale's Pasture	372	1 Jun 1699	34/182;38/143
PG	Beale's Meadows	1,088	10 Nov 1697	38/44
Cal	Belfast	200	11 Oct 1682	24/445;31/1
PG	Bread & Cheese	53	6 Jly 1698	38/1
Cal	Concord	406	20 Jly 1686	25/252
Dor	Danby	1,000	-- Jly 1684	25/147
Cal	Darnall's Grove	3,800	28 Jun 1682	25/6;31/8
Cal	Dundee	150	25 Jly 1684	25/128;38/113
PG	Chance	132	1 Nov 1701	34/362
PG	Enclosure	237	30 Dec 1698	34/178;38/143
Cal	Expedition of Beale	221	19 Jly 1686	25/252;33/352;34/352
Cha	Fox Hall	150	4 Sep 1686	25/272;33/532
PG	G---ing	77	1 Nov 1701	34/349
PG	Good Luck	355	30 Dec 1698	34/179;38/143
PG	Good Luck Addition	200	20 Jly 1700	30/366
PG	Gore	179	30 Dec 1698	34/180;38/143
Cal	Hog Pen	358	13 Sep 1694	27/214
Cha	Inclosure	1,503	2 Oct 1687	25/323;33/721
Cal	Kenerton Lodge	500	27 Aug 1688	25/429;34/19
Cal	Kenerton Lodge Addition	498	10 Nov 1695	40/86
PG	Lois Point	79	1 Nov 1701	34/366
Cal	Maiden's Dowry	700	10 Sep 1694	27/275
Cal	Major's Lot	800	1 Mar 1687	25/330;32/531
Som	Meadows	82	15 Sep 1694	27/133
Cal	Neale's Desire*	455	25 Jly 1684	25/128
[marginal note: "surreptitiously obtained."].				
Cal	Plummer's Pleasure	135	1 May 1684	25/33
Cal	Porke Hall	300	4 Aug 1685	25/170;32/356
Cal	Rover's Content	562	2 Nov 1688	25/429;34/19
Cal	St. Andrew's	980	4 Oct 1687	25/20,322;
Cal	St. Andrew's	980	4 Oct 1687	31/533;32/530
Cal	Serge (?Lerge)	1,031	26 Jun 1685	25/178;32/354
Beale, Thomas of Calvert Co:				
Cha	Beale's Adventure	500	3 Apr 1685	25/266;33/326
Beale, Thomas of Anne Arundel Co:				
Bal	Beale's Purchase	141	14 Jly 1700	34/217
Beale, Thomas:				
Dor	Beale's Hope	500	29 Oct 1684	25/146;33/12
Bal	Beale's Enlargement	284	1 Jun 1702	35/390
Bal	Level	100	3 Jun 1702	35/435
PG	Loving Acquaintance	312	[1697]	37/547
Beamont—See Beaumont.				
Beard, Lewis of Somerset Co:				
Som	Betty's Enlargement	100	20 Nov 1685	25/262;33/359
Dor	Hog Quarter	300	9 Oct 1695	37/70

County	*Name of Tract*	*Acreage*	*Date*	*Reference(s)*
Beard, Richard, Deputy Surveyor for Anne Arundel & Baltimore Cos:				
AA	Bare Neck	290	20 Jan 1687	25/273;33/388
AA	Fortaine	155	10 Feb 1699	34/155
AA	Huckleberry Forest	611	10 Jun 1687	25/315;33/564
AA	Pound	68	10 Jun 1687	25/315;33/573
Beard, Robert:				
StM	Beard's Choice	50	8 Dec 1680	24/205,266;28/317
StM	St. Margaret's Forest	100	29 Apr 1682	24/410;31/58
Bearfoot—See Barefoot.				
Beasley, John:				
AA	Beasley's Lot	109	20 Jly 1684	32/152
Beason, Stephen:				
Assignor of land in Dorset Co. in 1681.				24/343
Beaumont [Beamont], James:				
Transported 30 persons [unnamed] before Sep 1680.				28/83
Beaumont, Mr. Richard:				
Cha	Wallingfield	160	3 Oct 1684	25/241;33/286
Beavan(s)—See Bevan(s).				
Beck, Edward:				
Cec	Beck's Addition	100	5 May 1684	25/343
Cec	Beckworth	150	14 Oct 1680	25/10
Cec	Long Compton	90	1 May 1701	34/356
Beck, John:				
Cec	Beck's Addition	100	2 Jly 1687	25/332;33/712
Beck, Richard:				
Transported by Thomas Maisterman before Sep 1680				28/53
Beckles, Thomas:				
Knt	Beckles' Recovery	200	14 Apr 1686	25/202;32/435
Beckwith, Henry:				
Dor	Beckwith's Addition	50	12 May 1687	25/302;33/449
Bedell, Edward, gent:				
Bal	Bedell's Chance	600	9 Jun 1683	25/4
Bal	Bedell's Reserve	100	22 Aug 1683	25/85
Beech, Edward:				
PG	Beech Hall	706	1 Jly 1698	39/47
Beetenson, Edmond & Lydia—See under Baldwin, John.				
Beetenson, Edward:				
AA	Beetenson's Adventure	82	23 Sep 1680	28/47
Belcher, William:				
Transported by Samuel Smith of Virginia			1680	24/33
Dor	Betty's Delight	500	20 Apr 1686	25/203
Bell, Anthony:				
Som	Nonsuch	50	9 May 1695	37/63

County	Name of Tract	Acreage	Date	Reference(s)
Bell, Daniel:				
StM	Hopewell	200	6 May 1686	25/217;32/373
StM	St. William's	114	10 Nov 1695	40/468
Bell, Edward of Talbot Co., planter:				
Dor	Bunhill Fields	50	4 Apr 1683	24/545;32/35
Dor	Hexham	45	4 Apr 1683	24/545;31/521
Bell, John:				
Som	Bell's First Choice	200	10 Oct 1695	37/232
Bellayne, Nicholas:				
Cha	Bellayne's Addition	50	29 Apr 1682	24/410;29/311
Benger [Benjor], Robert:				
Bal	Benger's Horse Pasture	30	12 Sep 1683	25/55
Bal	Benjor's Priviledge	108	27 Jly 1680	28/37
Bal	Privilege Addition	59	6 May 1689	34/53
Bennett, Edward:				
Som	Fairham	150	30 Jly 1681	24/308;28/385
Som	Titchfield	150	22 May 1688	25/420;32/655
Bennett, John, gent:				
AA	Bennett's Chance	124	25 May 1684	25/106
AA	Bennett's Park	81	7 Oct 1687	25/347;33/694
Bennett, John:				
Cal	Bennett's Desire	200	29 Jan 1681	24/297;28/481
Cal	Bennett's Refuge	40	11 Jan 1683	24/451;31/32
Bennett, John, planter:				
Som	Turkey Cock Hill	125	4 May 1680	24/271;28/342
Bennett, Richard, gent:				
Tal	Darlington	280	25 May 1686	25/338
Bennett, Robert:				
Transported by John Bodden of Somerset Co. bef. Apr 1681.				28/129
Benson, Daniel:				
AA	Benson's Luck	250	26 Mar 1696	40/261
Benson, James, surgeon:				
Tal	Benson's Choice	90	29 Aug 1687	25/366;33/648
Tal	Benson's Enlargement	740	20 Mar 1696	37/431
Benson, Stephen of Talbot Co:				
Bal	Fox Hall	200	10 Nov 1695	34/80;40/66
Benson, William:				
Cec	William's Choice	100	16 Mar 1681	25/12
Benston, Francis of Virginia, cooper:				
Som	Benston's Lot	100	28 Oct 1673	24/235;29/170
Benton, Richard:				
Bal	Wignall's Rest	200	2 Apr 1684	31/261
Berry, James, tanner:				
Som	Hopewell	300	1 Apr 1684	25/139;30/222

County	Name of Tract	Acreage	Date	Reference(s)
Berry, William:				
Tal		600	1 Aug 1680	24/194
Tal	Poplar Neck	400	5 Aug 1680	24/196;28/295
Dor	Wakefield	50	16 Aug 1680	28/32
Besson, Stephen:				
Assignor of lands in Dorchester Co. in 1678.				24/166
Dor	Racoon's Quarter	100	14 May 1679	24/91
Betts, George, planter:				
Som	George's Adventure	364	10 Nov 1695	34/71;40/244
Som	St. Giles	200	12 Dec 1683	25/189;30/211
Betts, Robert, planter:				
Tal	Addition	100	25 Jly 1681	24/336
Tal	Betts' Chance	200	24 Feb 1680	24/227
Tal	Betts' Range	400	4 Apr 1685	25/230;32/340
Tal	Rattlesnake Ridge	150	26 Jly 1687	25/341;33/630
Tal	Tatnell	100	14 Feb 1685	25/172,228;30/170
Tal	Westbury	100	9 Oct 1683	25/48
Bettson, Christopher:				
Tal	Yorke	306	10 Nov 1695	37/374
Bevan [Beavan], Charles:				
Cal	Hiccory Thicket	600	15 Mar 1696	37/202
Beavan, Thomas:				
Bal	Beavan's Hazard	175	25 Oct 1698	39/10
Bevans [Beavans], John:				
Bal	Bevans' Hazard	100	25 Oct 1698	35/443
Bal	Midsummer Hill	201	10 Jun 1695	40/506
Bevin, Rowland:				
Som	Warwick	400	13 Aug 1680	24/260;29/25
Bewin, John:				
Bal	Haphazard	100	11 May 1683	25/2
Bewing, Thomas:				
Bal	---?---	100	20 Apr 1683	30/38
Bewsey, William, planter:				
AA	Heart	60	3 Aug 1681	24/350;31/100
Bigger [Biggar], James, gent:				
Cal	Back Lands	135	17 Aug 1694	27/156
Cal	Forest	1,045	25 Oct 1694	27/278
Bigger, John:				
Assignor of lands in Calvert Co. in 1679			24/93	
Cal	Something	220	28 Aug 1694	27/250
Cal	South Lowding	150	10 Nov 1695	37/208
Binkes, Thomas of the Cliffes, Calvert Co:				
Cal	Binkes' Choice	116	8 May 1682	25/82;32/393
Cal	Binkes' Folly	67	8 May 1682	24/411;31/1

County	*Name of Tract*	*Acreage*	*Date*	*Reference(s)*
Bird, John:				
Transported by John Abington of Calvert Co. bef. Aug 1680.				28/34
Bird, William:				
Dor	Axmouth	55	12 Feb 1683	24/541;30/108
Birkhead, Abraham, gent:				
AA	Birkhead Mills	100	5 Aug 1682	24/461;29/308
AA	Birkhead's Right	66	27 May 1684	25/104;33/99
Bishop, Aaron:				
Som	Aaron's Lot	50	15 Jly 1684	25/139;30/205
Som	Beckford	300	3 Dec 1679	24/56
Bishop, Francis:				
Tal	Bishop's Fields	170	20 May 1687	25/315,27/354; 33/584
Bishop, Henry Sr:				
Som	Exon	250	18 Jun 1683	29/296
Bishop, Henry:				
Som	Discovery	300	16 Jly 1683	29/475
Som	Dives	600	11 Jun 1683	29/466
Bishop, John:				
Som	Reserve	250	8 Oct 1681	24/446;29/472
Bishop, Richard:				
Tal	Mistake	40	10 Nov 1695	37/499
Bishop, Roger:				
Bal	Talbot's Lane	44	8 Apr 1687	25/311;33/506
Bal	Talbot's Search	50	8 Apr 1687	25/311;33/537
Bishop, William:				
Assignor of lands in Talbot Co. in Apr 1680.				24/291
Tal	Bishop's Outlet	800	27 Jun 1681	24/356;29/325
Tal	Dangerfield	200	12 Aug 1684	25/149
Tal	Fox Hill	170	15 Jly 1684	25/150
Tal	Mill Range	163	26 Mar 1680	24/343
Tal	Out Range	174	15 Jly 1684	25/150
Blackeston—See Blankenstein.				
Blackwell, Josias:				
Transported by Samuel Smith of Virginia before 1680.				24/33
Blackwell, Thomas:				
AA	Blackwell's Search	439	13 Oct 1694	27/330
AA	Desart	148	12 Jun 1696	34/124;40/387
Blackwood, Phineas:				
Dor	Hide	50	11 May 1682	24/434;31/394
Bladen, William of Anne Arundel Co., gent:				
PG	Fairfax Beale	200	1 Nov 1701	34/328
Blangy, Lewis:				
Knt	France	100	17 Sep 1682	24/478;31/197

County	Name of Tract	Acreage	Date	Reference(s)
Bland, Thomas, gent:				
AA	Bland's Quarter	200	14 Aug 1680	24/205;28/329
Blankenstein [Blackeston], Ebenezer:				
Bal	Ebenezer's Lot	200	13 Jly 1684	25/109;32/102
Bal	Ebenezer's Park	200	[8 Apr 1684]	25/33;31/516
Cec	Hopeful Unity	150	12 May 1682	24/454;29/517
Cec	St. Tanton's	500	17 Oct 1681	24/347;32/100
Blankenstein, William of St. Mary's City, gent:				
Cec	Blankenstein's Park	400	14 Nov 1685	25/184;33/262
Cec	Browning's Neglect	482	28 Mar 1685	25/254
StM	Elbert Field	500	10 Jun 1684	25/28;31/428
Cec	Forest	400	14 Nov 1685	25/183;30/267
Cec	Requital	400	10 Oct 1687	25/306;32/475
Blankhorn, Robert—See under Sharpe, William.				
Blay, Edward & Ann his wife:				
Knt	Staples' Warren	110	1 May 1700	34/174
Blay, Edward, carpenter:				
Cec	Blay's Addition	450	5 Sep 1679	24/93
Cec	Hopeful Unity	150	12 May 1682	24/454;29/517
Bloise, Thomas:				
Assignor of lands in Somerset Co. in July 1679				24/274
Som	Penny Wise	50	24 Jly 1679	24/247;28/365
Boaring—See Boring				
Boreman, John:				
Som	Boreman's Addition	250	1 Mar 1696	37/91
Boreman, William:				
Cha	Boreman's Addition	857	1 Jly 1701	34/300
Boarman, Maj. William of St. Mary's Co:				
StM	Boarman's Reserve	588	2 Nov 1685	25/191,216;33/199
StM	Hard Shift	115	10 Mar 1696	37/258
StM	Wardle	780	5 Jly 1686	32/256
Bodden, John:				
Transported 4 persons before Apr 1681.				28/129
Bodkin, James of Charles Co., gent:				
StM	Charlesborough Swamp	326	2 Jly 1683	25/6
StM	Wardner's Desire	50	[29 Mar 1683]	25/2
Bollen, John:				
Assignor of lands in Cecil Co. in 1679.				24/43
Bond, Benjamin:				
AA	Favour	123	27 Jun 1682	24/460;40/419
Bond, Peter:				
AA	Bond's Forest	301	16 May 1688	25/406;32/628

County	Name of Tract	Acreage	Date	Reference(s)
Bond, Thomas:				
Bal	Lucky Hole	100	3 Apr 1702	35/417
Bondwell, Abraham:				
Cec	James' Forest	100	5 Oct 1680	25/10
Bondy, Richard:				
Cec	Bondy's Folly	100	4 Apr 1684	25/342
Bonham, Matthew:				
Knt	Buck Hill	150	19 Sep 1682	24/478;31/49
Bonham [Bonnam], William:				
Tal	Barbara's Delight	170	28 May 1683	24/527;32/55
Tal	Bonnam's Addition	100	16 Nov 1685	25/229;32/366
Bonner, Henry of Anne Arundel Co:				
Granted land called Fortune in Charles Co. bef. Nov 1680;				24/198
Father of Thomas Bonner of Charles Co.				25/61
Bal	Bonner's Camp	1,000	1 Jun 1685	32/90
Bal	Bonner's Interest	500	17 Oct 1685	25/217;33/193
Bal	Bonner's Purchase	500	12 Oct 1685	25/217;33/191
Bonner, Thomas of Charles Co., son of Henry Bonner:				
Bal	Jennifer's Delight	250	28 Apr 1684	25/61
Boone, James:				
Tal	Oak Ridge	350	[20 Nov 1678]	24/144
Boone, John of Talbot Co:				
Tal	Boone's Hope	100	29 Aug 1679	24/219;28/452
Dor	Exchange	600	4 Feb 1687	25/337;33/620
Tal	Haddon	400	3 Feb 1687	25/298;33/549
Tal	Hickory Ridge	150	2 Nov 1680	28/100
Tal	Oak Ridge	350	2 Nov 1680	28/111
Tal	Partnership	500	27 Oct 1683	25/23;31/527
Boone, William:				
Som	Boone's Park	240	10 Nov 1696	38/27
Booth, John, carpenter:				
Assignor of lands in Dorchester Co. in Nov 1681.				24/360
Dor	Arcadia	206	25 Apr 1682	24/408;31/88
Dor	Chesterfield	290	6 Oct 1683	25/124;32/386
Dor	Forest of Delamore	200	28 Apr 1682	24/426;31/373
Boothby, Edward of St. Mary's Co:				
Tal	Boothby's Fortune	500	2 Jun 1685	25/174
Tal	Hackett's Choice	500	4 Dec 1684	25/153
Tal	Pleasant Spring	500	10 Jun 1685	25/174
Boothby, Edward:				
Bal	Fanny's Inheritance	893	10 Mar 1696	40/424
Boram, John:				
Tal	Boram's Range	177	10 Nov 1695	34/76;40/148

Boreman—See Boarman.

County	Name of Tract	Acreage	Date	Reference(s)
Boring [Boaring], John:				
Bal	Boring's Passage	50	1 Dec 1682	24/504;25/287; 30/49;33/370
Bal	Boaring's Range	50	26 Jly 1680	28/16
Borne—See Bourne				
Boston, Isaac:				
Som	Boston's Green	75	10 Nov 1695	34/65;40/210
Boswell, Robert:				
Dor	Good Hope	120	4 Apr 1685	25/203
Boteler, Maj. Charles:				
Assignor of lands in Calvert Co. in 1679.				24/134
Cal	Brooke Place	43	10 May 1682	24/411
Cal	Harry's Lot	200	26 Jly 1679	24/149;28/141
Cal	Point Broomfield	43	20 Aug 1683	29/347
Boteler, Mr. Edward:				
Cal	Beale's Benevolence	300	8 Jan 1684	25/86;32/233
Boullay, James, gent:				
Knt	Caress	500	21 Jun 1680	24/189
Knt	Chance	200	20 Jun 1680	24/190;29/197
Knt	Dining Room	500	25 Jun 1680	24/188;29/194
Knt	Vianen	300	25 Jun 1680	24/188;29/195
Bound, John:				
Som	Pembridge	300	7 Jun 1688	25/400;32/647
Bournam, Mathew:				
Cal	Cuckold's Mess	160	6 Dec 1688	25/426;34/17
Bourn(e), William:				
Dor	Berkley	50	1 Jun 1683	25/118;32/453
Dor	Bourne's Conclusion	100	15 May 1682	24/434;31/360
Dor	Bourne's Landing	100	3 May 1682	24/431;31/153
Dor	Bourn's Meadows	50	2 Jun 1683	25/119;33/250
Dor	Bucknell	200	4 Sep 1679	24/149;28/182
Cec	Borne's Forest	400	15 Apr 1696	40/480
Cec	Walnut Thicket	200	15 Apr 1696	40/479
Bowdy, Thomas:				
Cec	Bowdy's Folly	100	12 Aug 1694	27/145
Bowen [Bowing], Jonas, planter:				
Bal	Jonas's Addition	51	20 Aug 1687	25/348;32/545
Bal	Jonas's Chance	20	13 May 1679	24/296
Bal	Jonas's Outlet	129	10 Nov 1695	40/438
Bal	Jonas' Range	100	29 May 1684	25/99;32/451
Bowen, Richard:				
Cal	Bowen's Desire	50	25 Feb 1682	24/394;31/6
Bowes [Bowse], George, planter:				
Tal	Bowse's Range	227	1 Nov 1697	38/61

County	*Name of Tract*	*Acreage*	*Date*	*Reference(s)*
Tal	Hasco Green	210	27 Mar 1687	25/313
Tal	Kendell	273	1 Nov 1697	38/52
Tal	Maxfield	152	15 Jun 1686	25/247;33/341
Tal	Moorfields	280	24 Feb 1686	25/308
Tal	Sibland Addition	110	10 Nov 1695	40/319
Bowes, Henry:				
Dor	Boulton	50	27 May 1681	24/346;31/380
Bowner, Henry of Anne Arundel Co., gent:				
Bal	Bowner's Camp	1,000	9 Feb 1685	25/157
Bowrin, Edward:				
Transported by John Abington of Calvert Co. bef. Aug 1680.				28/34
Bowring, William:				
Som	Bowring's Choice	350	12 Jun 1683	25/23
Bowsey, George:				
Cal	Chance	50	8 Mar 1682	24/397;31/21
Boyd, Benjamin & Elizabeth his wife, former wife of Humphrey Jones, deceased:				
Assignors of lands in Anne Arundel Co. in 1681				24/400
Boyde, John, planter:				
AA	Boyde's Chance	60	30 Jun 1684	25/94;33/108
Boyden, William planter:				
Cha	Boyden's Adventure	120	6 Oct 1684	25/215;32/437
Cha	Discovery	32	21 Apr 1681	24/303;29/237
Bradbury, Jacob:				
Tal	Jacob's Beginning	100	8 Jun 1689	27/179;34/83
Bradshaw, William:				
Som	Bradshaw's Purchase	250	1 Sep 1688	27/12
Som	Tossiter [Towcester]	150	28 May 1681	24/327;29/1
Bramble, Samuel:				
Dor	Bramble's Addition	64	20 Feb 1687	25/304;33/422
Brand, Samuel, smith:				
Bal	Contest	100	22 Aug 1683	25/83;33/127
Brandt, Capt. Randolph:				
Deputy Surveyor for Charles Co:				
Transported 6 persons [unnamed] before Sep 1680.				28/86
Cha	[unnamed]	200	9 Feb 1682	28/376
Cha	Asher	450	30 Jly 1683	25/2;33/25
from lands escheated for want of heirs to Thomas Petite.				
StM	Barbados	75	29 Apr 1682	24/363;29/48
Cha	Greenwich	167	26 Mar 1684	25/380;32/590
Cha	Putney	115	12 Sep 1683	25/380;32/572
Branikham, Elizabeth:				
Transported by John Abington of Calvert Co. bef. Aug 1680.				28/34
Brannock [Bronnack], John:				
Dor	Chance	118	1 May 1701	34/343
Dor	Decision	130	1 Jun 1700	34/243
Dor	Ragged Point	440	1 Jun 1700	34/276;38/159

County	Name of Tract	Acreage	Date	Reference(s)
Brannock, Thomas:				
Dor	Adventure	91	3 Jly 1702	35/395
Dor	Barron Ridge	47	2 Jly 1702	35/383
Bratten, James:				
Som	Neighbour's Goodwill	200	26 Mar 1688	25/359;33/679
Brawner, Henry:				
Cha	Fortune	102	20 Jan 1688	25/376;32/586
Bray, George:				
Som	Clonmell	40	15 Apr 1697	38/114
Breeme, John:				
Tal	Jamaica	150	17 Mar 1680	24/230;29/189
Brent, Henry, gent:				
Cal	Pitchcroft	400	21 Apr 1682	28/474
Brerely, Thomas:				
Tal	Brerely's Delight	150	14 May 1679	24/122
[including 50 acres for his time of service].				
Brereton, Maj. Thomas:				
Som	Recovery	500	8 Dec 1676	24/233,251;28/449
Brereton, William, gent:				
Som	Island Marsh	50	9 Feb 1683	25/32
Som	Middle Neck	300	24 May 1688	25/424
Som	Mile End	250	10 Jun 1680	24/312;28/403
Som	Whitechapel Green	50	9 Feb 1683	25/32
Brewer, George:				
Tal	Rape Green	210	1 Oct 1687	33/574
Brewer, John:				
AA	Brewer's Chance	152	16 Mar 1685	25/194;33/402
Briant—See Bryant.				
Brice, William:				
Dor	Brice's Adventure	150	26 Feb 1681	24/294;28/477
Dor	Brice's Range	100	20 Apr 1682	24/424;31/400
Dor	Whittlewood	100	4 May 1682	24/431;31/351
Brigantine, Thomas:				
Cal	Brigantine's Adv.	24	23 Feb 1695	27/248
Bright, Francis:				
Knt	Saw Pit	78	10 Aug 1695	40/4
Brightwell, Richard:				
Cal	Blackwell	160	20 Sep 1683	25/19;32/31
Cha	B'well's Hunting Quarter	1086	10 Oct 1695	37/253
Cal	Brightwell's Landing	47	1 Feb 1695	27/253
Cal	Brightwell's Range	100	12 Sep 1688	25/429;34/100
Cal	Spinum Land	136	5 Feb 1695	27/269
Cal	Thatcham	123	28 Feb 1695	27/280

County	*Name of Tract*	*Acreage*	*Date*	*Reference(s)*
Brimar, James:				
StM	Weems	424	16 Sep 1687	25/320
Briscoe, John, planter:				
Cec	Chance	65	2 Jun 1682	24/467;29/483
Cec	Providence	159	1 May 1701	34/334
Brittingham, William:				
Som	Houlston's Choice	150	[15 Jly] 1684	25/137;32/289
Broad, John:				
Bal	Broad's Choice	173	10 Nov 1695	40/276
Broadrib, John:				
Tal	Bradford	100	7 May 1679	24/118
Tal	Larkington	250	17 Jun 1679	24/119
Tal	Stoke	200	6 May 1679	24/45
Tal	Warmister	200	7 May 1679	24/19
Broadway, Robert:				
Tal	Hazard	175	20 Mar 1696	37/392
Tal	Musketoe Range	51	20 Jan 1697	38/48
Tal	Plains	110	20 Mar 1696	37/344
Broadway, Samuel:				
Tal	Ramah	100	16 Jun 1686	25/248;30/311
Brockden, Richard:				
Cal	Concord	131	16 Oct 1685	25/187;33/225
Brockett, William:				
His time of service completed by 1679.				24/106
Brooke, Baker Esq., Surveyor-General appointed in 1671:				
StM	Summer Seat	95	1 Jun 1685	33/70
Cal	Westfield	140	19 Sep 1678	25/29;33/60
Brooke, Charles:				
Cal	Brooke's Chance	81	1 Apr 1694	27/239
Brooke, Elinor daughter of Col. Thomas Brooke:				
Cal	Brooke's Discovery	350	30 Aug 1683	29/420
Brooke, Leonard:				
Cal	Haphazard	140	19 Sep 1678	25/29;33/6
[land purchased on his behalf by Baker Brooke Esq].				
Brooke, Roger, gent:				
Cal	Brooke's Discovery	489	10 Nov 1695	40/90
Cal	Brooke's Reserve	1,100	8 Jly 1681	24/174;28/156
Brook, Roger Jr. of Calvert Co:				
PG	Timberland	154	1 Jun 1700	34/235;38/161
Brooke, Col. Thomas of Calvert & Prince George's Cos:				
Cal	Brooke's Chance	830	13 Jly 1680	24/176;28/45
Cal	Brooke's Chance Addition	70	10 Jun 1685	25/168;32/164
Cal	Brooke's Discovery	531	10 Dec 1695	25/198;29/420
Cal	Brookfield	4,351	3 Jly 1699	34/145

County	Name of Tract	Acreage	Date	Reference(s)
Cal	Brookfield Addition	239	6 May 1689	34/16
PG	Brookfield Wedge	2,692	20 Nov 1698	38/90
Cal	Brook Neck	150	30 Aug 1683	29/419
Cal	Dan	3,697	6 Sep 1694	27/223
Cal	Forest	547	5 Sep 1694	27/232
Cal	Gore	70	10 Jun 1680	24/176;28/46
PG	Hart's Delight	456	5 Dec 1699	34/154;38/110
Cal	Hogpen	230	12 Jun 1685	25/169
Cal	Prospect	52	5 Jan 1696	40/263
PG	Reparation	415	5 Dec 1699	34/153;38/111
Brookes, Basil, son of Roger Brookes of Calvert Co:				
Bal	My Lord's Gift	500	5 Aug 1684	25/112;33/62
Brooks, John:				
Dor		200	14 May 1679	24/123
Brooks, Roger of Calvert Co., gent:				
Bal	Brooks' Cross	1,500	23 Sep 1684	25/141;33/69
Brookes, Mr. Thomas:				
Cal	Pork Hall Addition	239	20 Mar 1689	25/427
Brooks, William:				
Completed his time of service before Aug 1681.				28/305
Brooksby, John:				
AA	Brooksby's Point	350	5 Oct 1680	24/192;28/257
Brooksher [Brodsher], James:				
Som	Bedlam Green	150	5 Oct 1681	25/27;32/136
Broome, John of Calvert Co., innholder:				
Bal	Broome's Bloom	1,000	5 Aug 1684	25/107;33/66
Broome, John, gent:				
Cal	Grange	450	15 Feb 1684	25/43
Broomfield, Thomas:				
Bal	Hazard	200	10 Dec 1695	40/538
Broughton, John:				
Som	Welsh Folly	300	12 Dec 1688	27/38
Brown, Abell of Anne Arundel Co., gent:				
Bal	Abell's Lot	500	15 Jly 1684	25/110;32/93
Brown, Ann:				
Transported by Thomas Browning of Cecil Co. by 1680.				24/105
Browne, Bartholomew, eldest son of James Brown deceased who was son of John Brown:				
	F---ley	1,900	-- --- 1683	31/180
Browne, Daniel:				
Cal	Browne's Lot	70	1 Jun 1699	34/242;38/145
Brown, Capt. (later Col.) David:				
Som	[unnamed]	350	10 Nov 1695	34/135;40/314
Som	Glascow	300	7 Mar 1688	25/356;32/532

County	*Name of Tract*	*Acreage*	*Date*	*Reference(s)*
Som	Hackilah	300	28 Mar 1688	25/359;33/667
Som	Meadow	80	10 Nov 1695	40/194
Brown, Elizabeth:				
Transported by John Abington of Calvert Co. bef. Aug 1680;				28/34
another by William Peirce of Cecil Co. bef. Nov 1681.				24/383
Brown, Gabriel:				
Transported by Thomas Browning of Cecil Co. by 1680.				24/105
Browne, James of St. Mary's Co:				
PG	St. Wynesburgh	500	10 Nov 1695	40/557
PG	Woodcock's Range	500	10 Nov 1695	40/556
Brown, John of Somerset Co:				
Transported himself bef. Dec 1681.				28/406
Som	Brown's Chance	55	20 Apr 1688	25/382
Brown, John, carpenter:				
Som	Carpenter's Enjoyment	150	4 May 1686	25/237;33/317
Brown, John, shoemaker:				
Tal	Brown's Lot	200	3 Dec 1684	25/169;32/188
Brown, John:				
Som	Fanning's Adventure		21 Jun 1684	25/66;30/136
Som	Turnstile	300	29 Nov 1679	24/30
PG	Brown's Chance	19	2 Apr 1702	35/438
Brown, Mr. Peregrine of London, merchant:				
Cec	Fork	500	23 Oct 1683	25/187;33/249
Cec	Level	500	18 Sep 1683	25/129;32/105
Bal	Turkey Point	1,000	19 Dec 1698	34/152
Brown, Richard:				
Completed his time of service by 1679.				24/119
Brown, Sarah Sr. & Jr:				
Transported by their husband & father John Brown of Somerset Co. before Dec. 1681.				28/406
Brown, Thomas:				
AA	Brown's Adventure	1,000	10 Oct 1694	27/300
AA	Brown's Chance	98	29 Mar 1687	25/312;32/489
AA	Brown's Folly	270	1 Jun 1680	28/13
AA	Browne's Forest	387	10 Mar 1696	34/129;40/331
AA	Diamond	200	28 Sep 1681	24/352;31/414
AA	Friendship	150	24 May 1681	24/349;31/97
Brown, William:				
Transported by his father John Brown of Somerset Co. before Dec. 1681.				28/406
Brown, William:				
AA	Brown's Fancy	200	7 Dec 1694	27/306
Som	Mount Hope	300	20 Oct 1684	25/212
Som	Sand Down	500	17 Jan 1685	25/261

County	Name of Tract	Acreage	Date	Reference(s)
Browning, Hester:				
Transported by Thomas Browning of Cecil Co. by 1680.				24/105
Browning, John:				
Transported by Thomas Browning of Cecil Co. by 1680.				24/105
Browning, John of Cecil Co., surgeon:				
Cec	Assignor of lands in Cecil Co. in 1679 & 1680.			24/169,354
Cec	Askmore	550	8 Sep 1687	25/351;32/660
Cec	Brownley	100	17 Nov 1680	25/11;30/208
Cec	Clifton	883	22 Mar 1681	24/282
Som	Colman's Adventure	500	26 Nov 1679	25/401
Cec	Morelow	150	8 Sep 1687	25/352;32/662
Cec	Round's	500	18 Mar 1680	24/105
Cec	Success	500	2 May 1680	24/88
Cec	Warren	450	22 Mar 1681	24/282
Browning, Thomas of Cecil Co:				
Son and heir of John Browning in 1680.				24/105
Bruffe, Thomas & Susanna his wife of Kent Co:				
Their time of service completed by 1679.				24/106
Bryant [Briant], Darby:				
Transported by William Jones of Bristol bef. Aug 1680.				7/31
Bryant, John:				
Bal	Serjant's Hall	500	19 Sep 1684	25/101
Budd, William of Baltimore Co:				
AA	Timber Neck	132	13 Oct 1694	27/315
Bulks, Thomas:				
Assignor of lands in Talbot Co. in 1678 for transportation of 11 persons.				24/140
Bullett, Joseph:				
Cha	Bullett's Adventure	30	17 Sep 1683	25/181
Burch, Oliver:				
Cha	Penray	46	1 Jun 1698	38/139
Burchell, Adam, planter:				
Bal	Eden's Addition	100	11 Jun 1685	25/288;33/513
Bal	Garden of Eden	150	18 Jun 1685	25/189;32/426
Burford, Thomas Esq:				
Dor	Burford's Close	500	4 Oct 1684	25/131;33/17
Dor	Burford's Hope	500	24 Oct 1684	25/130
Burgess, Edward:				
AA	Burgess' Right	153	28 Apr 1688	25/406;32/627
Burgess, George, Deputy Surveyor for Charles Co. in 1695.				37/173
Burgess, George of Anne Arundel Co., gent:				
AA	Bare Neck	290	14 Jun 1685	25/273
Tal	Brother's Annexion	1,000	29 Apr 1684	25/108,113
Bal	Dandy Hill	175	10 Apr 1695	27/332

County	*Name of Tract*	*Acreage*	*Date*	*Reference(s)*
Bal	Goodwill	200	8 Aug 1684	25/99
Bal	Burges' Camp	1,000	21 Sep 1683	25/108
AA	Health	236	16 Aug 1684	25/98
Bal	Tapley Neck	306	11 Apr 1695	27/335
Burges, Peter:				
Cal	Chance	100	22 Sep 1688	25/427;34/18
Cal	Woodbridge	200	16 Oct 1684	25/330;33/719
Burgess, Ursula:				
Administratrix of Col. William Burgess deceased; Assigor of lands in Anne Arundel Co. in Oct 1687.				25/347
Burges, Col. William:				
Assignor of lands in Anne Arundel Co. in 1679				24/98
Burgess, William of Anne Arundel Co., gent:				
Bal	Cub Hill	500	26 Mar 1696	40/370
Burk, Richard of London, gent:				
Bal	Readbourne	1,000	3 Feb 1685	31/508
Burkum, Roger:				
Som	Friend's Discovery	30	19 Dec 1694	37/54
Burle, Stephen:				
AA	Burle's Park	200	21 May 1683	25/7;31/451
AA	Locust Thicket	200	21 May 1683	25/7;31/441
Burman, Robert of London, merchant:				
Bal	Burman's Adventure	1,000	21 Mar 1686	25/216
Bal	Burman's Forest	350	12 Feb 1686	25/231,243
Bal	Industry	120	31 Oct 1684	25/151;33/101
Burnett, Richard & Elizabeth his wife:				
AA	Bell's Haven	55	3 Jun 1684	25/94
Burnham, William:				
Cha	Burnham's Beginning	85	23 May 1682	24/457;31/198
Burrall, John & Anne his wife, & Anne their daughter:				
Transported by John Viner bef. Sep 1680.				28/66
Burroughs, John:				
Tal	Burroughbridge	100	9 Mar 1686	25/212
Burrows, John:				
Cal	Long Looked For	250	1 Nov 1688	32/507
Burroughs, William & Ann his wife:				
AA	Cheney's Neck	80	1 Jun 1696	40/389
[Ann Burroughs being formerly married to Peter Barnett of Anne Arundel Co. and the mother of Ann Barnett].				
Burton, William:				
Tal	Carman & Burton	150	14 May 1681	24/337;31/250

County	Name of Tract	Acreage	Date	Reference(s)
Butcher, Adam:				
Guardian of son of Wm. Lowe of Charles Co., deceased, in March 1682.				24/404
See also under Lowe, William.				
Butler, George, gent:				
Dor	[blank]	600	20 Sep 1684	25/153
Dor	Butler's Adventure	400	26 Sep 1684	25/204
StM	Hebdon's Hole	700	16 Jan 1693	27/57
Butler, James of Ann Arndell Co:				
Bal	Jacob's Addition	225	18 Apr 1696	40/415
Butten, John, cooper:				
Dor	Butten's Content	66	5 Apr 1685	25/293;33/528
Dor	Turkey Point	350	29 Mar 1686	25/294;33/476
Dor	Wolverton	50	26 May 1682	24/459;29/274
Butteram, Nicholas of Calvert Co:				
AA	Landing	21	22 Oct 1684	25/144;33/119
Butwell, Richard:				
Dor	Turkey Ridge	100	22 Dec 1681	24/389;31/196
Buxton, Francis:				
Cal	Darby	200	26 Apr 1683	24/522;29/43;33/685
Byram, Thomas of Baltimore Co.—See under Thurston, Thomas.				
Cabarbe, Ann:				
Completed her time of service bef. Jan 1680.				24/20
Cable, John, planter:				
Cha	Bachelor's Rest	100	8 Jun 1681	24/293
Cade, Robert:				
Som	Ainee Down		20 Jly 1679	24/44
Som	Cade's Addition	234	20 Sep 1687	25/355;32/528
Som	Sandy Point	200	10 Sep 1679	24/57
Calvert, Benedict Leonard Esq:				
StM		2,400	21 Apr 1684	25/159
Calvert, Philip Esq:				
Tal	White Marshes	1,000	8 Feb 1682	28/418
Calloway, Peter, planter:				
Som	Callaway's Addition	50	18 Nov 1685	25/279
Som	Little Britain	200	27 Nov 1688	27/104
Som	New Recovery	288	30 Nov 1682	24/519;33/179
Callwell, John:				
Som	Callwell's Chance	27	10 Jly 1689	27/64
Som	Cloulett	380	10 Sep 1688	27/40
Calvert, Jane—See under Herman, Ephraim.				
Campbell, Maj. John:				
StM	Forest of Dean	100	6 Nov 1685	25/192;33/186
StM	Joining	50	18 Jan 1687	25/269;33/266

County	*Name of Tract*	*Acreage*	*Date*	*Reference(s)*
Cambell, John:				
Cec	Eyla	190	28 Feb 1684	25/30
Campbell, Rebecca, widow:				
Cec	New Garden	190	23 Nov 1685	25/243;30/303
Campbell, Walter:				
Dor	Dumbarton	76	10 Apr 1695	40/590
Cannon, James:				
Dor	Cannon's Chance	300	28 Jun 1688	25/409;32/696
Dor	Ickford	112	31 May 1696	37/409
Cannon, Stephen:				
Som	Cannon's Lot		8 Oct 1681	24/510
Som	Cannon's Peace	100	1 Jun 1700	34/275
Cantwell, Edward:				
Bal	Taylor's Hall	200	2 Oct 1698	35/360
Cape, John:				
Tal	Tranquility	185	10 Nov 1695	37/498
Capman, John:				
Som	Templecombe	200	22 Sep 1683	25/65;29/526
Capstan, Francis, planter:				
StM	Gilded Morton	150	24 May 1682	24/514
Carman, Thomas:				
Tal	Carman & Burton	150	14 May 1681	24/337;31/250
Carnell, Daniel of St. Mary's Co:				
Assignor of lands in Talbot Co. in 1679–1681.				24/212,387
Knt	Honest Dealing	400	10 Sep 1685	25/211;32/456
Cec	Anchor & Hope	500	10 Jan 1682	28/423
Cec	Yorkshire	500	10 Jan 1682	28/424
Bal	Carnell's Fortune	500	22 Sep 1680	28/53
Tal	Colne	400	10 Aug 1683	31/323
Carpenter, Simon, son of Simon Carpenter deceased:				
Anna	Catharina Neck	400	11 Apr 1683	29/208
Carpenter, Thomas:				
AA	George's? Park?	400	[1698]	39/60
Carpender, William:				
Tal	Carpender's Outlet	136	7 Nov 1684	25/103;32/116
Carr, Robert of St. Mary's Co:				
Bal	Carr's Forest	500	15 Aug 1696	37/281
Carroll, Charles of Anne Arundel Co., Esq:				
Cha	Carroll's Forest	500	3 May 1689	27/17
Bal	Ely O'Carroll	1,000	10 Feb 1697	37/339
AA	Fortaine	148	4 Dec 1696	38/134
AA	[2 houses in Annapolis]		10 Oct 1701	34/370
Carroll, James:				
Deputy Surveyor for Baltimore County in 1700.				38/153

County	*Name of Tract*	*Acreage*	*Date*	*Reference(s)*
Carter, George:				
Som	Carter's Lodge	350	18 May 1683	25/68;30/187
Carter, Henry:				
Tal	Carter's Addition	50	5 Oct 1695	40/30
Knt	Chance	50	10 Aug 1695	40/10
Carter, John:				
Som	Bricklehow	300	30 Aug 1679	24/262;29/8
Som	Long Hedge	250	25 Feb 1680	24/334;29/172
Tal	Copartnership	104	1 Jun 1700	34/264;38/160
Carter, Philip, planter:				
Som	Dorman's Purchase	150	29 Nov 1682	24/520
Som	Sarah's Neck	100	5 Jly 1680	24/265
Som	Whetstone	350	28 May 1681	24/315;29/73
Carter, Richard, merchant:				
Assignor of lands in Talbot Co. in Jun 1679.				24/215
Tal	Addition	68	1 May 1701	34/333
Tal	Bodkin	15	5 Oct 1687	25/363;33/660
Tal	Carter's Addition	21	1 Oct 1701	34/342
Tal	Carter's Forest	420	4 Oct 1687	25/364;33/649
Tal	Carter's Forest	326	10 Nov 1695	40/461
Tal	Carter's Outwork	19	28 Oct 1687	25/325;30/187
Tal	Carter's Shonce	139	10 Oct 1687	25/363;33/657
Tal	Craven	300	26 Jun 1688	25/413;32/689
Tal	Gore	170	4 Oct 1687	25/363;33/647
Carter, Valentine:				
Tal	Copartnership	104	1 Jun 1700	34/264;38/160
Carter, William:				
Cal	Norwich	300	3 Mar 1688	25/344;33/720
Carty, Charles:				
Transported by Thomas Maisterman bef. September 1680.				28/53
Carvile, John:				
Cec	Carvile's Prevention	26	25 Jly 1694	27/149
Carvile, Robert of St. Mary's City., gent:				
StM		1	9 Jun 1678	24/154
Cal	Catton	500	4 Oct 1681	24/354;31/39
StM	Inclosure	170	27 Oct 1686	25/269
Tal	[unnamed]	500	17 Jly 1682	25/6
Tal	Royston's Purchase	500	5 Oct 1683	25/89;29/518
Carvile, Thomas:				
StM	Salter's Load	800	12 Jan 1683	29/90
formerly estate of Edward Parker who died without heirs.				
Cary, Edward:				
Som	Cary's Advance	50	2 Jly 1683	25/31
Cary, Richard:				
Som	Cary's Chance	164	12 Mar 1688	25/357;32/524

County	Name of Tract	Acreage	Date	Reference(s)
Cary, Thomas:				
Som	Cary's Advance	50	14 Jly 1683	25/31;30/3
Casey, Thomas, planter:				
Cec	Kappagh	1,593}		
Cec	Crossayle	575}	14 Apr 1684	25/51,61;32/197
Castle, Ralph—See under Lowe, Susan.				
Catlin [Catlyn], Robert:				
Som	Branfield	100	19 Oct 1685	25/275
Som	First Choice	250	[22 Jun 1679]	24/165;32/231
Som	Long Ridge	135	10 Nov 1695	34/62;40/254
Som	Meadow	50	2 Oct 1695	37/101
Catterson, Francis:				
Dor	Catterson's Hamell	500	28 Oct 1684	25/146;32/113
Dor	Catterson's Range	200	8 Oct 1684	25/158;32/108
Catterton, Michael:				
Cal	Catterton's Lot	182	27 Dec 1686	25/292;33/591
Causey, John:				
Dor	Causey's Choice	100	18 Mar 1681	24/297;29/164
Dor	Causey's Lot	100	10 Nov 1681	24/360
Cavrup, William, Joane his wife, and William Cavrup, their son: Transported by John Viner before September 1680.				28/66
Cawley, John:				
Tal	Slaughterton	500	14 Mar 1683	24/522
Cayson, William:				
Dor	Dale's Right	100	18 Apr 1683	24/534
Celis, Stephen:				
Dor	Celis's Fortune	35	20 Oct 1679	24/170
Cely [Sely], Emmanuel, planter:				
Bal	Emmanuel's Hope	100	5 Aug 1684	25/92;33/128
Bal	Emmanuel's Hope	172	3 Jly 1702	35/381
Bal	Mates' Affinity	200	1 Mar 1684	25/40;30/36
Bal	Range	200	11 Nov 1686	25/290;33/510
Chabner, Jane:				
Transported by John Abington of Calvert Co. bef. Aug 1680.				28/34
Chaffy, Richard:				
	?	100	6 May 1689	34/20
Chaires, John, cooper:				
Tal	Bachelor's Adventure	150	26 Oct 1679	24/223;29/488
Tal	Chaires' Addition	100	15 Nov 1686	25/315;33/585
Tal	Rear Guard	400	25 Jun 1681	24/368;31/301
Chaldy, Richard:				
Cal	Chaldy's Delight	100	24 Aug 1688	25/428

County	Name of Tract	Acreage	Date	Reference(s)
Chambers, Richard:				
Som	Brown's Chance	55	27 Mar 1688	25/382
Som	Cackmore	200	30 May 1681	24/366;29/383
Som	James's Choice	150	24 May 1688	25/418;32/653
Som	Rowley Ridge	100	28 May 1681	24/315;29/13
Som	Vulcan's Forge	100	28 May 1681	24/315;29/52
Som	Wolf Pit Ridge	115	24 May 1688	25/418;32/654
Chandler, Job, gent:				
Transported himself, Anne his wife & Anne his daughter & others before 1651.				29/149
Chandler, Mr. William:				
Cha	Old Woman's Branch	200	3 Dec 1678	24/149
Chaney, Richard:				
PG	Chaney's Adventure	343	10 Aug 1696	37/475
Chaplin, Francis, planter:				
Tal	Newlin	140	20 Mar 1696	37/427
Tal	Whitechapel	100	19 Dec 1682	24/496;30/69
Chapman, John:				
Transported by Thomas Maisterman bef. Sep 1680.				28/53
Chapman, John of Prince George's Co:				
Bal	Chapman's Fellowship	150	5 Jun 1700	34/252;38/157
PG	Churtsey	365	25 May 1700	34/185;38/151
Chapman, Mathew, planter:				
Cec	[unnamed]	500	25 May 1683	24/554
Cec	Lee	14	19 Jly 1686	25/255;33/285
Chappell, Thomas:				
Som	Kingston	100	1 Oct 1681	24/379;29/427
Cheseldyne, Kenelme:				
StM	Dryden	483	1 Apr 1700	38/149
Chiseldyn, Reuben of St. Mary's Co:				
Assignor of lands in Somerset Co. in Aug 1681.				28/314
Cheseman, William, planter:				
Dor	Cheseman's Gore	50	24 Apr 1683	24/535;30/99
Dor	Poplar Ridge	290	16 Feb 1683	24/538;30/89
Cheshire, Richard, mariner:				
Tal	Cheshire's Delight	600	18 Jly 1684	25/161;33/95
Chester, Edward of Calvert Co:				
Transported himself and Elinor his wife by Aug 1681.				28/305
Chew, Ann:				
Transported by Thomas Dent of Somerset Co. by Apr 1681.				28/174
Chew, Joseph:				
Cal	Chew's Meadows	100	15 Mar 1696	37/203
Chew, Mr. Samuel:				
AA	Chew's Purchase	145	10 Nov 1694	27/348

County	Name of Tract	Acreage	Date	Reference(s)
AA	Chew's Vineyard	1,024	17 Apr 1689	27/307
AA	Resolution Manor	1,073	5 Apr 1689	27/304
Chew, William:				
Cal	Chew's Fortune	49	15 Jun 1694	27/218
Chillcott, Anthony:				
Dor	World's End	300	10 May 1688	25/435;34/287
Chilcot, James:				
Cal	Lavall	100	8 Aug 1670	24/67
Childe, Abraham, gent:				
AA	Childe's Reserve	62	6 Mar 1684	25/95
AA	Chilton	40	19 Oct 1681	24/354;31/94
Chinn, John:				
StM	Chinn's Purchase	50	10 Jun 1683	31/52
StM	Muriel's Choice	50	9 Feb 1687	25/324;33/609
Chiseldyn—See Cheseldyne.				
Chittle, William:				
Cal	Persia	110	17 Nov 1682	24/482;31/14
Chittom, John:				
PG	Chittom's Addn.	100	4 Nov 1699	38/156
PG	Weymouth	517	20 Apr 1698	34/158;38/149
Chockley, Richard, planter:				
Som	Chockley's Purchase	400	12 Jun 1683	25/71
Christen, Lawrence, planter:				
Cec	Christen's Addition	515	11 Mar 1686	25/216,333
Christian, John:				
Bal	Christian Deary	100	1 Jun 1700	34/273
Bal	Christian's Lot	100	1 May 1696	37/354
Christopher, John:				
Som	Battlefield	50	8 Feb 1683	25/22
Som	Marsham	100	4 Jly 1683	25/193;32/425
Clagett—See Clegatt.				
Clare, John George:				
Transported by Thomas Maisterman bef. Sep 1680				28/53
Clarke, Alexander:				
Cec	Stand Off	100	1 Oct 1701	34/321
Clarke, Andrew of Calvert Co:				
Cha	Meurs	500	24 Sep 1685	25/268;33/353
Clarke, Edward:				
Tal	Delicey	100	20 Mar 1696	37/403
Clarke, Gilbert:				
Cha	Aberdeen	428	15 Jan 1689	25/425;32/709
Clarke, Gilbert of St. Mary's CoL				
Bal	Clarke's Forest	500	18 Mar 1684	25/45

County	Name of Tract	Acreage	Date	Reference(s)
Knt	Killins Worth More	500	1 Oct 1683	25/69
Dor	Taylor's Promise	500	27 Oct 1684	25/148;30/124
Clark, James:				
Transported by Richard Edelen bef. September 1680.				28/82
Clarke, John:				
Som	Miserable Quarter	400	10 Dec 1698	38/107
Clarke, Neale:				
AA	Clarke's Enlargement	265	20 Jun 1686	25/274;33/438
AA	Clarke's Luck	60	14 Oct 1684	25/116;32/415
AA	Turkey Island	333	26 Mar 1696	34/131;40/350
Clarke, Richard:				
Transported by James Round of Somerset Co. by. Apr 1681.				28/129
Clarke, Robert:				
Som	Addition	100	9 Nov 1694	27/132
Clarke, Roger:				
Dor	Foxon is Defeated	150	10 Oct 1695	40/579
Dor	Old Bayley	10	30 Sep 1680	24/201;30/120
Clarke, William:				
AA	Clarke's Purchase	70	20 Jun 1686	25/347;33/732
Clarkson, Robert of Anne Arundel Co., gent:				
AA	Clarkson's Hope	600	28 Sep 1683	25/51;31/448
Bal	Clarkson's Purchase	600	24 Oct 1683	25/85
Bal	South Couton	245	8 Aug 1680	24/285;28/168
Clarkson, William:				
Cha	Clarkson's Purchase	192	18 Jly 1687	25/319;32/87;33/689
Clawson, Peter:				
Cec	New Amster	200	2 May 1687	25/351;33/710
Clay, Henry:				
Tal	Clay's Neck	100	24 Apr 1679	24/212,543;28/341
Cley, John:				
Som	Cley's Adventure	160	5 July 1695	37/89
Clayland, James, clerk:				
Tal	Bridgewater	300	6 May 1687	25/340;33/661
Tal	Clayland's Purchase	200	10 Nov 1696	38/85
Tal	Gloucester	300	6 Jun 1687	25/341;33/640
Tal	Parsonage	100	10 Aug 1681	24/374
Tal	Parsonage Addition	100	8 Aug 1683	29/396
Clegatt [Clagett], Thomas of Calvert Co., gent:				
Cal	Clegett's Design	376	3 Nov 1682	24/480;31/496
Bal	Clegatt's Forest	1,000	4 Aug 1684	25/140;32/566
Cal		700?	1 Aug 1698	39/2
	Godlington Manor	1,000	5 Jly 1686	32/261
Cleveland, William:				
Transported by Christopher Rousby of Calvert Co.				24/22

County	Name of Tract	Acreage	Date	Reference(s)
Cleverly, Thomas:				
Cal	Cleverly's Addition	200	10 Aug 1682	24/477;29/422
Cal	Cleverly's Fancy	200	10 Aug 1682	24/477;29/423
Cley—See Clay.				
Cliffen, Thomas:				
Som	Taymouth	200	22 Sep 1683	25/64;33/84
Clifton, Thomas, planter:				
Som	Hog Hill	100	28 Aug 1679	24/247;28/404
Som	Crowland	100	5 Oct 1687	25/390;34/48
Clipsham, Thomas:				
Cha	Assignor of lands in Charles Co. in 1678			24/141
Cha	Clipsham Mount	68	28 Sep 1680	28/48
Clocker, Daniel:				
StM	Lewis's Neck	30	26 Nov 1681	24/349
StM	St. Andrew's Freehold	50	26 Nov 1681	24/349
Clowter, Richard, planter:				
Cha	Bastable	100	13 Oct 1684	25/182;32/439
Clouds, Nicholas:				
Tal	Clouds' Adventure	500	15 Jly 1684	25/149;32/96
Tal	Conquest	394	18 Jly 1686	25/220;32/337
Tal	Noller's Delight	150	31 May 1696	37/445
Tal	Nollar's Desire	198	4 Jly 1685	25/305
Tal	Nollar's Enjoyment	500	16 Jly 1685	25/164;32/115
Tal	Salisbury	500	2 Jly 1685	25/163;32/120
Cluttom, John:				
PG	Cluttom's Addition	100	1 Jun 1700	34/201
Clyburn, John:				
Dor	Dubling	100	31 May 1696	37/442
Clymer, John:				
Tal	Grantham	50	[11 Jun 1677]	24/166;29/230
Coales, John, gent:				
Cal	Chance	107	5 Jly 1694	27/225
Coape, George, planter:				
AA	Coape's Hill	350	4 Aug 1681	24/350;31/95
Coapland, Lettice:				
Transported by Samuel Gibson of Calvert Co.				24/4
Coard, Joseph:				
Som	Coard's Lot	430	31 Aug 1688	25/387;32/640
Coates, Col. John:				
Cha	Clean Drinking	700	1 Oct 1700	34/215
Cobreath, John:				
Cal	Good Luck	300	22 Apr 1681	28/384
Cocke, John:				
Cec	Chance		[6 Mar 1682]	24/468;29/365

County	***Name of Tract***	***Acreage***	***Date***	***Reference(s)***
Cockey, William of Anne Arundel Co:				
AA	Cockey's Addition	25	23 May 1683	25/7;29/305;31/453
AA	Cockey's Addition	130	6 Aug 1681	24/351
Bal	Cockey's Trust	300	1 May 1696	34/138;40/373
AA	Cuckold's Point	100	10 Mar 1696	34/121;40/220
AA	Mutual Consent	50	20 Jun 1683	25/96;32/181
Cocks—See Cox.				
Cockshell, Richard, planter:				
Som	Bacon Quarter	200	5 Apr 1686	25/235;33/319
Coghill, James:				
PG	Little Worth	190	1 Oct 1696	38/65
Cole, Barnaby:				
Transported by William Peirce of Cecil Co. bef. Nov 1681.				24/383
Cole, Edward:				
StM	Cole's Adventure	150	1 Jun 1682	24/413;29/331
StM	Cole's Purchase	210	13 Jun 1689	27/284
Cole, George:				
Cal	Little Gunerby	42	20 Jun 1694	27/167
Cole, John:				
Bal	Cole's Addition	67	[1697]	39/38
Cole, Philip:				
Cha	Green Bank	66	27 Sep 1680	28/49
Cole, Robert:				
StM	Cole's Addition	50	10 Jun 1686	25/324;33/602
Cole, Thomas:				
Som	Whitby	150	10 Jun 1680	24/309;28/405
Cole, William:				
StM	Manley	50	19 Jan 1681	24/301;28/445
Coleborne [Coulborne], Robert:				
Som	Heart's Content	50	5 May 1677	24/238;28/368
Colebourne, William, gent:				
Som	Pomfret	1,400	13 Jun 1679	24/150;29/150
Coulborne, Col. William:				
Som	Ferrybridge	200	10 May 1685	25/180
Coleman, Ellis, merchant:				
Som	Retirement	200	1 May 1686	25/286;33/556
Som	Salem	250	19 Apr 1681	28/174;29/467
Colman, John of Bristol, England, merchant:				
Som	Colman's Adventure	500	26 Nov 1679	25/401
Collet, John:				
Granted land called Friendship in Cecil Co. bef. 1680.				24/185

County	*Name of Tract*	*Acreage*	*Date*	*Reference(s)*
Collier, Francis, on behalf of Francis Swanson, son & heir of Francis Swanson deceased:				
Cal	Swanson's Lot	1,303	3 Aug 1683	25/19
Collyer [Collier], Robert, planter:				
Som	Collyer's Good Success	320	15 Apr 1684	25/140;30/178
Som	Late Discovery	50	7 Nov 1686	25/263;33/366
Collins, Francis, planter:				
Tal	Collins' Pasture	50	17 Jly 1686	25/245;33/306
Collins, George:				
Som	Collins' Adventure	500	14 Aug 1680	24/288;28/392
Som	Prickles Cocked Hat	75	6 Jun 1688	25/392;32/632
Cal	Collins' Comfort	250	27 Apr 1681	24/299;29/324
Som	Woolhope	75	6 Jun 1688	25/392;32/633
Collins, Richard:				
Tal	Collins' Lot	200	3 Jan 1680	24/226;32/203
Tal	Freshford Addition	100	4 Jan 1680	24/226;32/166
Tal	Shotland	200	4 Jan 1680	24/226;32/204
Collins, Samuel:				
Som	Ham	50	25 Nov 1679	24/83
Som	Collins' Addition	223	24 Apr 1701	34/371
Collins, Thomas, gent:				
Tal	Castle Miles	200	2 Aug 1684	25/157;33/157
Tal	Collins' Own	91	10 Nov 1695	34/84;40/177
Tal	Collins' Range	300	4 Mar 1680	24/229;29/489
Tal	Collinston	120	16 Oct 1687	25/370;33/626
Tal	Corke House	200	29 May 1683	24/526;33/144
Tal	Discovery	220	10 Nov 1695	37/288
Tal	Fool Play	500	10 Nov 1695	37/286
Tal	Frankford	200	7 Mar 1687	25/308
Tal	Kelmanam Plains	300	4 Feb 1686	25/248,341;33/641
Tal	Partnership	400	10 Nov 1695	34/98;40/236
Tal	Ring's End	100	28 Jly 1686	25/245;30/325
Collins, Thomas, planter:				
Cec	Camel's Worth More	1,150	17 Jun 1682	24/472;31/248
Collins, Thomas of Chester River:				
Tal	Kilkenny	200	3 Jly 1685	25/173;32/214
Collins, William, planter:				
Som	Tradah	200	24 Nov 1685	25/238;33/327
Collinson, George:				
Tal	Rahaboth's Point	50	29 Oct 1680	24/197;28/335
Collyer—See Collier.				
Colman—See Coleman.				
Colson, Robert:				
Tal	Folly	100	30 Nov 1681	24/386;31/291

County	*Name of Tract*	*Acreage*	*Date*	*Reference(s)*
Colstone, John:				
Som	Far Kill Hummock	30	5 Oct 1681	24/529
Som	Fishing Island	20	6 Oct 1681	24/529
Combes, Abraham & Sarah his daughter:				
Transported by Clement Hill bef. Sep 1680				28/71
Combes, William:				
Tal	Security	200	17 Apr 1682	24/406;29/344
Comegys, Cornelius of Kent Co., gent:				
Granted land called New Forest in Kent Co. bef. 1680.				24/187
Knt		500	1 Jun 1680	24/187
Knt	Adventure	300	16 Jun 1680	24/190;29/116
Tal	Adventure	45	26 Jun 1685	25/163;32/122
Tal	Andover	100	3 Jly 1685	25/163;32/119
Knt	Comegys' Delight	400	15 Aug 1683	25/5
Knt	Comegys' Farm	300	24 Jun 1680	24/189;32/537;29/113
Knt	Comegys' Farm Addition	370	3 May 1687	25/334
Knt	Grove	400	24 Jly 1681	28/316
Tal	Poplar Plain	500	16 Jly 1685	25/162;32/123
Knt	Relief	130	2 May 1687	25/334
Knt	Sewell	1,224	[11 Jan 1681]	24/367;32/153
Tal	Timber Fork	500	16 Jly 1685	25/162;32/124
Knt	Viana	600	16 Aug 1683	25/5
Comegys, William of Kent Co:				
Tal	Gloucester	400	16 Jly 1685	25/163;32/109
Knt	Littleworth	15	10 Mar 1696	40/486
Connant, Robert:				
AA	Connant's Chance	25	17 Jly 1680	28/19
Connell, Daniel:				
Cha	Dalkeith	183	30 May 1688	25/373;33/690
Connell, James:				
Completed his time of service bef. Sep 1680.				28/128
Connelly, Patrick:				
Tal	Connelly's Park	200	6 May 1688	25/415;32/610
Conner, Hannah:				
Transported by Mark Cordea bef. September 1680.				28/51
Connor, James:				
Som	Coleraine	200	16 Feb 1683	24/530;30/149
Som	Stooping Pine	50	7 Oct 1685	25/234;33/259
Conner, Philip:				
Knt	Little Neck	55	16 Aug 1680	28/28
Conner, Philip Sr.:				
Som	Roscommon	100	3 May 1689	27/53
Som	Rumbling Point	100	20 Apr 1694	37/56
Constable, Henry of Anne Arundel Co:				
Bal	Range	240	23 Dec 1685	25/289;33/379

County	Name of Tract	Acreage	Date	Reference(s)
Cood, John of St. Mary's Co:				
PG	Second Thought	500	1 Nov 1701	34/355
Cook, Edward:				
Transported by William Thomas of Charles Co. before September 1680.				28/121
Cooke, John, planter:				
Bal	Cooke's Rest	100	10 Sep 1683	25/52;30/52
Tal	Hasely	200	11 Jun 1686	25/246;33/333
Cooper, Benjamin:				
Transported 20 persons [unnamed] bef. Sep 1680.				28/78
Cooper, Gabriel:				
Som	Orphan's Lot	500	13 May 1688	27/41
Cooper, John:				
Cal	Cooper's Lot	96	1 Jan 1683	24/451;31/9
Som	Golden Valley	250	24 Dec 1681	24/448
Cooper, Nicholas:				
Cha	Middle Green	94	10 Nov 1695	34/144;37/236
Cooper, Richard of Accomack, Virginia:				
Som	Cooper's Purchase	100	2 May 1689	27/124
Cooper, Samuel:				
Deputy Surveyor for Somerset Co.				
Som	Coram	500	1 Dec 1679	24/17
Som	Basham	200	10 Oct 1683	29/438
Som	Goshen	300	23 Jly 1681	28/244
Som	Malborough	150	22 Dec 1681	24/449
Som	Salem	350	25 Dec 1680	24/283;28/240
Cooper, William:				
Tal	Long Neglect	100	20 Mar 1696	37/401
Copes, John of St. Mary's Co:				
Transported himself, his wife Frances & son John before1683.				29/319
Coplyn, Elizabeth & Henry—See under Baldwin, John.				
Copshaw, Francis:				
StM	Gilded Morton	150	24 May 1682	24/411,514;29/319
Coppin, John:				
Tal	Coppin's Coppice	50	10 May 1683	24/527
Copus, John, planter:				
Bal	Copus' Harbour	100	6 Sep 1683	25/50;30/62
Corbin, Nicholas:				
Bal	Corbin's Rest	200	26 Jly 1680	28/24
Bal	Corsell Hill	100	6 Mar 1688	25/349;33/735
Cord, William:				
Som	Islington	200	13 May 1689	27/122
Som	Key	100	26 Mar 1680	24/257

County	*Name of Tract*	*Acreage*	*Date*	*Reference(s)*
Cordea, Mark, gent:				
StM	Hog Quarter	250	24 Sep 1680	28/51
StM	Hog Ridge	150	25 Sep 1680	28/50
StM	Cordea's Hope	1	[1684]	30/133
Corner, John:				
Transported by Thomas Window of Calvert Co. before August 1681				28/305
Cornwell, Nicholas, planter:				
Som	Cornhill	293	30 Mar 1686	25/279;33/376
Som	Cornwell's Addition	40	1 Oct 1687	27/107
Som	Peterborough	50	10 Nov 1695	40/296
Correy, William:				
Som	Fattar's Quarters	186	24 May 1688	25/421;32/656
Corss, James:				
Cec	Chance	50	11 Jun 1686	25/225;32/374
Corwin, William:				
Assignor of lands in Talbot Co. in May 1682.				24/411
Cosden, Stephen of Somerset Co:				
Transported himself before July 1681.				28/198
Cosden, Thomas:				
Cal	Lower Gronery*	440	9 Feb 1683	24/483
Cal	Punch	150	3 Feb 1682	24/392
Costin, Henry, planter:				
Tal	Costin's Chance	141	13 Jly 1683	25/38;33/78
Tal	Court Road	138	18 Mar 1686	25/221;33/208
Tal	Doctor's Gift	100	12 Apr 1679	24/211;28/272
Tal	Dullidge (Dulwich)	180	29 Apr 1687	25/324
Tal	Lambeth	100	10 Dec 1682	24/232,494;25/41;
Tal	Lambeth	100	10 Dec 1682	30/76,77;32/206
Tal	Lloyd Costin	500	20 Feb 1680	24/232;32/229
Tal	Newington	80	12 Jly 1683	25/38;30/78
Tal	Sarah's Lot	50	12 Apr 1679	24/211;28/227
Costin, Stephen, planter:				
Som	Bear Point	500	21 Nov 1679	24/9
Som	Costin's Trouble	450	[11 Jun 1679]	24/167;29/231
Som	Emmett's Discovery	260	10 Mar 1696	37/502
Cottman, Benjamin, planter:				
Som	Berkes	150	12 Jun 1688	32/565
Som	Chance	500	6 Jun 1683	29/286
Som	Cottman's Point	50	10 Jun 1680	24/311;29/75
Coulborne—See Coleborne.				
Coursey, Henry, gent:				
Tal	Coursey's Addition	150	27 Aug 1687	25/367
Tal	Neglect	400	25 Aug 1687	25/367;33/639
Coursey, Thomas of Talbot Co				
Cec	Coursey's Triangle	200	10 Aug 1695	40/33

County	Name of Tract	Acreage	Date	Reference(s)
Coursey, William:				
Deputy Surveyor for Kent & Cecil Cos.				
Coursey, William Jr:				
Deputy Surveyor for Talbot Co.				
Coursey, William:				
Tal	Coursey upon Wye	920	10 Nov 1695	37/340
Tal	Coursey's Addition	130	20 Mar 1696	37/378
Tal	Inclosure		3 Apr 1683	24/511;31/172
Tal	Long Neglect	60	31 May 1696	37/457
Coursey, William of Talbot Co:				
Cec	Coursey's Triangle	200	10 Aug 1695	40/33
Coursey, Maj. William:				
Tal	Eason's Addition	300	10 Aug 1683	29/400
Tal	Vaughan's Discovery	400	10 Aug 1683	31/280
Court, John Jr.:				
Cha	Court's Discovery	60	15 Mar 1683	24/505;33/20
Courtes, John:				
Cha	Thanet Housing	36	17 Jly 1697	38/137
Courtney, Thomas:				
StM	Creydon	100	15 Jun 1681	24/292,304;29/289
StM	Draper's Neck	500	28 Mar 1683	25/18;29/290
StM	St. Thomas	300	28 Apr 1682	24/409
Coverdale, Thomas:				
His time of service assigned to Thomas Dant bef. Sep 1680.				28/54
Covington, John:				
Som	Long Acre	200	4 Feb 1680	24/80
former estate of David Williams alias Williamson of Somerset Co. who died without heirs.				
Som	Sassafrax Neck	150	28 May 1681	24/323;29/30
Covington, Nehemiah:				
Som	Collins' Adventure Addn.	420	14 May 1688	25/425;32/711
Dor	Coventon's Chance	512	10 Nov 1695	37/349
Som	White Marsh	100	20 Feb 1675	24/236;29/181
Covington, Philip:				
Som	Covington's Meadows	460	10 Oct 1700	34/228
Cowley, Capt. George:				
Tal	Intention	100	1 Aug 1697	38/77
Tal	Plensly	100	28 Nov 1684	25/223;32/330
Cox, Anthony:				
Tal	Cox's Addition	70	10 Nov 1695	37/386
Tal	Cox's Chance	160	5 Nov 1695	39/12,15
Cox, Christopher, planter:				
AA	Cox's Forest	199	24 May 1683	25/8;31/512
Bal	Cox's Range	200	15 Nov 1686	25/290;33/558

County	***Name of Tract***	***Acreage***	***Date***	***Reference(s)***
Cox, Christopher Jr.:				
Som	Hearn Quarter	200	10 Nov 1695	40/279
Cox, Daniel:				
Dor	Bridge Neck Addition	90	2 Aug 1687	25/408;32/697
Cox, Edward:				
Knt	Cooper's Quarter	50	9 Jun 1681	25/15;29/520
Cox, Henry:				
Cal	Little Land	34	26 Sep 1694	27/252
Cal	Meadows	186	10 Nov 1696	38/24
Cal	Refuge	14	20 Jly 1696	37/479
Cox, James:				
Cha	Woodbridge	90	10 Dec 1684	25/188;32/474
Cox, John:				
Cec	Cox's Forest	500	20 Sep 1682	24/478;31/86
[including lands assigned by Abraham Wied for transportation of 24 persons].				
Cox, Rebecca, sister & heir of Daniel Clarke who died intestate:				
Som	Maidenhead	300	29 Mar 1683	29/203
Cox [Cocks], Thomas:				
Som	Alderbury	550	10 Oct 1695	37/134
Som	Aldermanbury	172	14 May 1688	25/425;32/710
Som	Cock Land	246	17 May 1688	27/228
Tal	Cox's Delight	110	14 Sep 1697	38/36
Som	Cox's Fork	300	18 Dec 1681	25/285;32/494
Som	Cox's Lot	100	9 Jly 1683	29/473
Som	Friend's Denial	300	14 Aug 1680	24/287;28/399
Som	Rum Ridge	300	14 Aug 1680	24/287;28/394
See also under Lewellin, Audry.				
Cox [Cocks], William of St. Mary's Co:				
Assignor of lands in St. Mary's Co. in 1680.				24/189
Knt	Kindness	50	24 Jun 1680	24/186;28/160
Cozens, John:				
PG	Londee	310	1 May 1699	34/189;38/143
Craig, Edward:				
Som	Scotch Ireland	300	10 Nov 1688	27/32
Cranford, Mr. James of Calvert Co:				
Cha	Cranford's Adventure	500	7 Apr 1685	25/165;32/171
Cal	Potts' Folly	15	27 May 1687	25/329;33/684
Crawley, John:				
Dor	Whetstone Park	50	29 Jly 1687	25/409;32/695
Craycroft, Ignatius:				
PG	Craycroft's Purchase	235	10 Oct 1698	38/147
PG	Little Addition	122	10 Oct 1698	38/72
Cal	Timber Neck	265	30 Jun 1694	27/246
Craycroft, John of Calvert Co				
Bal	Craycroft's Purchase	300	1 Sep 1698	37/530

County	*Name of Tract*	*Acreage*	*Date*	*Reference(s)*
Crayker, Samuel:				
Tal	Ramah	300	27 Oct 1680	24/266;29/97
Creed, Bennett of Calvert Co:				
Bal	Creed's Beginning	223	1 Nov 1701	34/346
Cressey, Susanna & Mary, orphans of Samuel Cressey of Charles Co. deceased:				
StM	Proprietor's Gift	150	12 Apr 1683	29/211
Crolee—See Crowley.				
Cromwell, Richard, planter:				
Bal	Cromwell's Addition	16	12 Jan 1687	25/288;33/557
Bal	Cromwell's Range	200	10 Dec 1695	40/436
Cromwell, William:				
Bal	Hunting Quarter	134	30 May 1683	31/213
Bal	Phillip's Fancy	61	1 Apr 1682	24/498;30/24
Cropper, John:				
Som	Golden Valley	50	10 Sep 1683	29/469
Som	Hog Quarter	150	20 Feb 1682	24/393;29/462
Som	Hogsnorton	200	9 Oct 1683	25/57
Som	Point Lookout	150	6 Oct 1683	25/56
Som	Sturbridge	150	20 Feb 1682	24/393;29/432
Cropper, Nathaniel of Accomack, Virginia:				
Som	Friends' Assistance	500	1 Oct 1687	25/394;32/637
Crosse, John:				
AA	Angle	70	12 Sep 1682	24/464;31/409
AA	Level	264	11 Sep 1682	24/465;29/510
Cross, William:				
Tal	Leicester Fields	200	27 Jly 1687	25/342;33/666
Crouch, John:				
Cec	Crouch's Addition	70	28 Sep 1694	27/161
Crowch, Robert:				
Som	Bedlam Green	150	5 Oct 1681	25/27
Som	Crouch's Desire	100	10 Nov 1695	40/173
Som	Whitechapel Green	100	10 Nov 1695	40/144
Crowder, Thomas:				
Cal	Crowder's Lot	60	10 Mar 1683	24/512;32/18
Crowe, Gourny:				
Dor	Addition	116	17 Aug 1686	25/304;33/400
Dor	Crow's Lodge	50	16 May 1681	24/292;28/469
Dor	Crow's Lodge Addition	44	12 Apr 1682	24/422;31/244
Dor	Crowe's Nest	100	[18 Nov 1677]	24/139;28/92
Dor	East Billeny	56	18 Apr 1682	24/423;31/140
Crowly, Dennis & Daniel:				
Bal	Crowly's Contrivance	200	11 Mar 1700	30/347;38/153
Bal	Crowly's First Venture	100	- Dec 1699	30/337;38/156
Crowley [Crolee], John:				
Som	Crolee's Folly	50	30 May 1683	25/78;30/176

County	*Name of Tract*	*Acreage*	*Date*	*Reference(s)*
Crump, William of Chester River, planter:				
Tal	Crump's Chance	150	13 Mar 1682	24/399;31/290
Tal	Crump's Forest	300	29 Sep 1687	25/370;33/644
Tal	Crumpton	50	17 May 1681	24/337;29/391
Tal	Crumpton	220	1 Mar 1687	25/368;33/622
Tal	Plain Dealing	200	25 Oct 1682	24/491;31/529
Tal	Shrewsbury	300	10 Apr 1684	25/173;32/463
Tal	Triangle	50	11 Apr 1685	25/224;32/343
Culhoone, John:				
Som	Mates' Enjoyment	100	22 Oct 1685	25/279;33/509
Cullen, James of St. Mary's, gent:				
AA	Beale's Gift	200	1 Nov 1701	34/354
Bal	Cullen's Addition	500	25 Sep 1683	25/49
Bal	Cullen's Lot	300	17 Jun 1683	24/523
Bal	Hopewell	381	15 Jan 1687	25/383;32/578
Cullins, James:				
Dor	Shadwell	500	24 Oct 1684	25/145
Culpepper, Michael:				
Cal	Wolf's Quarter	19	20 Sep 1696	38/33
Culver, Henry:				
Cal	---?---	118	10 Nov 1697	39/23
Cupman, John of Somerset Co:				
Transported himself and wife Sarah bef. Aug 1681.				28/273
Currer, John:				
Transported by Robt Menteship of Talbot Co. bef. Nov 1680.				28/111
Currer, William:				
Deputy Surveyor for territory called New Ireland in Nov 1687.				
Currey, William:				
Som	Haphazard	125	22 Apr 1695	37/41
Som	Middle Neck	200	2 Aug 1695	37/126
Curtiss, James:				
Som	Adventure	200	8 Nov 1695	37/46
Som	Horse Hammock	100	1 Jly 1700	34/305
Curtis, Martin:				
Som	Friendship	500	1 May 1688	25/395;32/642
Curtice, William:				
Tal	Springfield Grange	64	10 Nov 1695	37/319
Cusack, Michael of Anne Arundel Co., surgeon:				
Bal	Cusack's Forest	596	26 May 1685	25/186
AA	Garratt's Town	59	20 Jun 1685	25/169;32/414
Bal	Welfare	104	24 Jun 1685	25/289;33/458
Dale, David:				
Som	Dale's Adventure	400	4 Dec 1679	24/115
Dalken, Joseph:				
Assignor of lands in Calvert Co. in Dec 1681.				24/358

County	Name of Tract	Acreage	Date	Reference(s)
Dalton, John:				
Assignor of lands in Talbot Co. in 1679.				24/224
Daniell, John:				
StM	Daniel's Dream	150	10 Jun 1683	31/41
Daniell, Thomas:				
Dor	Daniell's Helicon	150	28 Apr 1682	24/425;31/425
Dor	Daniell's Security	100	27 Apr 1682	24/409;31/158
Dor	Daniells' Elizium	200	12 May 1682	24/434;31/369
Dannier, Thomas, planter:				
Cha	Rowley	200	[17 Dec 1680]	24/255;29/109
Dant, Thomas:				
StM	Peterborough	100	23 Sep 1680	28/54
including land for time of service of Thomas Coverdale of St. Mary's Co.				
Dare, William, gent:				
Cec	Dare's Desire	200	2 Dec 1680	25/12
Cec	Glance	200	2 Dec 1680	25/12
Cec	Lower Triumph	500	16 Sep 1680	24/185;25/160;28/337
Cec	Newcastle Back Landing	480	17 Jly 1683	25/253;30/260
Cec	Travellers' Refreshment	320	22 May 1684	25/342
Cec	Two Necks	600	28 Jly 1684	25/160
Darling, Thomas:				
Bal	Hab Nab at a Venture	350	6 May 1689	34/55
Darnall [Darnell], Col. Henry:				
Cha	Addition	948	5 Apr 1685	25/267;32/606
PG	Batie's Purchase	53	18 Sep 1698	38/8
Cal	Bring	1,900	22 Feb 1682	25/1
Cal	Concord	406	10 Jan 1687	25/252;32/607
Bal	Convenience	400	2 Oct 1684	25/102;32/603
Cal	Darnall's Delight	1,900	28 Jun 1683	29/417
Cal	Darnall's Grove	3,800	8 Mar 1682	24/398
Cal	Exchange	229	-- Nov 1694	37/489
Cal	Forest	712	10 Nov 1695	40/228
Cha	Girls' Portion	1,776	20 Sep 1687	25/319;33/724
AA	Hill's Chance	215	14 Sep 1698	38/31
Bal	Land of Promise	2,000	5 Oct 1683	25/48;32/600
PG	Long Lane	22	18 Sep 1698	38/7
Bal	Northampton	1,500	10 Dec 1695	37/246
Cal	Outlet	925	1 Jun 1685	32/604
Cha	Potomack Landing	250	6 Apr 1685	25/166;32/605
Cal	Prevention	200	3 Sep 1684	25/157;32/601
Bal	Reserve	1,000	2 Oct 1684	25/114;32/602
Cal	Strife	200	4 Jly 1680	24/236;30/172
Darnall, John Esq. of Calvert Co:				
Bal	Affinity	1,500	4 Oct 1683	25/39;32/7
Bal	Darnall's Camp	1,000	7 Jun 1683	25/4;32/6
Knt	Durnell's Farm	600	15 Aug 1683	25/37
Knt	Darnall's Lot	400	15 Aug 1683	25/102
Bal	Darnall's Sylvania	500	28 Sep 1683	25/83;32/3

County	Name of Tract	Acreage	Date	Reference(s)
Darnall, John:				
Cal	Partnership	1,500	9 Nov 1680	24/196
See also under Lowe, Susan.				
Darnall, Susanna of Calvert Co., widow of John Darnall:				
Cha	Henrietta Maria	500	1 Apr 1685	25/211;32/315
Darnall, Col. William:				
PG	Exchange	289	[1698]	39/58
PG	Northampton	1,500	[1698]	39/59
Darnell—See Darnall.				
Dashiell, James Jr.:				
Som	Anything	137	10 Nov 1696	38/39
Dasheile, James:				
Som	Becknam	150	10 Aug 1683	29/447
Som	Long Hill	300	15 Jly 1684	25/133;33/195
Som	Wolf Trap Ridge	50	4 Jly 1702	35/378
Davenport, Humphrey of Talbot Co:				
Tal	Bath Addition	300	5 Aug 1681	24/373;30/74
Knt	Hemberry	600	18 Jun 1681	24/341;29/494
Knt	Sutton	400	12 Jun 1681	24/340;31/193
Tal	Welsh Ridge Addition	300	4 Aug 1681	24/373;33/389
Davis, Edward:				
StM	Davis's Hazard	200	24 Jly 1694	27/222
Davis, Elizabeth:				
Som	Maidstone	70	7 Feb 1682	28/398
Davis, Elizabeth, daughter of William Davis of Somerset Co				
Som	Maidstone	70	10 Jun 1680	24/309
Davis, Henry:				
Dor	Davis's Venture	100	3 Jly 1702	35/368
Davis, Isaac of Anne Arundel Co:				
Bal	Davis's Pasture	200	1 Jun 1700	34/279
Davis, John:				
Som	Battlefield	50	10 Feb 1683	25/22;31/536
Som	Sallop	100	1 Jly 1683	25/22;31/538
Tal	Addition	350	10 Mar 1696	37/324
Tal	Davis's Outlet	50	20 Oct 1681	24/380;31/117
Tal	Davis's Range	600	6 Apr 1685	25/171;32/118
Tal	Knave Keep Out	50	19 Apr 1683	29/228
Tal	Parsonage	100	18 Jun 1679	24/214;29/243
Davis, John of Talbot Co:				
Transported himself bef. November 1680.				28/100
Davis, Capt. John:				
Tal	Davis Phersalia	350	31 May 1696	37/446
Davis, Philip of Kent Co:				
Cec	Dullean's Folly	300	1 Dec 1682	24/450;29/377
including 150 acres for his own and Michael Judd's time of service.				

County	Name of Tract	Acreage	Date	Reference(s)
Davis, Richard, planter:				
Som	Davis's Chance	100	30 Aug 1679	24/290;29/428
Som	Marsh Ground	200	8 Feb 1696	37/117
Davis, Samuel:				
Som	Inch	500	18 Sep 1684	25/262;30/249
Davies, Thomas, planter:				
Dor	Barrel Green	200	8 May 1680	24/182;28/3209
Dor	Dublin	50	3 May 1683	25/49,122
Som	Inlargement	100	20 Nov 1686	25/284
Som	Kirk Minster	225	10 Mar 1696	37/130
Som	Troublesome	260	10 Nov 1695	37/518
Knt	Providence	100	8 Aug 1683	25/41
Davis, Walter, planter:				
Dor	Davis's Chance	50	20 Feb 1683	24/539;30/84
Dor	Pilgrim's Rest	50	-- Apr 1680	24/182;28/286
Davies, Walter Jr:				
Dor	Barrel Green	200	8 May 1680	24/182;28/320
Davis, William of Somerset Co:				
Dead by Jun 1680 leaving a daughter Elizabeth.				24/309
Davon, John:				
Transported by Thomas Browning of Cecil Co. by 1680.				24/105
Dawkin, Joseph:				
Cal	Joseph's Place	200	13 Nov 1682	24/481;29/276
Cal	Joseph's Reserve	196	27 Nov 1682	24/482
Dawson, Anthony who married Rebecca, daughter of Henry Osbourne of Dorchester Co:				
Dor	Alexander's Place	650	5 Oct 1680	28/59
Dawson, Edward of Talbot Co:				
Dor	Addition	146	1 Jun 1700	34/198;38/158
Dawson, John:				
StM	Preston	60	7 Mar 1683	24/487;29/413
Dawson, Ralph:				
Dor	Fair Play	100	14 May 1679	24/91
Day, Edward:				
Som	Cox's Discovery	745	15 May 1688	27/134
Som	Day's Beginning	295	15 May 1688	25/423;34/47
Som	Grantham	1,000	3 May 1683	24/532
Som	Providence	1,100	8 May 1683	24/533
Day, Richard:				
Cal	Day's Fortune	100	7 Mar 1682	24/405;29/402
Deakes, Edward:				
Som	Buck Lodge	150	17 Jun 1684	25/148;33/230
Deane, William of Charles Co:				
Transported himself bef. September 1680.				28/48

County	Name of Tract	Acreage	Date	Reference(s)
Dean, William, planter:				
Dor	Dean's Choice	100	[26 Feb 1679]	24/148
Dor	Dean's Pasture	25	29 May 1683	25/118;32/382
Knt	Deane's Adventure	213	10 Nov 1695	40/494
Knt	Deane's Relief	50	26 Jun 1680	24/186;28/195
Knt	Middle Branch	200	2 Aug 1686	25/257;30/326
Deavour, John:				
AA	Rattlesnake Neck	300	22 May 1683	25/7;31/444
Deavour, Richard:				
AA	Deavour's Range	280	29 Mar 1683	29/156
Debt, William:				
Cha	Whitehaven	890	10 Nov 1695	40/109
Deele, John, labourer:				
Som	Oak Hall	200	16 Dec 1686	25/335;33/612
Dehymossa, Joannes:				
Tal	Copartnership	373	1 Feb 1698	38/63
Delap, Abraham:				
AA	Essex	250	10 Nov 1692	39/22
Demondesse, Mme. Katherine:				
Cec	Katherine's Delight	100	17 Mar 1681	25/13
Cec	Katherine's Lot	100	2 Dec 1680	25/12
Demus, Grace:				
Transported by Robert Grover of Anne Arundel Co. before 1683.				
Denahoe, Daniel, planter:				
Som	Denahoe's Choice	207	15 Feb 1688	25/355
Som	Denahoe's Second Choice	350	28 May 1681	24/322;29/59
Som	Merchant's Treasure	150	9 Jun 1679	24/164;28/198
Som	Unlooked For	50	28 May 1681	24/322;29/464
Dennard, Lewin for transportation of his son Lewin:				
Som	Stonidge	50	23 Aug 1681	24/245;28/282
Dennis, Edmond of St. Mary's Co., gent:				
Bal	St. Dennis	500	18 Sep 1684	25/101;30/142
Dennis, James:				
Bal	Dennis's Choice	300	1 Mar 1699	38/142
Bal	Good Endeavour	139	10 Oct 1695	40/525
Bal	Land of Nod	300	1 Mar 1699	34/156
Dennis, Peter:				
Tal	Peter's Rest	50	8 Jly 1679	24/218;28/464
Dent, Mr. Peter:				
Som	New Wood Hall	200	15 Jly 1695	40/44
Dent, Thomas of Somerset Co:				
Transported 3 persons before Apr 1681.				28/174

County	Name of Tract	Acreage	Date	Reference(s)
Dent, William of St. Mary's Co., gent:				
Cha	Baltimore's Gift	70	5 May 1681	24/293
Cha	Friendship	391	10 Nov 1695	37/182
Cha	Friendship	1,571	10 Nov 1695	40/100
Cha	Guisborough	370	10 Nov 1695	37/208
Cha	Halifax	95	22 Dec 1687	25/322;33/693
Cha	Hopewell	521	3 Jly 1699	38/91
Cha	Lodge	189	3 Jun 1702	35/367
Denton, Henry:				
Cec	Askmore	550	8 Sep 1687	25/351;32/660
Denton, Henry of St. Mary's Co., gent:				
Tal	Clowdent	200	29 Oct 1687	25/363;32/664
Bal	Denton	600	31 Jly 1686	25/215
Tal	Denton Holme	600	19 Nov 1686	25/259;32/663
Dor	Denton Valley	400	4 Jly 1688	25/409;32/661
StM	Hackett's Choice	500	2 Apr 1684	25/154;33/27
Tal	Irish Discovery	350	24 Jun 1687	25/366
Cec	Morelow	150	8 Sep 1687	25/352;32/662
Tal	Sebergham	800	24 Jun 1687	25/299;32/659
StM	Warnell	240	4 Sep 1686	25/269;33/257
Denton, James:				
Bal	Denton's Hope	311	29 May 1679	24/148
Denwood, Levin, merchant:				
Som	Denwood's Den	300	18 Dec 1686	25/282;33/425
Som	Denwood's Inclusion	21	6 Mar 1687	25/278;33/375
Desharoone, Michael, planter:				
Som	Bullary's	100	30 Mar 1695	37/226
Som	Nova Francia	300	27 Nov 1685	25/233;33/303
Devenish, Robert:				
Tal	Devenish's Chance	500	24 Apr 1688	25/415;32/687
Tal	Lambeth	250	24 Apr 1688	25/416;32/688
Devorill, John:				
Assignor of lands in Somerset Co. in Aug 1679				24/41
Diamond, George:				
StM	Diamond's Adventure	110	14 May 1695	40/27
Dickenson, Edward:				
Som	Dickenson's Hope	300	15 Dec 1679	24/63
Som	Goose Marsh	50	[24 Oct 1679]	24/245;28/264
Dickenson, Somerset:				
Som	Green Park	200	10 Nov 1695	34/67;40/250
Dickenson, Thomas:				
Cha	Dickenson's Delight	133	20 Mar 1688	25/377;32/555
PG	Hare Hole	300	1 Aug 1698	38/79
Dickenson, Walter of Talbot Co:				
Dor	Holbourn	1,000	28 Aug 1679	24/219;28/414
Dor	Mount Andrew	300	18 Jan 1682	24/222;28/450
Dor	Plow Yard	200	29 Aug 1679	24/219

County	*Name of Tract*	*Acreage*	*Date*	*Reference(s)*
Dickenson, William:				
Tal	Corn Whitton	200	10 Nov 1695	37/291
Tal	Crossedore Addn.	220	10 Nov 1695	37/293
Tal	Dickenson's Lot	216	14 Aug 1688	25/411;32/682
Tal	Dickenson's Lot Addn	95	10 Nov 1695	37/296
Tal	Dickenson's Plain	860	22 Aug 1688	25/411;32/684
Tal	Swan Brook	770	23 Aug 1688	25/412;32/685
Dickson—See Dixon.				
Dicks, Robert, son of Robert Dicks of Dorechester Co. deceased:				
Dor	Robert's Chance	50	2 May 1682	24/429;31/398,404
Digges, Col. William:				
StM	Baltimore's Gift	650	3 Aug 1682	24/475;29/18
StM	Baltimore's Gift Addn.	115	9 Nov 1682	24/481
Tal	Brandford	1,050	13 May 1682	24/341;28/486
Som	Cedar Neck	366	30 Apr 1688	25/383;32/608
Som	Coard's Lot	430	27 Apr 1688	25/387
Cec	Courster's Refreshment	1,600	14 Jly 1683	25/91
Cha	Digges' Addition	295	7 Jly 1683	25/90
Som	Digges' Point	475	30 Apr 1688	25/384;32/599
Cha	Digges' Purchase	402	16 Jly 1683	25/91
Cha	Elizabeth's Delight	1,000	15 Dec 1688	25/425;32/658
Som	Fair Meadow	438	1 May 1688	25/384
Som	Rochester	500	2 May 1688	25/395
StM	St. Peter's	10	8 Mar 1687	25/255
Som	Springfield	486	1 May 1688	25/385
Dine, John:				
Knt	Limbrick	100	10 Nov 1695	40/105
Dison, Thomas:				
StM	Dison's Chance	60	24 Jly 1694	27/209
StM	St. John's	115	10 Dec 1694	37/238
Divillard, Jacob, surgeon:				
Cec	Smoking Point	50	7 Oct 1682	24/479;31/275
Dixon [Dickson], Thomas:				
Som	Dam Quarter	100	12 Jun 1683	25/74;32/173
Cha	Dickson's Lot	104	28 Dec 1687	25/321;33/692
Som	Dixon's Lot	1,000	10 Nov 1695	37/523
Dickson, Walter of Talbot Co:				
Dor	Plow Yard	200	16 Jan 1682	29/151
Dixon, William of Talbot Co:				
Knt	Cumberland	600	18 Oct 1683	25/142;32/80
Knt	Cum Witton	360	[26 Jun 1683]	25/102;32/126
Tal	Dixon's Lot	100	26 May 1681	24/346;31/218
Tal	Dixon's Outlet	200	23 Aug 1687	25/341;33/645
Dobbs, John:				
Knt	Barnstaple Hills	100	5 Mar 1686	32/73
Knt	Dobbs' Adventure	36	10 Nov 1695	34/117;40/247

County	Name of Tract	Acreage	Date	Reference(s)
Dodd, Peter, sawyer:				
Tal	Dodington	200	4 May 1687	25/340;33/659
Doddridge, John:				
AA	Doddridge's Forest	200	6 Mar 1697	34/142;40/365
Doe, William, miller:				
StM	Bissing	100	30 Nov 1682	24/513
StM	Bissingham	100	6 Mar 1682	24/396;29/506
Dol(e)bury, William:				
Dor	Howard's Lot	120	20 Mar 1681	24/297;28/380
Dor	North Walsham	1,000	18 Mar 1680	24/268;28/374
Dor	North Yarmouth	614	19 Mar 1680	24/268
Dollahyde, Francis:				
Bal	Francis's Choice	200	1 Nov 1701	34/361
Dons, Edward, planter:				
Bal	Range	200	11 Nov 1686	25/290;33/510
Bal	Mates' Affinity	200	1 Mar 1684	25/40;30/36
Dorman, John, gent:				
Som	Beech & Pine	100	15 Dec 1686	25/280;33/446
Dorman, Matthew:				
Som	Dorman's Purchase	150	9 Jan 1683	24/520
Som	Turkey Ridge	100	23 Mar 1688	25/358;33/676
Dormer, Margaret:				
Transported by John Abington of Calvert Co. before August 1680.				28/34
Dorrell, Nicholas:				
Cec	Michum	100	1 Oct 1683	25/291;33/512
Dorrill, Paul:				
AA	Dorrill's Inheritance	300	27 Mar 1683	29/155
AA	Dorrill's Luck	76	28 Mar 1687	25/312;33/410
Dorrum, John:				
Bal	Levy's Tribe Addition	50	14 Apr 1681	25/14
Dorsey, Maj. Edward:				
AA	Long Reach	448	12 Mar 1695	27/303
AA	Major's Choice	599	15 Oct 1687	25/345;33/717
AA	Major's Fancy	186	12 Mar 1695	27/323
Dorsey, John:				
AA	Dorsey's Adventure	400	3 Feb 1688	25/346;33/733
AA	Dorsey's Search	476	26 Mar 1696	40/352
AA	Hockly in the Hole	842	17 Mar 1684	25/36;30/225
AA	Troy	763	12 Oct 1694	27/288
Dorsey, Joshua:				
AA	Dorsey's Addition	50	19 Oct 1683	25/96;32/433
Dossey, William, planter:				
Dor	Dossey's Chance	130	29 Apr 1683	24/538;30/95

County	Name of Tract	Acreage	Date	Reference(s)
Douch, Hugh:				
Cec	Douch's Folly	150	14 Oct 1682	24/480;31/272
Dougherty, Nathaniel:				
Som	Little Usk	100	[22 Sep 1680]	24/185;28/230
Som	Meadow	50	10 Nov 1685	25/265;33/368
Som	Woover	100	3 Oct 1681	24/515
Doughty, John:				
Assignor of lands in Talbot Co. in Dec 1678.				24/207
Doughty, Peter:				
Som	St. Germain's	50	1 Jun 1702	35/362
Douglas, John:				
Cha	Douglas's Delight	4	22 Apr 1681	24/150;28/188
Douglas, Reynold:				
Lands granted to him in 1679 for transportation of himself, Ann his wife, & Mary & Martha his children.				24/78
Dowell, Philip:				
AA	Philip's Pillaged Lot		1 Jun 1700	34/239
Dowly, Peter:				
Dor	Chesake	100	26 Feb 1689	37/17
Downes, James:				
Tal	Downe's Forest	300	14 Nov 1681	24/448;31/186
Downes, James, son of James Downes of Talbot Co. and devisee by the 1680 will of Elizabeth Hopkinson, devisee under the 1676 will of her husband Jonathan Hopkinson:				
Tal	Hopton	300	20 Dec 1681	28/491
Downes, Robert:				
Som	Downes' Chance	62	11 May 1689	27/89
Downing, William:				
Cal	Bachelor's Rest	100	11 Jan 1684	25/21;31/493
Dowty, Peter:				
Som	Paris	150	3 Dec 1679	24/8
Doyne, Joshua of St. Mary's Co:				
Dor	Range	100	2 Apr 1683	24/490;29/348
Dor	Tinnah Serah	1,000	4 Jun 1683	25/102,123;30/138
Doyne, Mr. Robert of Charles Co:				
Cha	Carrickfergus	181	18 Jly 1688	25/378;32/570
Bal	Constant Friendship	1,000	2 Nov 1685	25/202;32/438
Som	Fairfield	442	2 May 1688	25/386;32/613
Som	Spring Bank	500	2 May 1688	25/386;32/612
Som	Meadfield	400	21 Aug 1686	25/232;33/291
Draper, Lawrence:				
AA	Chelsea	117	26 Mar 1696	34/132;40/368
AA	Maiden Croft	128	17 Jun 1688	25/403;32/618

County	*Name of Tract*	*Acreage*	*Date*	*Reference(s)*
Dregas, Deveroe:				
Transported by Stephen Cosden of Somerset Co. before July 1681.				28/198
Drisdale [Drisdell], Robert, tailor:				
Bal	Drisdell's Adventure	123	12 Jun 1688	25/444;34/54
Bal	Drisdale's Habitation	200	18 Sep 1683	25/84;32/404
Driskell, Dennis:				
Som	Kingsale	350	10 Jly 1695	37/140
Drury, Robert:				
StM	Dry Dockin Addition	100	20 Oct 1683	25/36;31/483
Dryden, Henry:				
Cha	Duke's Delight	227	10 Nov 1695	37/234
Dryer, Samuel:				
AA	Dryer's Inheritance	254	10 Mar 1696	40/333
Dudley, Richard:				
Tal	Dudley's Chance	200	26 Jun 1679	24/217;28/427
Tal	Dudley's Choice	200	29 Jly 1681	24/371;25/307;29/380
Tal	Dudley's Cliffs	200	27 Mar 1687	25/307;33/582
Tal	Dudley's Desire	200	3 Jun 1682	24/469;31/111
Tal	Dudley's Domaine	200	12 Feb 1680	24/227;33/576
Tal	Dudley's Inclosure	104	10 Nov 1695	34/93;40/256
Tal	Pakedy Ridge	100	8 Jan 1680	24/227
Duke, James:				
Cal	Everbrich	51	20 Dec 1688	25/428;34/21
Cal	Mary's Widower	30	10 Feb 1687	25/329;32/547
Cal	Short Come Off	22	25 Jly 1694	27/244
Duke, Mary:				
Cal	Mary Dukedom	100	19 Dec 1681	24/358;31/24
Dukes, Robert:				
Som	Hog Hummock	100	28 May 1681	24/321;29/10
Duncan, Elizabeth, widow & executrix of James Duncan:				
Som	Beyond Expectation	500	10 May 1695	40/572
Dunken, Patrick:				
AA	Dunken's Luck	52	25 Feb 1685	25/188;33/399
AA	Neglect	30	14 May 1683	29/280
AA	Wardrope Ridge	100	12 May 1683	29/281
Duncan, Thomas:				
Som	Contentment	150	3 May 1686	25/264;33/354
Dunlap, Ninian:				
Som	Dunlap's Choice	100	1 Aug 1688	27/49
Dunn, John:				
Cec	Dunn's Folly	120	10 Jly 1696	37/470
Tal	Dunn's Range	200	18 Jun 1679	24/215;29/244
Durbin, Thomas:				
Bal	Hab Nab at a Venture	350	30 Jun 1688	25/440

County	*Name of Tract*	*Acreage*	*Date*	*Reference(s)*
Bal	Thomas's Addition	18	2 Apr 1682	24/498;30/37
Bal	Westminster	18	2 Apr 1682	24/498;30/50
Durden, John:				
AA?		50	8 Jly 1682	24/400
Duvall, John:				
AA	Duvall's Delight	1,000	10 Dec 1695	34/133;40/323
AA	Duvall's Range	708	16 Nov 1694	27/292
AA	What You Will	373	1 Jun 1700	38/153;30/344
Duvall, Mareen:				
Cal	Netland	200	22 Jan 1659	24/67
Eaglestone, Bernard:				
AA	Eaglestone's Range	206	23 Sep 1680	28/55
Ealor, Elizabeth:				
Transported by Francis Wine bef. Sep 1680.				28/116
Eames, Joseph:				
Som	Mates' Enjoyment	100	22 Oct 1685	25/279;33/509
Earle, Thomas:				
Tal	Discovery	530	[21 May 1696]	37/515
Early, John:				
Dor	Cheshire	24	29 Apr 1682	24/427;31/150
Eavens, John:				
Som	Troy	50	28 May 1681	24/316
Eccleston, Hugh of Somerset Co:				
Dor	Eccleston's Hill	200	10 Oct 1695	40/576
Dor	Retaliation	940	1 Sep 1701	34/338
Edelen, Richard, Deputy Surveyor for St. Mary's Co:				
Cha	Friendship	258	16 Jan 1688	25/376;37/371
Edge, Daniel:				
AA	Edge's Addition	50	22 Jun 1683	25/55;31/455
Edloe, Edward:				
Cal	Edloe's Adventure	300	10 Dec 1695	40/559
Edloe, Joseph, gent:				
Cal	Edloe's Addition	37	23 Jan 1681	24/256;29/94
Cal	Edlow's Hope	400	10 Jun 1685	33/117
Cal	Edlow's Lot	400	1 Jun 1685	33/241
Cal	Forest of Harvey	400	8 Aug 1681	24/197;28/305
Cal	Parke	300	17 Feb 1682	24/362;31/17
Edmunsun, Archibald:				
Bal	Beale's Camp	1,000	10 Nov 1695	37/384
Edmondson, John, attorney & merchant of Talbot Co., apprentice of John Horne of Talbot Co. in 1660:				24/485
Tal	Adventure	400	10 Dec 1679	24/86

County	***Name of Tract***	***Acreage***	***Date***	***Reference(s)***
Tal	Clifton	160	16 Aug 1680	24/172;28/421
Tal	Desire	200	2 Nov 1678	24/147,198
Tal	Desire's Addition	60	16 Aug 1680	24/172;28/420
Tal	Eastwood Point	40	17 May 1682	24/489
Tal	Heworth	700	25 May 1682	24/489
Tal	Hickory Ridge	150	[9 Feb 1678]	24/148;29/114
Tal	Pocoason	100	17 Aug 1680	24/172;28/422
Dor	Range	400	28 May 1682	24/437;31/90
Cal	Rocky Point	360	25 Jan 1683	24/451;31/69
Dor	Willenbrough	980	16 Mar 1680	24/266
Edmonson, William:				
Tal	Out Range Addn.	824	27 Jly 1696	37/527
Edwards, John:				
Dor	Edwards' Adventure	50	12 Nov 1680	24/257;29/135
Edwin, William:				
Knt	Edwin's Addition	240	10 Mar 1696	40/495
Elbart, Hugh:				
Bal	Dogwood Ridge	99	27 Dec 1687	25/349;33/716
Elder, John:				
Cha	Elder's Fancy	31	10 Jly 1695	37/275
Cha	Elder's Lot	179	10 Jly 1695	37/251
Eldersley, Henry:				
Assignor of lands in Cecil Co. in Nov 1680.				25/11
Cec	Folorn Hope	150	1 Oct 1697	38/148
Elgate, William Sr:				
Som	Blackwall/Blackwater	25	[5 May 1679]	24/244;28/275
Som	Elgate's Lot	100	10 Jun 1680	24/310
Som	Jeshimon	150	17 May 1688	25/424;32/713
Som	Supply	25	[5 May 1679]	24/244;28/388
Elgate [Elget], William Jr. planter:				
Som	Friends' Assistance	300	19 Dec 1685	25/236;33/358
Ellett, Edward:				
Tal	Ellett's Folly	100	26 Nov 1685	25/223;32/339
Tal	Ellett's Lot	276	10 Nov 1695	40/212
Elliot, Daniel:				
Cha	Bersheba	47	10 Nov 1695	37/245
Cha	Dan	209	10 Oct 1695	37/235
Elliot, Henry:				
Dor	Henry's Choice	50	7 May 1682	24/433;31/368
Elliott, John:				
Tal	Elliott's Addition	100	29 May 1681	24/337;31/287
Ellyott, William:				
Som	Point Patience	143	1 Jly 1695	37/231
Ellis, James of Anne Arundel Co., gent:				
Bal	James' Park	500	28 Sep 1683	25/111;33/50

County	Name of Tract	Acreage	Date	Reference(s)
Ellis, John:				
Knt	Ellis's Chance	1,000	10 Nov 1695	40/124
Ellis, Peter, gent:				
Bal	Expectation	350	25 Sep 1683	25/39;30/50
Bal	Parker's Court	150	25 Sep 1683	25/84;30/42
Ellis, Robert:				
Tal	Wrexham's Plains	500	1 Nov 1679	24/224;29/261
Ellis, Thomas:				
Cha	Mount Arrarat	140	10 Nov 1695	38/72
Elmes, William:				
Cec	Ashby Green	200	31 May 1696	37/449
Elsie [Elzey], Arnold:				
Som	Partners' Choice	150	1 Mar 1684	25/58
Elsie [Elzay], Peter:				
Som	Chance	50	2 Oct 1683	25/28
Som	Gladstones' Adventure	150	17 Sep 1687	25/300;33/599
Som	Gladstones' Choice	150	17 Sep 1687	25/301,326;33/601
Elston, Ralph:				
Tal	Byldon	100	17 Jun 1679	24/116
Tal	Exchange	100	28 Mar 1682	24/403;29/409
Emerson, John:				
Tal	Ephraim's Hope	100	20 Dec 1688	27/191;34/87
Tal	Vincent's Lot	43	26 Jun 1688	25/412;32/690
Tal	[3 tracts]	398	1 Apr 1697	38/58
Emerton, Humphrey:				
AA	Emerton's Addition	20	25 Jun 1680	28/38
AA	Emerton's Range	130	28 Jun 1680	28/42
Emery, Arthur, planter:				
Tal	Emery's Addition	50	18 Sep 1684	25/225;32/348
Tal	Emery Paxton	372	4 May 1687	25/313;33/581
Tal	Emery's Neglect	125	6 Dec 1682	24/493
Emery, George:				
			10 Oct 1695	40/474
Cec	High Park	222	10 Nov 1695	40/476
Emmett, Abraham, planter:				
Som	Brent Marsh	400	2 Apr 1686	25/266;30/259
Som	Lymson	200	5 Apr 1688	25/423;34/49
[assigned from John Emmett]				
Som	Partners' Contentment	500	2 Apr 1686	25/278;33/441
Emmett, John:				
Som	Enlargement	300	18 Sep 1684	25/261; 33/357,381
Som	Pander's Neglect	200	20 May 1680	25/27;33/224
Cha	Seaman's Delight	504	10 Apr 1695	37/158
English, Dennis:				
Cec	Sinclare's Purchase:	100	1 Aug 1679	24/72

County	Name of Tract	Acreage	Date	Reference(s)
Inglish, Edward of Cecil Co::				
Cec	Cheapside	500	20 Sep 1683	25/107
Inglish, James:				
Som	Sulekirke	50	15 Jun 1683	25/55
English, John:				
Cec	Rumford	200	19 Jun 1683	29/321
Ennals, Bartholomew, gent:				
Dor	Addition	63	21 Nov 1677	24/183
Dor	Angle	87	21 Nov 1677	24/183;28/381
Dor	Bartholomew's Neck Addn.	63	26 Nov 1681	28/374
Dor	Gore	265	10 May 1687	25/303;33/409
Dor	Howard's Lot	120	20 Mar 1681	24/297;28/380
Dor	Island	50	13 Dec 1681	28/382
Dor	North Walsham	1,000	18 Mar 1680	24/268;28/374
Dor	North Yarmouth	614	19 Mar 1680	24/268;28/382
Ennalls, Mr. Thomas:				
Dor	Cam? Garden	64	10 Nov 1697	39/25
Dor	Ennall's Chance	119	10 Nov 1697	39/26
Dor	Norage	300	10 Nov 1697	39/27
Dor	Partnership	1,170	10 Nov 1697	39/23
Ensom, Robert of Talbot Co:				
His time of service completed by 1679.				24/119
Erickson, Matthew of Kent Co:				
Knt	Erickson's Islands	20	26 Sep 1681	24/304;29/235
Knt	Mary's Portion	150	10 Jun 1682	25/1;31/479
Knt	Matthew's Enlgmnt.	155	10 Nov 1695	40/103
Knt	Sarah's Portion	150	25 Sep 1681	24/304;28/434
assigned from Elizabeth, relict & administratrix of John Erickson deceased.				
Evans, Anthony:				
StM	Poplar Hill	63	8 Mar 1682	24/406;31/62
Evans, Benjamin:				
Cal	Good Luck	100	8 Sep 1688	25/431;34/22
Evans, Charles:				
StM	Evans' Lot	26	10 Aug 1687	25/320;33/608
Evans, Edward:				
StM	Content	99	8 Mar 1688	25/380;32/560
StM	Evans' Reserve	100	[16 Feb 1679]	24/148;28/201
Som	Harry Gate	500	15 Dec 1683	25/131;30/179
Cha	Poole	215	10 Jun 1695	37/249
Evans, Job of Anne Arundel Co:				
Bal	Beale's Purchase	141	10 Jly 1700	34/216
Bal	Friend's Discovery	1,000	12 Jun 1694	27/313
Evans, John, planter:				
Som	Fox Hall	50	14 Feb 1683	25/81;30/248
Som	Little Monmouth	100	21 Sep 1681	28/269
Som	Troy	50	1 Apr 1682	29/077

County	*Name of Tract*	*Acreage*	*Date*	*Reference(s)*
Evans, John of St. Mary's Co:				
Cha	Salcom	300	21 Sep 1685	25/267;30/308
Evans, Obadiah:				
Cal	Rich Neck	121	22 Jan 1684	25/79
Evans, Richard of Calvert Co:				
Cha	Barbador	250	30 Mar 1685	25/164;30/192
Cal	Evans's Range	800	1 May 1696	37/199
Cha	Green's Delight	200	1 Jun 1686	25/226;30/193
Evans, Robert of Talbot Co:				
Dor	Poplar Ridge	290	16 Feb 1683	24/538;30/89
Tal	Stamford Point	100	17 Jun 1679	24/110
Evans, Thomas:				
Transported himself.				31/274
Evans, Walter of Calvert Co:				
Cha	Evans' Range	100	16 Mar 1685	25/164;32/428
Cha	Little Worth	78	10 Mar 1696	37/173
PG	Nameless	230	30 Dec 1698	30/351;38/144
Cha	Stony Hill	98	3 Apr 1685	25/266;30/271
Evats, Nathan:				
Granted land called New Forest in Kent Co. before 1680.				24/187
Everden, Thomas:				
Som	Everden's Lot	500	16 Jly 1689	27/2
Everenden, Thomas:				
Som	Flat Land	850	10 Jun 1696	37/460
Everet, Joseph:				
Knt	Hatchbury	50	[15 Apr 1682]	24/400;31/219
Everet, Philip:				
Knt	Hatchbury	50	[15 Apr 1682]	24/400;31/219
Everat, Richard:				
AA	Stony Hills	36	10 Jan 1696	34/126;40/328
Everett, Thomas of Calvert Co., planter:				
Bal	Bennett's Range	50	15 Dec 1683	25/86;33/121
Fairbank [Farebank], David, planter:				
Tal	Bradford	62	10 Aug 1686	25/296;33/486
Tal	Farebank's Chance	195	1 Oct 1700	34/302
Tal	Jones's Hole	36	10 Nov 1695	37/373
Tal	Wisbech	60	10 Aug 1686	25/339;33/658
Tal	Yorke	100	17 Jly 1680	24/174;28/180
Fanning, John of Charles Co., gent:				
Bal	Buck Range	750	19 Oct 1681	24/502;30/126
Cha	Fanning's Adventure	100	10 Jly 1683	24/524
Cha	Saturday's Work	250	2 Oct 1680	24/178;29/205

County	*Name of Tract*	*Acreage*	*Date*	*Reference(s)*
Farewell, Richard, gent:				
Som	New Wood Hall	200	10 Nov 1686	25/277
Farguson—See Ferguson.				
Farmer, Samuel:				
Tal	Rogue Keep Off	50	10 Nov 1695	34/97
Farn, Thomas of Dorchester Co:				
His time of service completed in 1680.				24/85
Farnell, Thomas, planter:				
Som	Bower	200	17 Jun 1684	25/107
Som	Good Neighbourhood	200	24 Nov 1686	25/235;33/342
Farrow, Charles:				
Tal	Maxfield	100	10 Nov 1695	34/94;40/229
Faulkes—See Foulkes.				
Falkner, John:				
Cha	Chairman's Purchase	200	1 Jun 1685	33/35
Faulkner, Martin:				
AA	Martin's Rest	150	23 Sep 1680	28/64
Faulkner, Thomas, carpenter:				
Tal	Faulkner's Folly	100	4 Jly 1679	24/218;33/154
Tal	Faulkner's Levels	150	5 Oct 1687	25/370;33/627
Tal	Faulkner's Square	200	5 Oct 1687	25/371;33/651
Faucett, John:				
Som	Long Lot	80	30 May 1689	27/75
Fawsett, Rhodah:				
Som	Golden Valley	250	6 Dec 1681	24/448
Febus, George:				
Som	Cow Quarter	60	6 Dec 1688	27/30
Som	Little Worth	200	1 Jun 1689	27/127
Felkes, Edward:				
Bal	Felkes' Range	200	14 Aug 1688	25/443;34/57
Bal	Felkes' Rest	200	2 Dec 1688	25/443;34/56
Bal	Good Hope	200	12 Aug 1696	40/508
Felpes—See Phelps.				
Fendall, James of Brighthelmstone, England, mariner:				
Tal	Brighthelmstone	100	[2 Jly 1682]	24/554
Fenwick, Thomas:				
Som	Cow's Quarter	500	14 Apr 1686	25/276;33/443
Som	Dumfries	500	5 May 1687	25/336;34/51
Som	Fenwick's Choice	500	12 Apr 1686	25/276;32/493
Som	Scottish Plot	400	4 May 1687	25/336;32/708
Ferguson, George, carpenter:				
Dor	Betty's Lot	100	[20 Oct 1678]	24/145;28/97

County	*Name of Tract*	*Acreage*	*Date*	*Reference(s)*
Dor	Edinbrough	100	29 Apr 1682	24/427;31/370
Dor	Farguson's Forest	150	12 Jun 1683	25/120;32/410
Ferris, Charles, planter:				
Tal	Dancey	440	14 Feb 1687	25/230;32/329
Ferry, Capt. John:				
Bal	Ferry's Range	289	30 Nov 1697	38/16
Bal	Long Point	50	10 Nov 1695	38/81
Ficksimons, Nicholas:				
Bal	Cordwainers' Hall	300	10 May 1696	37/412
Fiddeman, Richard, planter:				
Tal	Fiddeman's Choice	100	26 Nov 1685	25/295;33/485
Tal	Fortune	121	10 Mar 1696	37/497
Fillpotts—See Philpotts				
Finch, Guy:				
Cal	Woodbridge	118	15 Sep 1684	25/128
Finley, James:				
Cha	Leith	100	25 Jun 1685	25/167;33/90
Fish, Edmund:				
Tal	Stapleton	77	27 Jun 1688	25/412;32/668
Fish, James:				
Transported by William Peirce of Cecil Co. before November 1681.				24/383
Fishborne, Ralph:				
Tal	Fishborne's Landing	104	1 Dec 1694	37/34
Tal	Fishborne's Lot	150	12 Aug 1680	24/171;29/200
Fisher, Alexander:				
Dor	Barren Point	40	8 Nov 1680	24/279;28/501
Dor	Elson	50	8 Nov 1680	24/279;28/495
Dor	Little Worth	10	8 Nov 1680	24/279;28/411
Fisher, Edward, cooper:				
Dor	Fisher's Landing	50	3 May 1682	24/431;31/156
Dor	Fisher's Title	100	27 Apr 1682	24/425;31/379
Dor	Weston	50	15 May 1682	24/455
Fisher, Edward of St. Mary's, planter:				
Tal	Nuthead's Choice	300	4 Apr 1687	25/295;33/371
Fisher, Mary:				
Transported by William Peirce of Cecil Co. bef. Nov 1681.				24/383
Fisher, Samuel:				
Transported by John Edmondson bef. Nov 1680				28/57
Fisher, Thomas, gent:				
Tal	Freshford	2,000	29 Sep 1685	25/219;33/467
Tal	Long Range	147	7 Aug 1688	25/411;32/674
Fisher, William:				
Assignor of lands in Cecil Co. in 1680.				24/66

County	*Name of Tract*	*Acreage*	*Date*	*Reference(s)*
Fitch, Edmond, planter:				
Tal	Fitch's Range	74	15 Aug 1684	25/297;33/456
Floyd, James:				
AA	Floyd's Adventure	320	10 Mar 1696	40/307
Floyd, James of Baltimore Co:				
AA	Floyde's Beginning	230	24 May 1683	25/8;31/513
Floyd, John:				
AA	Floyd's Chance	60	17 Jun 1686	25/249;30/272
Fluellin, Samuel:				
Som	Clear of Cannon Shot	100	25 Nov 1685	25/265;33/369
Som	Clear of Cannon Shot	50	1 Nov 1696	38/74
Som	Flewellin's Purchase	50	10 Nov 1696	38/116
Som	Milk More	50	1 Nov 1696	38/70
Flyharty, John & Margaret:				
	Transported bef. Aug 1680 by William Jones of Bristol.			28/31
Forbas, Alexander:				
Tal	Condeewhire	77	1 Jun 1700	34/229
Tal	Primus	96	1 Jun 1700	34/192;38/152
Forbus, James & Elizabeth—See under Sharpe, William.				
Foord, Abraham:				
PG	Lemster	127	1 Jun 1700	34/197;38/157
Forde, Thomas of Ann Arundell Co:				
Bal	Rockford	300	25 Jun 1680	28/14
Foorde, William:				
	Assignor of lands in Dorchester Co. in 1679.			24/200
Forrest, Jane of Calvert Co:				
	Transported by Samuel Gibson.			24/4
Forrest, John:				
Cal	Forest	225	18 Jun 1680	28/39
Forrester, John:				
Dor	[unnamed]	245	6 Oct 1684	25/292;33/435
Fort, John:				
	Transported by John Richens bef. Oct 1680.			28/97
Foscue, Simon of Accomack, Virginia:				
Som	Sand Down	500	9 Jan 1686	25/261;33/337
Foskin, Simon:				
Som	Basingstoke	400	10 Nov 1695	40/185
Fosse, John:				
StM	Shocke Park	100	15 Feb 1683	24/487;29/354
Fossitt, William:				
Som	New Invention	425	1 Jan 1695	37/80
Foster, John:				
Dor	Crooked Billet	15	10 Nov 1695	37/265

County	Name of Tract	Acreage	Date	Reference(s)
Foulkes, Margaret, daughter of Thomas Foulkes:				
Dor	Milverton	50	25 Dec 1681	24/416;31/344
Foulkes, Nicholas:				
Dor	Taunton	200	28 Dec 1681	24/417;29/410
Foulkes, Thomas:				
Dor	Foulkes' Content	100	28 Apr 1682	24/426;31/159
Dor	Foulkes' Delight	250	25 May 1682	24/438;31/362
Dor	Ill Favoured Coomb	50	26 May 1682	24/440;30/104
Dor	Welcome	100	28 May 1682	24/438;31/177
Fountain, Nicholas, planter:				
Som	Double Purchase	80	20 Oct 1680	24/307;28/409
Som	Newfound Land	20	20 Oct 1680	24/307;28/387
Som	Nova Francia	100	30 Aug 1679	24/290;29/480
Fowke, Amy of Somerset Co:				
Transported by Thomas Dent bef. Apr 1681.				28/174
Fowle, Roger:				
StM	Fowle's Discovery	100	16 Oct 1680	24/185
Fowler, Edward:				
Som	Walbrooke	260	10 Oct 1695	37/58
Fowler, John:				
Cal	Fowler's Delight	100	24 Dec 1683	25/20;31/534
Foxcroft, Capt. Isaac of Northampton Co., Virginia:				
Som	Supply	750	15 Jly 1684	25/135;32/289
Foxon, James:				
Dor	Bellgrave	66	7 Apr 1697	35/402
Frampton, Robert, planter:				
Tal	Frampton	122	24 Feb 1686	25/246
Frances, Capt. Thomas:				
AA	Brustrey Neck	390	7 Oct 1683	25/106
Francis, Thomas of Ann Arundell Co., gent:				
Cec	Francis' Enlargement	500	6 Apr 1681	25/14;31/442
Bal	Francis's Freedom	1,000	[29 Sep 1693]	40/469
Bal	Holland's Lot	400	15 Sep 1678	24/162;29/260
Francis, Thomas & Mary—See under Young, Samuel.				
Frank, John Peter:				
Som	Lozenge	100	4 Jun 1688	25/397
Freake, Henry:				
Som	Fladders	50	2 Jly 1683	25/31
Freeborne, Thomas:				
AA	Freeborne's Enlargement	80	17 Oct 1694	27/328
AA	Freeborne's Progress	600	10 Dec 1695	40/321
Freeman, Ann:				
PG	Freeman's Lot	221	1 Jun 1699	34/194;38/145

County	Name of Tract	Acreage	Date	Reference(s)
Freeman, Henrick, planter:				
Cec	Matson's Range	30	9 Oct 1682	24/479;31/264
Freeman, John:				
Som	Freeman's Contentment	400	30 Apr 1686	25/277;33/521
Som	Teague's Content	160	15 Jly 1695	40/62
Som	Unpleasant	240	15 Jly 1695	40/60
Freeman, Joseph:				
Som	Freeman's Discovery	500	22 Sep 1683	25/64
Freer, John:				
Transported by Thomas Maisterman bef. Sep 1680.				28/53
Frisby, James, gent:				
Cec	Baltimore Field	33	1 Nov 1696	38/29
Cec	Dulleam's Folly	300	1 Dec 1682	24/450
Cec	Frisby's Farm	300	7 Oct 1681	24/347;28/419
Cec	Frisby's Forest	170	4 Jun 1682	24/469;29/300
Cec	Frisby's Meadows	1,000	30 Nov 1682	24/506,552;31/299
Cec	Frisby's Purchase	50	27 Feb 1683	24/551;31/302
Cec	Hopeful Unity	150	12 May 1682	24/454
Frisby, William:				
Knt	Swan Island	18	4 Aug 1686	25/256;30/281
Frith, Henry:				
Tal	Frith's Fortune	58	10 Nov 1695	37/301
Frizell, James of Ann Arundell Co:				
Bal	Knavery Discovered	400	1 Nov 1701	34/329
Frizell, John, planter:				
Som	Frizell's Enjoyment	150	12 Nov 1685	25/236;33/323
Som	Hungry Quarter	200	7 Oct 1695	37/44
Frezell, John:				
Dor	Galloway	50	9 Nov 1679	24/164;29/242
Frisell, William:				
AA	Friendship	30	3 May 1682	24/410;29/484
Fry, Francis, planter:				
Bal	Hazard	100	29 Sep 1682	25/1;30/67
Fugat, James:				
Bal	Fugat's Fork	300	14 Sep 1683	25/37
Bal	North Yarmouth	200	14 Sep 1683	25/37;30/127
Fuller, Edward, planter:				
Tal		50	[15 Oct 1680]	24/200
Tal	Old Woman's Folly	50	16 Oct 1680	24/207;28/304
Fuller, John, planter:				
Bal	Buck's Range	148	6 Feb 1688	25/345;33/709
Bal	Fuller's Outlet	100	11 Jan 1686	25/244;30/304
Bal	Huntington	300	1 Sep 1698	38/123
Furatt, Peter, planter:				
Bal	Peter's Addition	100	29 Dec 1685	25/244;30/306

County	*Name of Tract*	*Acreage*	*Date*	*Reference(s)*
Furlong, Edward:				
Som	Apes Hole		2 Dec 1679	24/51
Furnice [Furniss], William, planter:				
Som	Fair Spring	300	29 Jly 1680	24/273;28/542
Som	Hopewell	300	17 Dec 1683	25/139
Furrs, John:				
Som	New Recovery	288	28 Nov 1682	24/519
Gabb, Joyles of Calvert Co:				
Transported by Thomas Window bef. Aug 1681.				28/305
Gadsby, John:				
AA	Gadsby's Adventure	33	20 Dec 1694	27/301;34/115
Gaines, William:				
Bal	Waltowne	156	2 Jun 1682	24/502
Gaither, John:				
AA	Abington	364	10 May 1701	34/375
AA	Polecat Hill	391	21 Feb 1684	25/184;33/380
AA	Roundabout Hill	120	16 Jun 1686	25/274;33/396
Galloway, Richard of Anne Arundel Co:				
Dor	Barren Island	700	3 Sep 1698	34/150
AA	Favour	115	20 Jun 1682	24/460;30/234
Galloway, Samuel:				
AA	Gift	115	20 Jun 1682	24/460;30/233
Galloway, William:				
Cec	Galloway's Choice	200	9 Apr 1684	25/342
Cec	Galloway's Farm	286	14 May 1695	40/22
Gamling, James:				
Cha	Pasture	129	5 May 1686	25/271;33/455
Gant, Thomas:				
Cal	Bullwick	213	28 Dec 1688	25/426;34/23
Gardiner [Gardner], Edward:				
AA	March	110	7 Jun 1673	25/257;33/280
Gardiner, Mr. Luke:				
StM	Gardiner's 2nd Addn.	250	10 Nov 1695	40/127
StM	Gardiner's 3rd Addn.	119	5 Oct 1695	40/5
StM	Gardiner's 4th Addn.	400	5 Oct 1695	40/19
StM	Fourth Addition	83	30 Jly 1695	27/350
StM	Gardiner's Chance	155	1 Oct 1700	34/255
Gardiner, Marjery, widow of Richard Gardiner:				
Cal	Marjery	200	15 Jly 1694	27/294
Cal	Parting Path	300	10 Nov 1694	27/296
Gardner, Mary:				
AA	Luck	155	27 Aug 1684	25/143;33/169
Gardiner, Richard:				
Transported 5 persons [unnamed] bef. Sep 1680.				28/71

County	Name of Tract	Acreage	Date	Reference(s)
StM	Collewood	100	1 Jun 1685	33/38
Cal	Margery	200	10 Jan 1681	24/238
Gardner, Richard, son & heir of Luke Gardner deceased:				
StM	St. John's Landing	300	1 Jun 1687	33/560
Garland, William:				
Transported by Mark Cordea bef. Sep 1680.				28/51
Garret, John:				
Som	Hopewell	100	27 Jun 1679	24/263
Gary, Richard:				
StM	Hard Shift	50	13 May 1684	25/107;33/32
Gary, Stephen, gent:				
Dor	Gary's Rest	400	17 Nov 1679	24/184;28/325
Gary, William:				
Tal	Dirty Weeden	100	25 Jun 1689	27/181
Tal	Dirty Weeden Addition	100	10 Nov 1695	37/390
Tal	Fortune	52	10 Nov 1695	40/181
Tal	Gary's Delight	50	22 Dec 1678	24/207
Tal	Knightley's Addition	50	22 Dec 1678	24/207
Gase, Thomas & Ann his wife:				
Transported by Robert Menteship bef. November 1680				28/111
Gaskins, William:				
Tal	Gaskins' Pasture	50	27 Mar 1682	24/403
Gassaway, Maj. Nicholas:				
Bal	Gassaway's Addition	280	24 Oct 1683	25/83;33/96
Gates, Jane, wife of Joseph Gates, & Jane Gates their daughter:				
AA	White's Ford	1,000	20 Jly 1693	27/147
Gates, Mary:				
Transported by John Abington of Calvert Co. bef. Aug 1680.				28/34
Gates, Robert, carpenter:				
StM	Gates' Swamp	192	2 Sep 1687	25/350;32/523;33/701
StM	New Branford	375	27 Jan 1687	25/323;33/604
StM	St. Michael's	100	28 Jan 1687	25/323;33/610
Gatton, Thomas:				
Cha	Hiccory Plains	300	20 Dec 1695	37/197
Gawthering, Matthew:				
Cal	Fried Bacon	7	20 May 1687	25/330;32/514
Geffe, Thomas:				
AA	Geffe's Increase	180	3 Jly 1684	25/95
Gelley—See Jelley.				
Genty, Joseph:				
Dor	Genty Marsh	510	10 Nov 1695	37/495
George, Samson:				
Cec	Small Hope	8	2 Aug 1686	25/328;33/729

County	*Name of Tract*	*Acreage*	*Date*	*Reference(s)*
Gery, Lawrence:				
Som	Pander's Neglect	200	18 May 1680	25/27
Gibbs, Edward:				
Som	Cox's Choice	300	16 Dec 1686	25/281
AA	Jornston Hill	115	10 May 1687	25/346;33/731
Gibbs, William:				
AA	Gibbs' Folly	200	5 Jly 1684	25/116;32/312
Gibson, Batt:				
Transported by John Abington of Cal Co. bef. Aug 1680.				28/34
Gibson, Michael:				
Bal	Gunn's Lot	500	8 Jun 1683	25/3
Gibson, Miles, gent:				
Bal	Ann's Lot	500	[10 Aug 1684]	30/65
Bal	Delph's Neglect	120	13 Mar 1684	25/49;30/23
Bal	Gibson's Marsh	200	20 Jun 1683	30/44
Bal	Gibson's Neck	200	3 Sep 1683	25/40
Bal	Gibson's Park	800	19 Sep 1683	25/58
Bal	Gibson's Ridge	500	19 Sep 1683	25/42;30/63
Bal	Portugall's Purchase	100	20 May 1683	29/413
Gibson, Thomas, planter:				
Cha	Gibson's Pound	42	3 Oct 1684	25/242;30/278
Gilbert, John:				
Knt	[unnamed]	98	10 Aug 1695	40/7
Gilbert, Thomas:				
Bal	Gilbert's Adventure	150	10 Nov 1695	34/102;40/217
Giles, William:				
Som	Silas's Lot	450	9 Aug 1695	37/217
Gilley—See Jelley				
Girling, Richard:				
Tal	Buckland Marsh	50	26 Sep 1683	25/44;31/529
Gist, Christopher:				
Bal	Low Neck	100	11 Jun 1683	25/3;30/18
Givan, James:				
Som	Dungivan	200	19 Jun 1689	27/98
Som	Green	150	1 Mar 1689	27/54
Givan, Robert:				
Som	Flower Field	165	4 Jly 1702	35/380
Som	Givan's Last Choice	200	19 Jun 1689	27/90
Som	Givan's Lot	150	1 Mar 1689	27/112
Gwin—See Gwyn.				
Gladstones, John:				
Som	Dublin	300	24 Apr 1684	25/127;30/220

County	Name of Tract	Acreage	Date	Reference(s)
Gladstones, John of Dorchester Co:				
Som	Gladstones' Adventure	150	15 Jun 1682	25/300
Som	Gladstones' Choice	150	2 Nov 1682	25/301,326
Som	Gladstones' Delight	100	3 Jun 1682	25/112
Som	Gladstower	100	3 Jun 1682	25/50
Som	Taylor's Hills	200	3 Jun 1682	25/50
Glass, John:				
Transported himself, his wife Joyce and daughter Elizabeth before October 1681.				28/93
Glover, Daniel:				
Tal	Hope	200	6 Nov 1684	25/190
Goddard, George:				
Som	Cramburne	350	28 May 1681	24/320;29/61
Som	Windsor	100	15 Jly 1684	25/134;30/185
Goddard, John:				
StM	Heart's Delight	200	12 Feb 1686	25/398;32/611
Goddard, Thomas:				
Assignor of lands in Talbot Co. in Oct 1680.				24/266
Goddard, Mr. Thomas of London:				
Dor	Betty's Delight	500	22 Apr 1686	25/203;32/195
Godden, John, gent:				
Som	East Gate	500	28 Apr 1687	25/388;32/704
Som	Spittlefields	500	12 Jun 1683	25/280;32/485
Som	Rochester	2,900	10 Feb 1683	25/87;33/613
Som	Upner	250	28 Apr 1687	25/337;32/706
Godfrey, George:				
Cha	Trooper's Rendezvous	250	15 Jun 1672	25/210
Patent to issue to Thomas Jenkins of Charles Co.				
Godscross, John:				
Cal	Neglect	41	21 Sep 1694	27/216
Godwin, William, planter:				
Tal	Godwin's Addition	90	28 Feb 1687	25/368;33/642
Goffe, Thomas:				
AA	Goffe's Increase	180	12 Aug 1682	24/463;33/116
Golby, Richard:				
Cha	Aithey's Folly	72	4 Feb 1687	25/272;32/485
Gold, Edward:				
Som	Beverley	200	13 May 1689	27/72
Som	Gold's Delight	450	8 Sep 1695	37/133
Goldsborough, Robert:				
Tal	Controversy	500	10 Nov 1695	37/348
Tal	Discovery	96	10 Nov 1695	40/158
Goldsmith, George of Cecil Co:				
Granted land called Friendship before 1680.				24/185

County	*Name of Tract*	*Acreage*	*Date*	*Reference(s)*
Bal	Goldsmith's Rest	600	3 Jly 1682	25/2;32/97
Bal	Inlargement	200	25 Apr 1680	29/256
Goldsmith, George, son & heir of George Goldsmith deceased:				
Bal	Surveyor's Point	500	25 Apr 1683	29/255
Goldsmith, John:				
Som	Golden Quarter	150	15 Jun 1683	25/54;30/7
Gouldsmith, William:				
Som	Bear Den	100	23 Mar 1688	25/358;33/674
Goodman, Edward:				
Bal	Goodman's Adventure	250	14 Jly 1679	24/74
Bal	Norfolk	200	10 Jun 1683	31/225
Goodman, George:				
Transported by Francis Wine bef. Sep 1680.				28/116
Goodrick, George of Charles Co.—See under Ashford, Michael.				
Goodridge, Timothy:				
Tal	Timothy's Lot	300	26 Nov 1680	28/57
Goosey, John:				
Dor	Cante	100	16 Nov 1677	24/205;29/227
Dor	Gander's Labyrinth	195	3 Feb 1682	24/419;31/38
Goosey, Mr. Samuel:				
Cal	Goosey's Addition	150	27 Dec 1684	25/156;30/209
Cal	Goosey's Come Again	70	1 Aug 1685	25/164;33/123
Cal	Hard Fortune	162	27 Dec 1684	25/154;32/434
Gooty, Joseph:				
Dor	Joseph's Lane	50	9 Apr 1683	29/206
Gordon, Daniel:				
Transported by Job Chandler, gent, bef. 1651.				29/149
Gordon, Thomas, planter:				
Som	Addition	250	27 Nov 1685	25/232;33/308
Som	Gordon's Delight	100	14 May 1689	27/74
Som	Gordon's Lot	200	19 Jun 1689	27/125
Som	Thomas's Court	500	[25 Oct 1685]	25/232;33/273
Gormuckson, Michael:				
Bal	Passage	232	10 Nov 1695	37/425
Gorsuch, Charles, planter:				
Bal	Abington	100	12 Jun 1682	24/501;30/61
Bal	Good Endeavour	40	10 Nov 1695	34/130;40/266
Bal	Huntington	146	12 Jun 1682	24/503;30/45
Bal	Welcome	100	28 Oct 1684	25/154;32/352
Gorsuch, Charles of Talbot Co:				
Bal	Willin	398	30 May 1683	31/240
Gorsuch, Lovelace:				
Tal	Dickenson's Plain	860	22 Aug 1688	25/411;32/684

County	*Name of Tract*	*Acreage*	*Date*	*Reference(s)*
Tal	Gravelley's How	150	29 Jly 1681	24/372;31/334
Tal	Poplar Ridge	150	12 May 1679	24/39
Tal	Poplar Ridge Addition	200	29 Jly 1681	24/370;31/229
Tal	Swan Brook	770	23 Aug 1688	25/412;32/685
Gosnell [elsewhere Goswell], William of Anne Arundel Co:				
Bal	Gosnell's Adventure	199	25 May 1683	25/8;30/140
AA	Gosnell's Choice	250	6 Mar 1695	27/295
Gotee, John:				
Dor	Bourburke	100	19 Jly 1681	24/200;28/301
Dor	Bow Court	100	[8 Dec 1679]	24/183
Dor	Callis	150	12 Feb 1680	24/182;28/343
Dor	Frankling	100	18 Jly 1681	28/309
Dor	Graveling	100	12 Oct 1679	24/183
Gouly, Joseph:				
Dor	Gouly's Marsh	510	10 Nov 1695	37/289
Goustree, Richard:				
Dor	Richard's Delight	100	25 Mar 1694	37/16
Gover, Robert of Anne Arundel Co:				
Cal	Gover's Addition	167	14 Jun 1694	27/11
AA	Gover's Frewin	419	2 Jun 1683	29/283
including lands for transportation of 4 persons.				
Cal	Gover's Expedition	88	14 Jun 1694	27/346
AA	Gover's Hills	70	8 Jly 1680	28/20
Gower, George, blacksmith:				
Cha	Gower's Addition	28	15 Dec 1684	25/242;33/275
Grace, Nathaniel:				
Tal	Adventure	327	10 Nov 1695	34/104;40/164
Granger, Christopher:				
Knt	Chance	50	19 Jun 1681	24/367;31/188
Granger, James:				
Transported by William Thomas of Charles Co. before September 1680.				28/121
Grason, Robert Jr:				
Tal	Robert's Infancy	65	10 Nov 1695	37/398
Gray, James:				
Som	Wing	600	[3 Jan 1679]	24/148;29/177
Gray, John, planter:				
AA	[blank]	17	15 Jan 1684	25/220
Cha	Gray's Addition	100	15 Mar 1683	24/504;33/15
AA	Gray's Adventure	184	24 Jly 1685	25/250
AA	Gray's Chance	64	15 Jan 1685	25/230
AA	Gray's Increase	300	6 Jly 1681	28/147
AA	Gray's Lot	239	24 Jly 1689	25/251;30/253
AA	Gray's Luck	361	4 May 1688	25/404;32/622
AA	Happy Choice	331	3 Jly 1684	25/326,426; 33/611
AA	Roper Gray	480	4 Aug 1681	24/350;31/410

County	*Name of Tract*	*Acreage*	*Date*	*Reference(s)*
Gray, Joseph:				
Som	Rest	150	7 Jan 1684	25/132;32/291
Som	Wing	600	[3 Jan 1679]	24/148;29/177
Gray, Miles:				
Som	Gray's Improvement	150	10 Nov 1695	40/167
Gray, Richard:				
Knt	Hobson's Choice	100	12 Jly 1683	25/141;33/89
Green, Edward:				
Som	Parker's Adventure	400	8 Oct 1698	38/100
Som	Partner's Desire	300	10 Nov 1697	38/38
Green, George:				
Bal	Little Britain	200	1 Sep 1696	38/12
Green, John:				
Tal	Green's Adventure	300	25 Jun 1679	24/220;29/265
AA	Green's Beginning	70	4 Sep 1682	24/463;29/513
Green, Joseph:				
Cal	[unnamed]	400	10 Jan 1696	27/357
Green, Leonard:				
StM	Green's Content	100	27 Oct 1682	24/480
StM	Proprietor's Gift	50	8 Feb 1682	28/360
Green, Samuel:				
Tal		150	1679	24/39
Green, Thomas of Calvert Co:				
Cha	Cuckold's Delight	200	13 Apr 1686	25/240;30/320
Cal	Green Spring	100	11 Jan 1684	25/21;31/531
Green, William:				
Dor	Beaver Dam Neck	105	30 Sep 1684	25/205;32/446
Dor	Cow Quarter	100	10 Nov 1682	24/543;30/90
Som	Greenland	500	29 Jly 1683	25/81;32/237
Som	Green's Recantation	200	28 Nov 1679	24/52
Som	Hog Quarter	700	21 Nov 1679	24/102,154
Som	Marrish Island	200	11 Dec 1679	24/13
Greenbury, Nicholas:				
AA	Middle Burrow	11	26 Mar 1688	25/345;32/513
Greenfield, James:				
Cal	Beale's Gift	500	3 Aug 1688	27/18
Greenfield, Thomas:				
Cal	Compass Hill	50	19 Dec 1679	24/166
Cal	Gedling	200	15 Jun 1680	28/9
Cal	Golden Race	181	10 Nov 1695	40/89
Cal	Merry Greenwood	454	12 Sep 1685	25/192;32/282
Cal	Podda	100	19 Dec 1679	24/165
Cal	Stock Bardolph	119	10 Nov 1695	40/92
Cal	Stoke	42	3 Sep 1688	25/431;34/12
Cal	Whinisacre	50	30 Sep 1680	28/70
Cal	Woodborough	225	15 Jun 1680	28/8

County	Name of Tract	Acreage	Date	Reference(s)
Greenwood, John:				
Cec	Greenwood's Advancement	100	12 Aug 1694	27/145
Greere, Archibald of Kent Co., gent:				
Knt	Killins Worth More	500	26 Apr 1684	25/69
Greer, James:				
Cec	Greer's Range	100	6 May 1687	25/333;33/708
Grenisse, James:				
AA	Greeniston	700	29 Sep 1681	24/352,513
Gresham, John of Anne Arundel Co., gent:				
AA	Fortune	54	6 Apr 1687	25/316
Bal	Gresham College	500	27 Oct 1684	25/154;32/92
Griffin, Lewis, orphan son of Lewis Griffin deceased:				
Dor	Cutters' Hall	50	2 Jun 1683	25/118;32/464
Dor	Griffin's Chance	50	1 Aug 1701	34/297
Griffin, William:				
Cha	Hills	113	15 Mar 1689	25/433;34/5
Griffith, Henry:				
Dor	Bandon	400	26 May 1688	25/435
Dor	Griffeth's Chance	200	9 Sep 1684	25/150
Dor	Griffith's Purchase	400	11 May 1688	25/435
Griffith, Samuel:				
Cal	Welshpool	330	1 Sep 1681	28/222
Griffith, William:				
AA	Griffith's Lot	197	4 Oct 1695	27/320
Cha	Griffith's Fancy	100	10 Oct 1695	37/248
Griggs, John & Mary, executors of Richard Keen of Calvert Co., who died before Sep 1680.				28/78
Grimes, Margaret:				
Transported by Samuel Gibson of Calvert Co.				24/4
Grimes, William:				
AA	Graves' Enlargement	187	10 Nov 1695	34/105;40/264
Groome, Moses:				
Bal	Groome's Chance	300	28 Apr 1687	25/299;33/452
Cal	Loving Acquaintance	105	27 Jly 1684	25/128
Groome, Samuel, merchant:				
Tal	Buck Range	50	24 Nov 1678	24/196
Tal	Ratcliffe	3,250	8 May 1679	24/112
Gross, Ann, daughter of William Gross of Baltimore Co:				
Bal	Ann's Dowry	200	22 Sep 1683	25/99;32/353
Gross, Nicholas:				
AA	Eagle's Nest	40	29 Mar 1679	24/164;28/177
Grosse, William:				
Tal	Ashby's Addition	200	21 Jan 1689	25/416;34/33
Tal	Gross's Addition	24	22 Apr 1684	25/113;30/160

County	*Name of Tract*	*Acreage*	*Date*	*Reference(s)*
Grundy, Robert:				
Tal	Grundy's Addition	73	8 Aug 1694	37/25
Tal	Grundy's Adventure	171	10 Apr 1697	38/53
Tal	Grundy's Lot	46	29 Aug 1694	37/24
Tal	Thripley's Fortune	391	28 Aug 1694	37/23
Tal	Yorkshire	280	10 Apr 1697	38/56
Grunwin, Thomas of St. Mary's Co., gent:				
Bal	Cullen's Addn	200	25 Sep 1683	30/141
Bal	Cullen's Lot	300	17 Jun 1683	30/129
Gubbins, Mary:				
Transported by Francis Wine bef. Sep 1680.				28/116
Guggeon, Lawrence:				
AA	Burntwood Common	50	1 Jly 1684	25/104;30/224
AA	Orphans' Addition	85	1 Jly 1684	25/95;32/150
Guggeon, Robert:				
AA	Burntwood Common	50	1 Jly 1684	25/104;30/224
AA	Orphans' Addition	85	1 Jly 1684	25/95;32/150
Guider—See Gwyther.				
Guisnam?, Thomas:				
StM	Bampfield	150	5 Oct 1695	40/1
Gullet, William:				
Som	Gullet's Assurance	100	15 Jun 1683	25/52;29/524
Som	Gullet's Hope	50	20 Jly 1683	25/24
Gullock, Thomas:				
AA	Vale of Pleasure	46	13 Nov 1684	25/117;32/216
Gundry [Gunry], Benjamin:				
Cec	Hopeful Unity	150	12 May 1682	24/454;29/517
Cec	New Hall	485	19 Mar 1682	24/547
Gundry, Gideon:				
Cec	New Hall	485	19 Mar 1682	24/547
Gunnell, George:				
Bal	Gunnell's Division	60	24 Jun 1680	28/14
Gunton, Timothy:				
Cal	Muffett's Mount	16	18 Aug 1685	25/177;30/195
Gurden, Adrian:				
Som	Whitechapel Green	50	17 Feb 1683	25/32;30/157,213
Gwyn [Gwin], Henry:				
Cal	Maiden's Delight	65	15 Oct 1685	25/213;32/368
Gwyther [Guider], Nicholas, formerly of Maryland:				
Cha	Baltimore's Gift	70	before 1681	24/293
Guider, Thomas of St. Mary's Co:				
Tal	Guider's Lot	200	6 Nov 1685	25/221;32/391

County	Name of Tract	Acreage	Date	Reference(s)
Gwyther [Gwither], William of St. Mary's Co:				
Tal	Guider's Range	500	6 Nov 1685	25/222;30/171
StM	St. Barbary's	200	8 Mar 1682	24/405;29/415
Haborne, James:				
Cec	Haborne's Farm	200	15 Jly 1683	25/40
Hack, Mr. Peter:				
Cec	[unnamed]	470	7 Sep 1683	25/19
formerly surveyed for George Hack of Accomack, Virginia,				
Cec	Hack's Addition	150	7 Sep 1683	25/20;32/138
Hacker, John:				
Tal	Hacker's Adventure	250	10 Nov 1695	34/81;40/252
Hackett, Michael:				
Tal	Hackett's Chance	250	24 May 1681	24/365;29/403
Tal	Hackett's Delight	150	5 Mar 1680	24/229;31/283
Tal	Highgate	300	4 Mar 1680	24/229;31/293
Tal	Highgate Lane	100	5 Mar 1680	24/229;31/212
Tal	Sparke's Choice	450	18 Jly 1681	24/369;31/114
Hackett, Nicholas:				
Dor	Fairfields	396	24 Oct 1684	25/204
Dor	Hacket's Choice	500	28 Oct 1684	25/149
Tal	Hacket's Field	143	8 Apr 1684	25/104
Dor	Hackett's Neck	105	20 Oct 1684	25/214;33/245
Dor	Hacket's Stay	500	29 Oct 1684	25/150
Dor	Lambert's Marsh	300	16 Aug 1685	25/193,214;33/234
Hackett, Nicholas of Talbot Co:				
Dor	Sheele's	510	4 Dec 1682	25/16,130
Hackett, William, carpenter:				
Tal	Barton	150	5 Mar 1680	24/230;31/115;29/190
Tal	Contest	50	2 May 1687	25/313;33/572
Tal	Hackett's Lot	150	10 Mar 1686	25/211;33/190
Tal	Southampton	150	10 Mar 1686	25/247;30/275
Tal	Woolverhampton	500	29 Jun 1681	24/368;29/384
Haddaway, Peter:				
Tal	[unnamed]	200	5 Jun 1683	24/526
Tal	Point & Marsh	50	18 Jun 1683	25/50
Hadder, Warren:				
Som	St. Martin's Desert	300	4 May 1688	25/400,423;32/715
Hadduck, Benjamin of Calvert Co				
Cha	Hadduck's Hill	500	25 Apr 1685	25/166;32/184
Cha	Seaman's Delight	500	14 May 1685	25/167;33/92
Hager, Robert:				
Assignor of lands in Charles Co. in Dec 1682.				24/512
Hagley, John:				
Cec	Indian Range	300	18 Jly 1683	25/129;32/81

County	*Name of Tract*	*Acreage*	*Date*	*Reference(s)*
Hagoe, Thomas:				
StM	Good Intent	650	11 May 1695	27/351
StM	St. Jansen	200	27 Sep 1680	28/84
Hale, Henry:				
Bal	Parker's Increase	225	25 Dec 1695	37/492
Hale [Haile], Nicholas:				
Bal	Haile's Adventure	56	10 Nov 1695	40/512
Bal	Hale's Fellowship	200	10 Nov 1695	39/51
Haile, William:				
Cal	Haile's Adventure	150	8 Mar 1682	24/398;29/398
Cal	Haile's Rest	200	8 Feb 1682	24/362;31/494
Haillings, Thomas:				
Tal	Adventure	100	26 Apr 1683	29/252
Tal	Bachelor's Hope	150	26 Apr 1683	29/250
Hall, Benjamin:				
Cha	Hall's Lot	338	1 Oct 1701	34/312
Cha	Strife	235	1 Oct 1700	34/211
Hall, Charles, planter:				
Som	Hall's Adventure	250	29 Jly 1680	24/273;29/56
Som	Hall's Hummocks	100	22 Dec 1680	24/307;28/395
Som	Hall's Pasture	100	2 Jly 1688	25/390;32/630
Som	Partners' Desire	325	10 Nov 1697	39/16
Hall, Elisha:				
Cal	Hall's Addition	24	1 Nov 1701	34/365
Hall, Henry:				
AA	Bachelor's Choice	100	1 Dec 1701	34/379
Bal	Hall's Palace	300	10 Nov 1695	40/64
Hall, Henry, planter:				
Som	Middleton	300	[16 Sep 1675]	24/146
Hall, James:				
Tal	Edward's Hopewell	100	7 Nov 1679	24/225;29/258
Tal	Greenland	50	22 May 1682	24/456;31/174
Tal	Hall's Harbour	500	30 Apr 1684	25/113;32/104
Tal	James's Folly	50	21 Aug 1677	24/306;32/38
Tal	James's Look Out	51	10 Aug 1684	31/525
Hall, Jasper [Gespher]:				
Tal	Couple Close	100	12 Apr 1686	25/437;34/34
Tal	Glayde's Addition	71	1 Jly 1698	38/51
Hall, John of Baltimore Co., planter:				
Bal	Acquilla's Inheritance	732	1 Jun 1700	34/246
AA	Coad's Hill	140	12 Jun 1688	32/558
Bal	Cranberry Hall	1,547	10 Mar 1697	38/94
Bal	Hall's Hope	45	16 Jly 1684	25/155;32/564
Bal	Hall's Purchase	400	[1700]	38/160
Bal	Hall's Ridge	218	30 Jan 1688	25/348;33/707
Cal	Holland's Purchase	300	1 Nov 1686	25/231
Bal	Hopewell Marsh	55	6 Jly 1684	25/151;32/563

County	Name of Tract	Acreage	Date	Reference(s)
Hall, John & Martha his wife:				
Bal	Hall's Rich Neck	400	1 Jun 1700	34/245
Hall, John of Talbot Co:				
Dor	Fat Point	100	28 Sep 1683	25/123;32/454
Hall, Joshua:				
Cal	Hall's Chance	26	16 Feb 1695	27/241
PG	Range	101	10 Nov 1697	39/28
Hall, Josiah:				
AA	Hall's Parcel	100	6 Aug 1681	24/351;31/66
Hall, Nicholas :				
Bal	Mereman's Lot	210	29 Jun 1688	25/437
Hall, Phenix, planter:				
Som	Castle Fine	200	10 Nov 1695	34/70
Som	Digden Bottom	200	18 Nov 1685	25/278;33/372
Hall, Richard of Talbot Co., blacksmith:				
Dor	Hall's Fortune	200	24 Oct 1682	24/548;30/68
Hall, Mr. Richard:				
Cal	Spittall Addition	196	1 Apr 1686	25/213;32/375
Hall, Thomas:				
Cal	Forge	50	20 May 1688	33/540
Som	Castle Fine	200	10 Nov 1695	40/248
Som	Laugton	150	10 Aug 1683	29/463
Tal	Northumberland	61	10 Apr 1698	38/108
Hall, William:				
Som	Hall's Lot	450	18 May 1689	27/94
Hallit, Jacob:				
AA	Hallit's Lot	50	1 Jly 1680	28/17
Halsoe, Thomas:				
Som	Warrington	200	28 Feb 1681	24/307;28/396;32/264
Haly, Darby:				
Cec	Chance	200	7 Dec 1697	37/528
Hambleton, Gawman:				
Cal	Hambleton's Park	87	18 Feb 1687	25/329;32/516
Hambleton, William, gent:				
Tal	Hambleton's Addition	100	18 Apr 1687	25/368;33/634
Hamer, John:				
Tal	Hamer's Lot	200	2 Jun 1685	25/191
Hamer, Thomas, planter:				
Tal	Hamer's Choice	200	2 Jun 1685	25/195;32/303
Hamilton, Gavin of Calvert Co:				
Cha	Hamilton	150	13 Apr 1686	27/1
Hamilton, John:				
Assignor of lands in Dorchester Co. in 1679.				24/184

County	Name of Tract	Acreage	Date	Reference(s)
Hamlin [Hamlyn], George:				
Som	Andrews	300	16 Dec 1683	25/131;30/243
Som	Key	100	26 Mar 1680	24/257
Som	Winchester	800	12 Dec 1678	24/162
Hammon, Philip:				
Som	Jersey	500	30 Aug 1680	24/239;28/363
Hammond, Andrew:				
Tal	Hammond's Delight	168	10 Nov 1695	40/463
Hammond, Daniel:				
StM	Lewgar's Plains	430	1 Jly 1682	24/474;31/42
Hammond, Edward:				
Som	Chashbury	700	1 Oct 1681	25/70
Hamond, Henry:				
Som	Castle Haven	200	5 Apr 1673	24/550
Hammond, Maj. John:				
AA	Addition	22	16 Sep 1685	25/252;30/314
Hammond, Maj. John:				
AA	Hammond's Forest	362	1 May 1696	34/141;40/378
AA	Hammond's Pasture	118	6 Apr 1688	25/404;32/623
AA	Rich Neck	284	20 Mar 1685	25/183;40/375
Hammond, Capt. Thomas:				
Bal	Hammond's Addition	29	1 Dec 1698	34/157;38/141
Hancock, Thomas:				
Bal	Bachelor's Hope	50	[1696]	39/53
Handy, Samuel:				
Som	Handy's Choice	175	1 Aug 1696	38/75
Som	Handy's Meadow		8 Oct 1681	24/511;31/486
Hanker, Thomas:				
Cec	Worton Meadows	200	22 Jun 1681	24/500
Hankins, William:				
Bal	Hankins' Ridge	100	8 Jly 1679	24/162
Hanslap, Henry, gent:				
AA	Come by Chance	214	3 Nov 1682	24/513
AA	Hanslap's Range	300	20 Aug 1680	24/176;28/211
AA	Ayno	400	29 Sep 1682	24/466;31/408
Hanson, Hans [Hance], gent:				
Knt	Grazing Point	150	7 Jly 1681	24/369;31/192
Knt	Hanson's Choice	100	3 Oct 1680	24/254;29/100
Harbert, Elinor:				
AA	Harbert's Choice	146	26 Mar 1690	34/126;40/346
Harbinger, William:				
Transported by Francis Wine bef. Sep 1680.				28/116

County	Name of Tract	Acreage	Date	Reference(s)
Hardrope, Richard:				
Cal	Seaman's Delight	100	4 Jun 1684	25/35;32/27
Hardy, Henry:				
Cha	Hardy's Purchase	150	14 May 1681	24/279;28/488
former estate of Thomas Percy escheated for want of heirs.				
Harebottle, John:				
AA	Tryall	164	22 Oct 1698	38/95
Harle, John:				
Dor	Harle's Fortune	40	2 May 1682	24/429;31/383
Harles, James:				
Dor	Harles' Chance	26	19 Sep 1684	25/203;33/247
Harlings, Thomas:				
Tal	Adventure	100	30 Nov 1676	24/252
Tal	Bachelor's Hope	150	30 Nov 1676	24/252
Harman, Augustine, gent:				
Cec		4,100	27 Sep 1683	25/19;32/79
Cec	Bohemia Manor	6,000	8 Oct 1681	24/361;29/15,38
Cec	Little Bohemia	1,000	14 Aug 1682	29/16,40
Cec	Misfortune	1,339	14 Dec 1678	24/365;29/7
Harman, Henry:				
Som	Bagshot & Bon Won?	200	10 Oct 1695	37/107
Dor	Carter?	380	14 Oct 1701	34/296
Som	Twitnam	200	8 Dec 1688	27/25
Harness, Jacob:				
AA	Harness's Gift	51	28 May 1684	25/33
Harness, Judith:				
AA	Harness's Gift	51	28 May 1684	25/33
Harny, Timothy:				
Som	Timothy's Choice	250	10 Nov 1696	38/120
Harper, Edward:				
Transported by John Abington of Calvert Co. before August 1680.				28/34
Harper, Edward, planter:				
Som	Beckles	200	[11 Jun 1679]	24/163;29/239
Harper, John:				
Dor	Harper's Increase	43	10 Oct 1695	40/598
Harper, William, planter:				
Som	Harper's Discovery	200	28 May 1681	24/316;29/3
Som	Harper's Increase	100	2 Oct 1683	25/28
Som	Harper's Outlet	48	[12 Oct 1677]	24/163;29/201
Som	Middle Plantation	175	18 May 1683	25/70;32/246,360
Som	Norfolk	500	[11 Jun 1679]	24/163;28/528
Harper, William Jr:				
Dor	Harper's Lot	50	23 Nov 1694	37/14

County	Name of Tract	Acreage	Date	Reference(s)
Harpin, Thomas, planter:				
Dor	Creek's End	50	20 May 1682	24/436;31/345
Dor	Knivar Heath	120	2 Mar 1684	24/540;34/503;30/88
Dor	Salisbury Plain	100	14 Nov 1679	24/184;29/263
Harrington [Herrington], Cornelius:				
Bal	Rosindale	50	10 Nov 1698	38/44
Bal	Seneca	50	10 Nov 1695	37/383
Harrington, Richard:				
Transported himself.				31/274
Harris, David, planter:				
Som	Heart's Content	300	21 Nov 1685	25/234;33/355
Harris, Elizabeth, dau. & heir of Edward Jones of Cecil Co., deceased:				
Cec	Abram's Promise	300	3 Jun 1702	35/406
Harris, George:				
PG	Rum Point	8	12 Mar 1700	30/339;38/155
Harris, James, son & heir of Edward Jones of Cecil Co., deceased:				
Cec	Neglect	240	23 Mar 1702	35/410
Harris, John:				
AA	Harris's Beginning	122	5 Dec 1695	27/338
Harris, Moses:				
Tal	Harris's Range	400	8 Aug 1684	25/268;33/351
Tal	Rumsey Forest	300	27 Jun 1688	25/412;32/681
Harris, Richard:				
Som	Curvurth	200	18 Sep 1684	25/177
Som	Friends' Assistance	100	3 May 1686	25/275;33/444
Harris, Samuel:				
AA	Harris's Adventure	449	1 May 1700	39/44
Harris, William:				
Knt	Addition	150	14 Sep 1688	25/437;34/35,434
Knt	Father's Gift	150	23 Jly 1686	25/258;30/313
Knt	Holy Land	425	10 Mar 1696	40/487
Harris, William of Calvert Co., planter:				
Bal	Friendship	600	11 May 1684	25/34
Bal	Harris's Trust	300	6 Aug 1684	25/95;32/390
Cal	Illingworth's Fortune	265	20 Feb 1684	25/90;32/248
Harris, William:				
Tal	Long Neglect	39	14 Oct 1699	38/109
Knt	Maiden's Lot	50	[15 Apr 1682]	24/400;33/14
Knt	Millford	50	27 Jun 1685	25/195;33/231
Knt	Poplar Farm	400	10 Jun 1682	24/413;31/202
Knt	Poplar Hill	200	20 Jun 1680	24/186;28/416
Harrison, [blank], son & heir of James Harrison deceased:				
Tal	Scarbrough	1,400	9 May 1682	24/411

County	Name of Tract	Acreage	Date	Reference(s)
Harrison, Henry:				
Transported by William Moure bef. Sep 1680.				28/56
Harrison, James, planter:				
Tal	Dover Marsh	150	7 Jly 1680	24/172;28/458;
Tal	Dover Marsh	150	10 Nov 1695	34/78;40/162
Harrison, John:				
Cha	Harrison's Adventure	252	23 Mar 1688	24/146;25/378;
Som	Harrison's Adventure	600	[12 Jun 1679]	28/109;29/9; 32/592
Som	Harrison's Venture	200	28 May 1681	24/323
Som	Middle Town	175	18 May 1683	25/65
Cha	Providence	215	8 Feb 1688	25/378;32/568
Harrison, Joseph, orphan under guardianship of Thomas Shuttleworth:				
Cha	Baltimore's Gift	50	20 Nov 1680	24/267;29/82
Harrison, Miles:				
Transported himself before 1680.				24/20
Harrison, Richard:				
AA	Harrison's Lot	13	20 Sep 1687	25/347;32/521
Cal	Harrison's Addition	65	6 May 1689	34/24
Cal	Harrison's Enlargement	425	1 Jun 1700	34/188;38/155
Cal	Pork Hall Addition	65	22 Nov 1688	25/427;34/19
Harrison, Robert:				
Tal	Haphazard	120	10 Nov 1695	34/86;40/239
Harrod, Patrick:				
Dor	Entrim	100	10 Nov 1680	24/280;28/461
Hartley, Joseph:				
StM	Whitehaven	164	20 May 1697	38/49
Hartley, Thomas:				
Transported by John Richens bef. Oct 1680				28/97
Hartrupp, Richard:				
StM	Hickory Hill	100	5 Oct 1682	24/453;29/349
Harwood, John:				
Dor	Harwood's Chance	150	1 Jly 1702	35/357
Hasfurt, George:				
Assignor of lands in Somerset Co. in 1679.				24/235
Hast, Arthur:				
Dor	Hast's Content	500	17 Sep 1687	25/350;33/714
Hast, Daniel & Catherine his wife:				
Transported themselves before February 1682.				28/394
Haste, Daniel:				
Som	Anderson's Invention	200	15 Jly 1695	40/58
Som	Fortune	100	30 May 1682	28/482
Som	Greenwich	50	30 Aug 1680	24/278;28/232
Som	Might Have Had More	50	10 May 1682	28/522
Som	Second Purchase	300	15 Jly 1695	40/57
Som	Tossiter	150	20 May 1682	28/482

County	Name of Tract	Acreage	Date	Reference(s)
Hathaway, John, gent:				
Bal	Ah Ha at a Venture	200	7 May 1687	25/310;33/522
Bal	Ah Ha Cow Pasture	194	3 May 1687	25/310
Bal	Hathaway's Trust	150	28 Mar 1685	25/182
Hatton, John:				
Tal	Bentley Hay	50	29 Oct 1681	24/383;31/238
Tal	Hatton Garden	50	29 Oct 1681	24/383;31/125
Tal	Hatton's Hope	100	29 Mar 1682	24/404;29/360
Tal	Jane's Prograce	70	10 Nov 1695	37/400
Hatton, William:				
Cha	Rich Hill	320	1 Mar 1688	25/376;32/580
Haveringham, Christopher, gent:				
Tal	[unnamed]	200	26 Sep 1686	25/307
Hawker, John:				
Tal	Hawker's Meadows	460	10 Mar 1697	38/55
Hawkins, Henry:				
Granted land called the Fork in Kent Co. before 1680.				24/187
Cha	Hawkins' Addition	238	23 Jan 1688	25/376;32/596
Cha	Hawkins' Barrows	171	10 Jan 1688	25/375;32/591
Cha	Hawkins' Lot	266	25 Jan 1687	25/272;33/470
Cha	Hawkins' Purchase	1,000	15 Nov 1684	25/238;33/293
Hawkins, John:				
Transported by John Quigley of Cecil Co. by 1679.				24/93
Tal	Baron Neck	227	12 Jun 1694	37/31
Tal	Braunton's Addition	314	10 Nov 1695	40/170
Tal	Contention	450	30 Jun 1681	24/340;29/179
Tal	Hawkins' Farm	500	7 Jan 1680	24/278
Tal	Jasper Lot	770	22 Nov 1694	37/32
Hawkins, William of Baltimore Co:				
Bal	Hawkins' Addition	203	10 Nov 1695	34/143;40/317
AA	Hawkins' Choice	134	23 May 1683	25/8;30/30
Hayes, John:				
Bal	Mount Hayes	317	10 Nov 1695	34/109;40/67
Hayman [Heyman/Haymund], Henry, planter:				
Som	Haymund's Choice	50	18 May 1680	24/333
Som	Henry's Enjoyment	50	19 Nov 1686	25/263;33/256
Haynes [Heines], John:				
Dor	Vale of Easum	100	-- Jan 1682	24/422;29/399
Dor	Worchester	150	25 Apr 1682	24/484
Hayward, Thomas:				
Dor	Hayward's Farm	50	13 Jan 1695	37/21
Haywood, William:				
Cec	Boston	40	10 Dec 1700	34/301
Heape, Francis:				
Som	[unnamed]	300	5 Sep 1687	25/360;33/668
Som	Rotten Quarter	100	10 Nov 1695	34/61

County	*Name of Tract*	*Acreage*	*Date*	*Reference(s)*
Heard, John:				
StM	Coventry	100	19 Oct 1680	24/201;28/318
StM	Heard's Choice	150	22 Oct 1681	24/348;29/449
Heard, William:				
StM	Heard's Purchase	115	[12 May 1697]	38/111
Heare, Arthur of Dorchester Co:				
Completed his time of service completed in 1679				24/49
Hearne, William:				
Som	Key	100	26 Mar 1680	24/257
Som	New Yarmouth	200	12 Jun 1683	25/74;32/377
Heath, Abraham:				
Som	Dudley	50	28 Sep 1681	24/378;29/444
Som	Heath's Quarter	100	15 Jly 1684	25/134;30/182
Som	Rowley Hill	100	30 May 1683	25/52
Heath, James of Kent Co:				
Cec	Heath's Chance	200	15 Jun 1700	34/186
Knt	Heath's Discovery	23	1 Nov 1701	34/347
Tal	Heath's Forest	150	3 Jly 1699	30/363
Tal	Heath's Heath lands*	533	3 Jly 1700	30/361
Cec	Wright's Rest	150	7 Oct 1700	34/206
Heath, Thomas:				
Bal	Black Sedge	50	14 Jly 1680	25/9;30/26
Heathcote, Nathaniel of Anne Arundel Co., gent:				
Bal	Heathcote's Cottage	500	22 Mar 1679	24/161
Heatherington, Richard:				
Tal	Adventure	327	10 Nov 1695	34/104;40/164
Tal	Heath'ton's Delight	50	10 Nov 1695	37/299
Hedge, Thomas:				
Bal	Benjamin's Choice	254	25 Sep 1683	25/38;30/60
Bal	Broad Street	40	28 Aug 1683	25/49;30/31
Heigh, James:				
Cal	James's Addition	21	3 Apr 1702	35/375
Heines—See Haynes.				
Hely, Clement:				
StM	Hely's Lot	104	4 Nov 1687	25/320;33/607
Hempsted, Nicholas:				
Bal	Jerusalem	318	25 May 1687	25/310;33/577
Hemsley, Philemon: Deputy Surveyor for Talbot Co:				
Tal	Chance	300	[1696]	40/568
Tal	Fair Place	136	10 Nov 1695	37/520
Hemsley, William of Talbot Co., Deputy Surveyor for Cecil Co., father of William Hemsley, Deputy Surveyor for Talbot Co.				
Hemsley, William:				
Tal	Addition	63	24 Aug 1688	25/410;32/669

County	Name of Tract	Acreage	Date	Reference(s)
Tal	Farm	348	24 Aug 1688	25/410;32/673
Tal	Friendship	87	[29 Jly 1694]	37/6
Knt	Goose Haven	500	10 Aug 1683	25/143;32/468
Tal	Hemsley's Addition	520	31 May 1696	37/459
Tal	Hemsley's Arcadia	1,030	10 Nov 1695	37/363
Tal	Hemsly's Britannia	600	10 Nov 1695	40/196
Tal	Hemsley's Brittland	40	3 May 1696	37/3
Tal	Hog Hole	260	[8 Apr 1696]	37/7
Cec	Hopeful Unity	150	16 Oct 1682	24/454;29/517
Tal	Little Britain	150	20 Sep 1688	27/155
Tal	Neglect	300	10 Nov 1695	40/199
Tal	Plain Dealing	600	1 Aug 1681	24/303
Tal	Plain Dealing	175	10 Nov 1695	40/140
Tal	Ruadely	200	3 May 1689	27/34
Tal	Sam's Fields	102	5 Apr 1695	37/5
Tal	Triangle	55	5 May 1689	27/138
Tal	York Fields	466	10 Nov 1695	40/134
Henderson [Hinderson], James:				
Som	Barron Lot	110	20 Dec 1688	27/14
Som	Double Purchase	1,100	5 Mar 1680	24/443;32/283
Som	Haphazard	70	10 Nov 1695	34/59;40/207
Henderson, John:				
Som	Chestnut	100	1 Dec 1696	38/118
Som	Henderson's Chance	70	20 Sep 1688	25/422
Som	Henderson's Conv.	120	1 Jun 1700	34/226
Hendrickson, Hendrick:				
Cec	Hendrick's Addition	100	11 Sep 1679	24/87
Hensley, Edmund:				
Bal	Edmund's Camp	200	10 Sep 1698	38/121
Hepworth, John of Talbot Co:				
Transported himself bef. November 1680.				28/100
Som	Hepworth's Pasture	48	10 Jun 1689	27/68
Herbert, Humphrey:				
Dor	John's Purchase	50	1 Jun 1700	34/266;38/154
Herbert, William:				
Transported by Mark Cordea before Sep 1680.				28/51
Cal	Chance	200	1 Jly 1685	27/268
Herrman, Casparus:				
Cec	Level	900	23 Feb 1688	27/184
Herman, Ephraim:				
Cec	St. Augustine's Manor	1,000	1684	31/312
Assigned by Jane Calvert, relict & executrix of Philip Calvert Esq., Chancellor of Maryland, deceased.				
Herman, Francis:				
Transported by Francis Wine bef. Sep 1680.				28/116

County	*Name of Tract*	*Acreage*	*Date*	*Reference(s)*
Herman, Henry:				
Transported by Francis Wine bef. Sep 1680.				28/116
Herring, John:				
Bal	Herring's Lot	29	9 May 1687	25/312;33/552
Herring, John, carpenter:				
AA	Herring's Purchase	205	26 Jan 1685	25/194
Herrington—See Harrington.				
Hewitt [Hewett], John, gent:				
Som	Conveniency	400	24 Nov 1685	25/265;30/256
Som	Conveniency	13	10 May 1689	27/70
Som	North Wales	200	21 May 1689	27/7
Som	Poole Hambleton	100	21 May 1689	27/9
Som	South Wales	200	16 May 1689	27/99
Heyman—Se Hayman.				
Hicks, Thomas, carpenter:				
Dor	Bartholomew's Close	165	10 Nov 1695	40/453
Dor	Forest	100	10 Nov 1695	40/451
Dor	Poplar Neck	75	30 Sep 1683	25/124;32/402
Hide, Edward:				
Dor	Hide's Chance	34	21 Nov 1678	24/284;29/493
Hide, Thomas:				
Cal	Cuckold's Rest	100	2 Mar 1682	24/395;31/23
Higginbotham, George:				
Cec	Hill Top	100	[8 Oct 1681]	24/387;31/166
Higham, Francis:				
Cal	Higham's	10	13 Feb 1688	25/344;33/722
Cal	Smith	50	5 Apr 1688	25/430;34/25
Highe, George:				
Som	Dixon's Kindness	100	10 Oct 1695	37/65
Som	Sunken Ground	100	2 Oct 1695	37/78
Hiland—See Hyland.				
Hilgore, Robert:				
Transported by John Edmondson before Nov 1680.				28/57
Hill, Abell:				
AA	Hillington	50	29 Mar 1683	29/204
Hill, Clement of St. Mary's. Deputy Surveyor-General;				
Transported Abraham Combes and his daughter before September 1680.				28/71
Bal	Hill's Camp	1,000	18 Mar 1684	25/47;30/131
Hill, Clement Jr:				
PG	Compton Bassett	740	1 Jun 1700	34/261;38/161
Hill, Cybell:				
AA	Hillington	50	26 Jly 1676	24/177

County	*Name of Tract*	*Acreage*	*Date*	*Reference(s)*
Hill, Francis:				
Transported by William Moure before Sep 1680.				28/56
Hill, Jacob of Somerset Co:				
Transported himself & assigned land by 1679				24/247,28/404
Hill, John, planter:				
Som	Agreement	100	15 Jun 1683	25/72;33/187
Som	Bay Bush Hall	100	4 Jun 1681	24/318;29/69
Hill, Mary of Somerset Co:				
Transported by her husband Jacob before Feb 1682.				28/404
Hill, Capt. Richard of Anne Arundel Co:				
AA	Addition	60	2 Jly 1684	25/104;33/321
AA	Angle	7	2 Jly 1684	25/103;30/305
AA	Little Worth	132	25 Jly 1685	25/189;30/180
AA	Mill Meadow	240	13 Sep 1682	24/465;31/418
AA	Tolly's Point	140	26 Apr 1684	31/319
purchased from Richard Tolly deceased, son and heir of Richard Tolly deceased.				
Bal	Hill's Forest	1,000	4 Oct 1683	25/40;31/443
Hill, Mr. Richard:				
Som	Addition	325	29 Aug 1684	25/175
Som	Conclusion	146	20 Apr 1687	25/355;32/509
Som	Cumberland	100	24 Sep 1687	25/353
Hill, Samuel:				
Cec	Green Spring	200	24 Oct 1680	25/11
Hill, William:				
Tal	Hill's Addition	50	8 Sep 1679	24/220;28/500
Cec	Hill's Adventure	68	14 Oct 1680	25/10
Tal	Hill's Outlet	100	[25 Jly 1679]	24/219;28/439
Hillen, Nathaniel, carpenter:				
Cec	Hillen's Adventure	600	11 Dec 1680	25/12
Cec	Nanny's Choice	200	4 Oct 1682	24/551
Cec	St. Margaret's	200	15 Apr 1682	24/551
Cec	St. Martin's	200	16 Apr 1682	24/550
Hillary, Thomas:				
Cal	Farm	235	24 Apr 1683	31/30
Cal	Three Sisters	1,000	11 Jan 1684	25/20;32/14
Hilling, Nathaniel:				
Cec	Hilling's Grove	44	6 Sep 1694	27/152
Hynson [Hinson], Col. John:				
Knt	Bounty	200	10 Nov 1696	38/19
Knt	Hynson's Division	876	1 May 1701	34/380
Knt	Lord's Gift	3,000	10 Aug 1695	27/362
Hynson, Nathaniel:				
Knt		200	17 --- 1698	38/98

County	*Name of Tract*	*Acreage*	*Date*	*Reference(s)*
Hinton, Mr. Thomas:				
Cec	Hinton's Adventure	200	1 Oct 1683	25/19
Hinton, Thomas:				
Cal	Adjunctive	10	25 Jan 1683	24/451;31/11
StM	Ambersly	65	20 Jan 1682	28/431
Cec	Manchester	245	13 Oct 1682	24/505
Hixon, James, son of Henry Hixon:				
Cha	Ardington Hall	125	24 Jly 1683	24/524;31/516
Hobbs, Thomas:				
Som	Abington	300	10 May 1683	25/51;32/135
Hobson, James:				
Cec	Luck	100	19 Jun 1683	31/266
Hodges, John:				
Transported by Mark Cordea before Sep 1680.				28/51
Hodgson, John:				
Cec	Ridmore Supply	350	[3 Sep 1678]	24/147;29/219
Hodgson, Nicholas:				
Cec	Bridge Point	20	17 Jly 1683	25/142;32/250
Hodson, John:				
Dor	Hodson's Adventure	300	[15 Dec 1680]	24/147;29/236
Dor	John's Lane Addition	50	17 Mar 1681	24/297;31/144
Hoggins, Edmund:				
Som	Barron Neck	100	10 Nov 1695	37/381
Holbrooke, Thomas, planter:				
Som	Harrington	200	28 May 1681	24/317;29/60
Holder, John:				
Som	Snow Hill	200	10 Nov 1695	34/64;40/206
Holland, Francis:				
AA	Holland's Addition	47	16 Oct 1687	25/348;32/539
Holland, George of Anne Arundel Co., Deputy Surveyor for Cecil & Baltimore Cos:				
Bal	Collett's Neglect	300	4 Jun 1683	31/242
AA	Denton	380	10 Dec 1679	24/71
Cec	Friendship	200	30 Sep 1680	28/107
Cec	Friendship	412	14 Mar 1681	24/296;29/294
Bal	Holland's Park	150	14 Oct 1683	25/41;31/435
AA	Oblong	70	31 May 1683	31/236
See also under Larkin, John.				
Holland, Richard:				
Som	Durham Down	77	16 Jun 1684	25/177;30/169
Holland, William, gent:				
Cal	Holland's Purchase	300	15 May 1686	25/216
Holleager, Philip, gent:				
Cec	Addition	100	1 Nov 1683	25/28;

County	Name of Tract	Acreage	Date	Reference(s)
Cec	Addition	100	1 Nov 1683	31/519;32/398
Cec	Addition	300	24 Sep 1685	25/217
Cec	Forest	200	10 Nov 1695	40/80
Cec	Forest	500	10 Dec 1695	40/481
Cec	Mill Fork	808	14 May 1695	27/341
Cec	Philip's Choice	400	10 Nov 1683	25/186;32/251
Cec	Pasterinhole	500	29 Feb 1684	25/28
Cec	Prior's Neglect	150	23 Sep 1685	25/217
Cec	Pryor's Neglect	250	23 Jun 1681	24/500;31/465; 32/421
Cec	Rich Level	800	6 Nov 1680	25/11;30/122
Cec	Stanaway	200	19 Jun 1683	31/267
Cec	Stannaway	400	15 Feb 1697	40/473
Holliday, Mr. Thomas:				
Cal	Addition	51	10 Nov 1695	37/491
Cal	Holliday's Choice	500	24 Aug 1688	27/81
Cal	Tewksbury	184	15 Jun 1685	25/167;32/169
Cal	Upper ---tten	181	10 Jan 1684	25/21;32/11
Hollingworth, Charles:				
Tal	Smith's Forest	140	10 Nov 1695	37/356
Hollingworth, John:				
Tal	Fox Harbour	150	5 Mar 1680	24/230;31/207
Tal	Jerusalem	400	2 Jun 1685	25/192;33/189
Hollinsworth, Charles of Talbot Co:				
Knt	Mount Hope	100	13 Jly 1683	25/43;33/81
Knt	Neysborough	100	13 Jly 1683	25/141;32/317
Hollingsworth, George:				
Cha	Brother's Expectation	250	10 Mar 1696	34/131;40/270
Hollingsworth, George, planter:				
Bal	Brothers' Unity	100	10 Mar 1696	40/335
Hollingsworth, William:				
Tal	Solomon's Friendship	100	31 Jly 1689	27/355
Hollis [Hollice] [Holls], William, planter:				
Bal	Geffery's Neck	130	10 Nov 1695	38/82,126
Bal	Hollis's Chance	43	7 Jly 1680	28/10
Bal	Hollis's Refuse	143	10 Nov 1695	40/552
Bal	Islington	22	8 Jly 1680	28/10
Bal	Planter's Neglect	63	29 May 1683	31/226
Holloway, James:				
Cec	Middle Grounds	200	10 Oct 1695	40/470
Holls—See Hollis				
Holmewood, Robert:				
Transported by Robert Grover of Anne Arundel Co. before 1683.				
Holmsworth, William:				
Tal	Solomon's Friendship	100	14 May 1695	34/90

County	Name of Tract	Acreage	Date	Reference(s)
Holson, Henry, planter:				
Som	Derby	200	21 Apr 1684	25/362
Holson, Thomas, planter:				
Som	Liverpool	500	27 Nov 1685	25/266;30/257
Holt, Elizabeth:				
Transported by Robert Grover of Anne Arundel Co. bef. 1683.				
Holt, Henry:				
Dor	Bachelor's Hope	150	27 Sep 1680	28/78
Homes, Richard:				
Tal	Buck Roe	680	10 Nov 1695	34/77;40/240
Homewood, James:				
AA	Homewood's Enlargement	100	26 Mar 1696	34/128;40/361
Homewood, Thomas :				
AA	Homeword's Outlet	60	24 Mar 1685	25/183;33/405
AA	Homewood's Search	78	1 Jun 1700	34/263;38/163
Hooke, Jeremiah of Somerset Co:				
Transported himself, his wife Ann & children Jeremiah, Roger & Mary Hooke & others before February 1682.				28/402
Hook, Joseph of Somerset Co:				
Transported by John Bodden before Apr 1681.				28/129
Hooker, Thomas:				
AA	Corrant	31	25 Jun 1683	29/320
AA	Hooker's Chance	154	2 Jun 1683	31/93
Bal	Maiden's Dowry	248	10 Mar 1696	40/521
Bal	Samuel's Hope	500	10 Nov 1695	34/139;40/273
Hoop, Francis:				
Som	Rotten Quarter	100	10 Nov 1695	40/234
Hooper, George of Dorchester Co., planter:				
Transported by John Richens before Oct 1680.				28/97
Dor	Bansbury	64	27 Dec 1679	24/179;28/301
Dor	Hooper's Endeavour	150	26 Apr 1680	24/180;28/285
Dor	Horsey Down	50	13 Jly 1681	28/330
Dor	Vale of Misery	100	29 May 1683	25/43;30/82
Hooper, George, cooper:				
Dor	William's Lot	25	29 May 1683	25/120;33/242
Hooper, Henry, gent:				
Dor	Elizium Fields	100	8 Oct 1679	24/170;29/129
Dor	Hooper's Adventure	65	22 Oct 1679	24/170;29/126
Dor	Hooper's Fortune	150	-- --- 1679	24/171;29/127
Dor	Hooper's Lot	100	11 Sep 1683	25/121
Dor	Hooper's Outlet	100	11 Sep 1683	25/43;30/101
Dor	Hooper's Range	150	19 Dec 1681	24/416;31/387
Dor	Horne Harbour	50	19 Oct 1679	24/170;29/130
Dor	Turkey Ridge	50	-- --- 1679	24/171;29/128

County	Name of Tract	Acreage	Date	Reference(s)
Hooper, Jane:				
Transported by Thomas Maisterman before Sep 1680.				28/53
Hope, George:				
Bal	Hope's Lot	200	10 Nov 1695	40/428
Bal	Hope's Recovery	31	10 Nov 1695	34/106;40/71
Hopewell, Francis:				
StM	Force Putt	100	10 Jan 1682	24/357
Hopewell, Mr. Hugh:				
Cal	Chunk's Delight	11	18 Apr 1683	24/520;32/20
Cal	Hopewell's Adventure	95	18 Apr 1683	24/521;32/17
Hopewell, Joseph of Calvert Co:				
Cec	Hereford	300	5 Nov 1680	25/11;31/533
Cal	Hereford	200	1 Nov 1680	24/252;29/259
Knt	Hopewell	300	6 Jly 1682	25/91;32/400
Hopewell, Richard of Calvert Co:				
Tal	Bloomsbury	400	19 Nov 1686	25/259;33/312
Cec	Hereford	300	5 Nov 1680	25/11;31/533
Cal	Hereford	200	1 Nov 1680	24/252;29/259
Knt	Hopewell	300	6 Jly 1682	25/91;32/400
Tal	Irish Discovery	350	20 Sep 1687	25/366;33/702
Hopkins, Joseph:				
Cec	Hopeful Unity	150	12 May 1682	24/454;29/517
Hopkins, Robert:				
Bal	Hopkins' Lot	81	10 Mar 1696	40/337
Hopkins, Samuel:				
Som	Baball	300	10 Nov 1697	39/34
Som	Nunn's Green	350	20 May 1682	24/447;29/454
Som	Stockley's Adventure	300	26 Jly 1696	37/479
Som	Vines' Neck	500	1 Nov 1697	38/115
Hopkins, Thomas:				
Tal	Hopkins' Point	100	22 Dec 1684	25/189;32/362
Hopkins, William:				
AA	Content	100	6 Jly 1681	28/153
AA	Friendship	150	24 May 1681	24/349;31/97
AA	Hopkins' Addition	100	6 Jly 1681	28/144
AA	Hopkins' Forbearance	142	9 Aug 1681	24/349;31/413
AA	Little Brushy Neck	150	30 Jly 1682	24/461
Horne, John of Talbot Co.—See under Edmondson, John.				
Horne, William:				
Bal	Harnisham	50	18 Jun 1681	24/497
Bal	Horne's Fancy	40	24 Jly 1688	25/442
Bal	William & Mary	50	10 Nov 1695	40/528
Horne, Winifride:				
StM	Maiden's Lot	100	5 Apr 1682	24/405
adjoining land of Edward Horne.				

County	Name of Tract	Acreage	Date	Reference(s)
Horseman, Thomas:				
Som	Carlisle	100	24 Nov 1686	25/263;33/320
Som	Chance	140	10 Jly 1695	37/220
Som	Fladders	50	3 Jly 1683	25/31
Som	Kendall	100	2 Jly 1683	25/30
Horsey, Isaac:				
Som	Unity	100	12 Jun 1683	25/74;32/297
Horsey, Nathaniel:				
Som	Unity	100	12 Jun 1683	25/74;32/297
Horsey, Samuel:				
Som	Unity	100	12 Jun 1683	25/74;32/297
Horsey, Stephen, gent:				
Som	Horsely Down	150	10 Jun 1680	24/312;29/71
Som	Horsey's Fancy	150	1 Jun 1700	34/224
Som	Undue	300	11 Jly 1683	29/437
Hosier, Henry:				
Knt	Bristol	150	15 Jun 1681	24/367;29/293
Hoskins, Philip, planter:				
Cha	Addition	20	8 Jun 1683	24/523;31/511
Cha	Hoskins' Lot	187	14 Dec 1687	25/322;33/688
Houlston, Robert:				
Som	Houlston's Choice	150	[15 Jly] 1684	25/137;32/289
Houp, Walter:				
Cha	Houp's Addition	154	7 Mar 1688	25/382;32/597
Cha	Hoop Yard	500	20 Jly 1686	25/240;30/276
Howard, Cornelius of Anne Arundel Co:				
Bal	Howard's Addition	50	20 May 1698	38/35
Howard, Edmond, gent:				
Som	Beach Pine	100	3 Nov 1685	25/280
Som	Beckford	500	18 May 1681	24/332;28/355
Som	Entrance	850	25 Apr 1683	24/521;31/306
Som	Spalding Woods	600	30 May 1683	25/23;31/487
Som	Yorkshire	400	[25 Feb 1681]	24/249;28/336
Howard, Elinor, relict of John Howard deceased:				
AA	Good Mother's Endeavour	285	1 Jun 1698	37/539
Howard, John of Anne Arundel Co:				
AA	Howard's Discovery	50	1 May 1697	39/18
AA	Howard's Hills	150	7 Sep 1665	24/71
Bal	Howard's Point	31	2 Jun 1702	35/374
AA	Howard's Search	121	10 Dec 1696	38/13
Howard, John:				
Dor	John's Choice	64	2 Apr 1685	25/293;33/546
Dor	Howard's Neglect	44	20 Jly 1687	25/407;32/698
Howard, John Jr:				
AA	Howard's Luck	190	26 Oct 1694	27/309

County	*Name of Tract*	*Acreage*	*Date*	*Reference(s)*
Howard, Joshua:				
Bal	Howard's Square	150	10 Feb 1699	39/1
Howard, Mary, spinster:				
AA	Maiden	40	29 Sep 1682	24/466;31/417
Howard, Mathew, gent:				
AA	Howard's Addition	22	28 Sep 1682	24/466,25/403; 29/299;32/619
AA	Howard's Adventure	500	19 Oct 1681	24/354;29/374
AA	Howard's Pasture	200	18 Jly 1683	25/97;33/112
AA	Howard's Range	270	17 Jly 1683	25/56;31/459
AA	Poplar Plain	500	17 Jly 1683	25/83;32/83
Howard, Peter:				
StM	Howard's Mount	200	16 Jly 1687	25/322
Howard, Philip:				
AA	Howard's Addition	70	21 Jun 1683	25/83;33/113
AA	Howard's Hills	150	10 Dec 1679	24/71
Howard, Roger:				
Cec	Cuckold's Hope	100	28 Jun 1687	25/330;32/527
Howard, William:				
Bal	Howard's Park	107	10 Nov 1696	38/21
Howden, Judith, wife of Thomas Wyatt (*sic*):				
Tal	[unnamed]	400	22 Jun 1683	24/528
Howden, Mary:				
Tal	[unnamed]	400	22 Jun 1683	24/528
Howell, John, gent:				
Cec	Beaver Dam	50	30 Jun 1682	24/474;31/407
Cec	Cranberry Neck	150	3 Oct 1682	24/479;29/405
Cec	Hopeful Unity	150	12 May 1682	24/454;29/517
Cec	Howell's Adventure	100	1 Jun 1682	24/466;31/426
Cec	Howell's Range	150	15 Jun 1682	25/254;33/324
Cal	Huckleberry Hills	50	1 Jun 1685	32/311
Howell, Lewis of Cecil Co:				
Assigned to John Howell lands granted for his time of service.				24/474
Howell, Nathaniel:				
Cec	Howell's Addition	40	4 Jly 1687	25/331;32/529
Hubbert, Humphrey:				
Dor	Bridsdill Deale	77	[6 Nov 1678]	24/146;28/96
Dor	Hubbert's Choice	7	[6 Nov 1678]	24/146;28/101
Huddock, Thomas:				
Transported by Mark Cordea before Sep 1680				28/51
Hudson, Henry:				
Som	Nonsuch	130	1 Jan 1696	37/103
Hudson, John, planter:				
Dor	Hudson's Addition	130	26 Jun 1682	24/473;31/395

County	Name of Tract	Acreage	Date	Reference(s)
Hudson, John, gent:				
Dor	John's Pound Addn.	50	15 Oct 1683	25/125;30/159
Dor	Little Britain	85	20 Oct 1683	25/125;32/234
Hudson, William of St. Mary's Co:				
Cha	Hudson's Range	500	6 Apr 1685	25/166;32/161
Huggett, Thomas:				
Som	Carpenter's Folly	190	29 Apr 1687	25/353;32/542
Som	Wolf's Den	500	30 Apr 1687	25/354;32/512
Hull, Richard:				
Som	Holdfast	400	25 Oct 1688	27/136
Hulls, Merwell:				
Cha	Bures' Gift	100	28 May 1680	24/191;28/319
Cal	Hulston	100	25 Jly 1681	28/300
Humphreys, Thomas:				
Transported by Samuel Smith of Virginia by 1680.				24/33
Humphreys, Thomas, cooper:				
Som	Greenhill	50	10 Jun 1680	24/309;28/390
Hungerford, William:				
Cha	Hungerford's Choice	28	22 Dec 1687	25/321;33/615
Hunt, Benjamin, gent:				
Dor	Bedminster	150	14 Apr 1683	24/536;30/147
Dor	Benjamin's Mess	23	25 Feb 1681	24/301;28/462
Dor	Winsor	198	28 Mar 1685	25/293;33/590
Hunt, John, planter:				
Tal	Dunned St. Andrew	200	17 Jly 1680	24/172;28/191
Hunt, Woolfram, physician:				
AA	Hunt's Range	200	20 Oct 1683	25/40;31/449
Hunter, William:				
Cha	Huntersfield	392	10 Nov 1695	37/369
Hurlock, Abraham:				
Tal	Abraham's Chance	50	29 Mar 1680	24/233
Tal	Abraham's Lot	200	15 May 1679	24/212;33/147
Hurlock, George, planter:				
Tal	Addition	50	6 Nov 1685	25/228;32/346
Tal	Bloomsbury	200	28 Feb 1687	25/364;33/656
Tal	Yarnton	200	8 Nov 1685	25/295
Hussey, Thomas, gent:				
Cha	Discovery	150	13 Jun 1681	24/292
Cha	Hussey's Addition	438	16 Jan 1688	25/381
Cha	Hussey's Adventure	100	8 Nov 1687	25/321
Cha	Hussey's Lodge	33	24 Mar 1688	25/374
Cha	Hussey's Lot	103	26 Jan 1688	25/374

Hutchison—See Hutchinson.

County	*Name of Tract*	*Acreage*	*Date*	*Refe[illegible]*
Hutchins [Hutchings], Charles:				
Dor	Camberwell	344	24 Apr 1682	24/407;31/[illegible]
Dor	Cyprus Swamp	62	16 Nov 1686	25/302;33/460,5[illegible]
Dor	Cyprus Thicket	37	16 Nov 1686	25/30[illegible]
Dor	Epping Forest	500	- Mar 1682	24/420;31/165
Dor	Holly Swamp	100	23 Apr 1682	24/424;31/366
Dor	Luck by Chance	105	28 Apr 1682	24/426;31/358
Dor	Pasture Neck	74	22 Apr 1682	24/424;31/83
Dor	Smithfield	400	30 May 1683	31/169
Hutchings, Francis:				
Cal	Murtle Point	250	30 Jly 1694	27/255
Hutchinson, Thomas, tanner:				
Tal	Barmestone	106	28 Jun 1683	25/125;32/221
Tal	Beaverly	522	28 Jun 1683	25/49
Tal	Beaverly's Addition	230	29 Sep 1683	25/170;32/321
Tal	Hull	200	28 Jun 1683	25/39
Tal	Hull's Addition	100	10 Oct 1683	25/22
Tal	Hutchinson's Addition	150	20 Nov 1682	24/491;31/514
Tal	Hutchinson's Discovery	300	6 Jun 1682	24/413
Tal	Hutchinson's Point	72	22 Aug 1683	25/202;30/163
Dor	Irish Hope	50	4 Jly 1681	24/442;31/130
Tal	Lord's Gift	450	29 May 1682	24/489
Hutchison, William:				
Cha	Aix	422	16 Jan 1688	25/372;33/691
Cha	Apple Hill (moiety)	552	22 Mar 1688	25/371;33/698
Cha	Arran	300	11 Jly 1688	25/398;32/615
Cha	Belfast	130	22 Mar 1688	25/401;32/614
Cha	Carlyle	148	10 Nov 1695	37/170
PG	Carrick	462	1 May 1698	38/150
Cha	Carrickfergus	181	16 Jan 1688	25/374
Cha	Convenience	240	10 Nov 1695	37/156
Cha	Dalkeith	183	26 Mar 1688	25/373
Cha	Fortune	500	4 Aug 1686	25/271;33/295
Cha	Fox Hall	150	28 Jun 1685	25/272
Cha	Friendship	856	10 Nov 1695	40/9[illegible]
Cha	Friendship	1,571	10 Nov 1695	40/100
Cha	Garden	155	29 Mar 1688	25/37[illegible];32/574
PG	Hazard	167	1 Apr 1699	3[illegible]/202;38/142
Cha	Leads	100	1 Jun 1686	25/258;33/297
Cha	Mount Pleasant	164	10 Nov 1695	38/77
Cha	Oxmontown	438	10 Dec 16[illegible]	37/168
Cha	Partnership	100	10 Nov 1695	37/215
Cha	Piscatoway Forest	693	10 Jun 1688	25/382;32/571
Cha	Saugwhar	350	26 Mar 1688	25/372;33/695
Cha	Strife	1,30[illegible]	10 Nov 1695	40/98
Cha	Vineyard	150	10 May 1696	37/150
Cha	Whitehaven	737	10 Apr 1696	37/164
Hyland [Hiland], John of Cecil Co., planter:				
Transported Mary his wife & 2 other persons before 1680				24/66
Bal	Highlands	2,300	8 Oct 1684	25/159;32/76

	Name of Tract	Acreage	Date	Reference(s)
[illegible]	Fryers Hill	250	10 May 1680	24/66
ec	Lower Triumph	500	16 Sep 1680	24/185
ec	Triumph	460	16 Sep 1680	25/9,160
Cec	Upper Triumph	500	30 Jly 1684	25/159
Hynson—See Hinson.				
Hythe, Elizabeth:				
Cal	Maid's Delight	200	22 Sep 1680	28/73
Imback, Andrew:				
Tal	Plain Dealing	470	10 Nov 1695	37/8
Impey, Thomas of Talbot Co., gent:				
Tal	Delmore End	500	24 Apr 1685	25/226;32/364
Tal	Knivar Heath	500	30 Apr 1686	25/248
Tal	Padan Aran	500	27 Apr 1686	25/248
Cec	Winfield	500	15 Sep 1683	25/50;32/40
Ingle, William:				
Som	Chance	100	6 Oct 1685	25/276
Inglish—See English.				
Ingram, James:				
Som	Moorfields	130	5 Jly 1695	37/219
Som	Mount Pleasant	150	24 May 1684	25/422;34/50
Som	Poor Fields	150	13 Oct 1695	37/97
Som	Smithfield	100	1 Mar 1683	25/63;33/85
Ingram, John, planter, son of Robert Ingram:				
Som	Kellam's Folly	550	30 May 1682	24/412
Inlowes, Henry:				
Bal	Low Lands	33	7 Mar 1688	25/348;33/723
Bal	Oblong	150	20 Jun 1687	25/311;33/570
Innis, John:				
Bal	Come by Chance	257	10 Jly 1695	40/505
Innis, Nathaniel:				
Som	Cannardee	300	18 May 1681	24/331;29/479
Som	Innis's Addition	100	4 May 1686	25/276;33/545
Innis, William:				
Som	Cannardee	600	2 May 1680	24/246;28/190
Innis, William Jr:				
Som	Deale	600	13 Jly 1683	29/424
Insley, Andrew of Hunger River, planter:				
Dor	Andrew's Cove	100	11 Sep 1679	24/99
Dor	Andrew's Desire	248	[14 Feb 1680]	24/241;29/183
Dor	Andrew's Fortune	126	[14 Feb 1680]	24/242;29/185
Dor	Betty's Chance	75	4 Dec 1682	25/17;30/148
Dor	Betty's Desire	50	5 May 1687	25/305;33/418
Dor	Betty's Hope	50	[16 Jun 1678]	24/161;30/144
Dor	Hampton	120	1 Jun 1683	25/121;33/238
Dor	Long Acre	150	6 May 1679	24/49

County	*Name of Tract*	*Acreage*	*Date*	*Referen*
Isaac, Joseph:				
Cal	Giant's Range	100	24 Feb 1682	24/394;31/
Isaack, Richard:				
PG	Plummer's Pleasure Addn	46	25 Mar 1701	34/359
Isaacs, Ann:				
Transported by William Moure before Sep 1680.				28/56
Jackson, Isaac, cooper:				
Bal	Jackson's Venture	350	3 Jun 1685	25/182
Jackson, James, planter:				
Bal	Bears' Thicket	100	10 Dec 1695	40/527
Bal	Jackson's Chance	150	4 Dec 1685	25/288;33/503
Jackson, John:				
Tal	Fortune	100	19 May 1682	24/456;31/243
Jackson, Richard:				
Cal	Neglect	50	8 Mar 1686	25/213
Jackson, Samuel:				
Som	Small Lot	100	2 Dec 1682	29/193,441
Som	Venture	300	2 Nov 1682	24/509
Jackson, Thomas:				
Tal	Barbara's Choice	80	10 Sep 1695	38/62
Jackson, Thomas of Plymouth, England, merchant:				
Tal	Boothby's Fortune	500	23 Sep 1685	25/174;33/59
Bal	Clark's Forest	500	29 May 1684	31/427
Tal	Pleasant Spring	500	28 Dec 1685	25/174
Jackson, William:				
Tal	Jackson's Boys	46	20 Mar 1696	37/394
James, Charles of Cecil Co:				
Transported by Thomas Browning by 1680.				24/105
Cec	Carrola	150	30 Oct 1694	27/158
Cec	Hall's	300	[14 Feb 1685]	30/123
Cec	Hopeful Unity	150	12 May 1682	24/454;29/517
Cec	Mayford	100	7 Jly 1687	25/331;32/541
James, Edward of Talbot Co:				
Knt	James's Choice	300	13 Jan 1699	34/154;38/134
James, Gilbert, planter:				
Som	Wormington	50	20 Oct 1676	24/234;28/229
James, John:				
Cec	Good Hope	300	10 Sep 1683	29/515
Cec	Hopeful Unity	150	12 May 1682	24/454;29/517
AA	James's Fancy	55	15 Nov 1684	25/144;32/139
Cec	James's Inspection	47	20 Nov 1694	27/141
Cec	Poole	200	5 Jun 1682	24/470;29/516
Cec	Potton	50	10 Aug 1684	31/462

[Cou]nty	Name of Tract	Acreage	Date	Reference(s)
[Ja]nes, Joseph of Holland Creek, Talbot Co:				
Tal	Hickory Ridge	150	2 Nov 1680	28/100
Tal	Oak Ridge	350	[20 Nov 1678]	24/144;28/111
James, Thomas:				
Dor	Golden Quarter	213	19 Mar 1685	25/151
Cha	Little Deane	103	10 Apr 1696	37/166
James, Thomas, carpenter:				
Bal	James' Forecast	50	19 Nov 1686	25/289;33/507
Bal	James' Park	200	3 May 1687	25/310;33/527
Janner, John:				
StM	Salisbury Plain	100	29 Nov 1680	24/360
Jary, Stephen, gent:				
Assignor of lands in Dorchester Co. in 1679.				24/142
Jeams, William:				
PG	Jeams' Choice	200	10 Aug 1696	37/466
Jeffe, Thomas:				
AA	Jeffe's Increase	180	5 Oct 1683	31/176
Jeff, William:				
AA	Jeff's Search	39	5 Jun 1688	25/405;32/626
Jeaforson, John of Dorchester Co:				
His time of service completed by 1679.				24/49
Jefferson, Richard:				
Som	Cock Land	200	14 Feb 1683	25/132;33/227
Jelley [Gilley], John:				
Som	Addition	100	1 Sep 1687	33/385
Som	Gilley's Addition	100	21 Nov 1685	25/275
Som	Gilly's Adventure	100	4 May 1700	34/176
Gelly, Robert of St. Mary's Co., gent:				
Bal	Good Endeavour	500	15 Oct 1686	25/257;33/289
Jenifer, Jacob:				
Bal	Jacob's Choice	733	17 Oct 1681	24/501
Bal	Middle Jennifer	97	20 Jly 1680	28/35
Jenkins, David:				
Dor	Saw Box	50	7 Jly 1696	37/357
Jenkins, Francis:				
Deputy Surveyor for Somerset Co. appointed in June 1676:				
Som	Basslegg	150	17 Jun 1684	25/147;33/196
Som	Bawn Hill	200	17 Jun 1684	25/147;33/174
Som	Castle Green	300	9 Oct 1683	25/187;32/277
Som	Forked Neck	300	15 Jly 1684	25/136;33/176
Som	Hog Neck	300	9 Oct 1683	25/76;33/194
Som	Jeshimon	150	9 Oct 1683	25/80;32/285
Som	Mayfields	500	9 Oct 1683	25/75;33/173
Som	Middlesex	150	17 Jun 1683	25/114;32/272

County	*Name of Tract*	*Acreage*	*Date*	*References*
Som	Morris's Advisement	150	9 Oct 1683	25/70
Som	Newington Green	500	9 Oct 1683	25/75;32/504
Som	Old Bury	400	28 May 1681	24/329;29/65
Som	Spring Hill	1,000	13 Aug 1680	24/260;28/162
Som	Wakefield	300	28 May 1681	24/329;29/167
Jenkins, Robert, planter:				
Dor	West Redding	200	21 Apr 1683	24/535;30/81
Jenkins, Thomas of Charles Co., planter:				
Cha	St. John's	250	10 May 1686	32/207
Cha	St. Thomas	77	10 Aug 1695	37/242
Cha	Trooper's Rendezvous	250	15 Jun 1672	25/210
Patent issued at instance of George Godfrey.				
Jenkinson, Emanuel of Talbot Co., merchant:				
Tal	Beginning	300	4 Aug 1680	24/285;28/401
Dor	Brotherly Kindness	250	6 May 1683	24/548,25/122
Tal	Upland	300	29 Jly 1681	24/371;31/296
Jenkinson, Nathaniel:				
StM	Married Man's Hope	32	21 Aug 1694	27/197
Jenner, John:				
Som	Fort Neck	400	10 Nov 1695	37/534
Som	Jenner's Lot	200	14 Apr 1689	27/28
Som	Magdalen's Choice	100	1 May 1696	37/532
Johns, Richard of Calvert Co., gent:				
Bal	Groves	1,150	23 Sep 1683	25/82;33/52
Johnson, Albert:				
Tal	Albert's Delight	200	29 Jun 1681	24/356;31/326
Johnson, Anthony:				
Bal	Johnson's Interest	360	10 Jan 1696	40/519
Johnson, Bernard:				
Cal	Dove's Branch	200	14 Jun 1681	28/436
Johnson, Cornelius, planter:				
Som	Cox's Choice	300	18 Dec 1686	25/281;32/484
Som	Cox's Mistake	200	29 Sep 1683	29/342
Som	New Holland	600	13 May 1685	25/178;32/585
Som	Rotterdam	400	8 Dec 1688	27/26
Johnson, Daniel:				
Bal	Johnson's Island	60	5 Jun 1702	35/372
Johnson, Elizabeth:				
Transported by Samuel Gibson of Calvert Co.				24/4
Another transported by William Peirce of Cecil Co.				24/383
Johnson, Henry:				
Tal	Johnson's Adventure	100	31 May 1696	37/441
Johnson, James of Somerset Co:				
Assigned lands in September 1681 to his brother John Johnson.				4/355
Som	Bedlam Green	150	5 Oct 1681	25/27
Som	Longvile	50	20 Aug 1683	29/457

County	*Name of Tract*	*Acreage*	*Date*	*Reference(s)*
Johnson, John:				
Transported by John Abington of Calvert Co. before August 1680				28/34
Johnson, John, planter:				
Tal	Denby's Addition	27	25 Jly 1686	25/245;33/346
Bal	Johnson's Rest	450	10 Sep 1683	25/85,155;33/135,136
Som	Bridgewater	200	30 Dec 1681	30/156
Johnson, John, labourer:				
Som	Longvill	50	28 Sep 1681	24/355
Johnson, Odbert:				
Tal	Hope	100	25 Feb 1680	24/228;31/133
Johnson, Robert:				
Som	Huntington	350	18 Jun 1683	25/53;30/11
Som	Johnson's Hope	300	4 Jun 1681	24/319;29/55
Cal	Johnson's Lot	344	8 Dec 1687	25/344;33/726
Joyce, Francis:				
Som	Lutterworth	100	10 Sep 1684	25/176;32/381
Jones, Andrew, nephew and heir-at law of James Jones of Somerset Co., deceased, who died testate leaving a widow Sarah Jones who also died:				
Som	Becknam	150	20 Nov 1681	24/384
Jones, Andrew:				
Som	Jones's Adventure	500	22 Mar 1684	31/257
Som	Poplar Ridge	200	22 Mar 1684	31/259
Jones, Charles, bricklayer:				
Assignor of lands in Somerset Co. in Aug 1681.				24/373
Jones, Charles of Baltimore Co., planter:				
Cec	Charles' Camp	100	2 Apr 1685	25/218;32/396
Jones, David:				
Bal	Jones's Chance	130	12 Jun 1682	24/501;30/32
Bal	Jones's Venture	80	12 Jun 1682	24/503;30/54
Bal	Long Point	250	16 Jun 1682	24/503;30/66
Bal	Ranger's Lodge	500	15 Jun 1681	24/502;30/56
Bal	Stony Banks	50	16 Jun 1682	24/503
Jones, Edward:				
Deputy Surveyor for Cecil Co.				24/46
Jones, Edward, surgeon:				
Cec	Coldin	170	18 Jly 1680	25/9
Cec	Friendship	412	4 Jan 1681	24/546;29/294
Cec	Mesopotamia	340	23 Apr 1684	25/30
Cec	Pasture Point	18	2 May 1687	25/330;33/715
Cec	Prosperity	250	16 Jly 1685	25/181
Cec	Shrewsbury	180	8 Nov 1680	25/11
Jones, Edward:				
AA	Tryal	164	15 Apr 1685	25/252

County	*Name of Tract*	*Acreage*	*Date*	*Referen*
Jones, Elizabeth of Anne Arundel Co:				
relict of Humphrey Jones by August 1681.				24/3
Jones, Griffin of Talbot Co:				
Cec	Griffin	1,000	25 May 1683	24/528
Jones, Humphrey of Anne Arundel Co:				
Dead by August 1681 leaving a widow Elizabeth.				24/303
Jones, Humphrey:				
Bal	Jones's Addn.	100	1 Aug 1696	37/467
Jones, Humphrey, planter:				
Knt	Britain	200	7 Jun 1685	25/186
Jones, John, planter:				
Knt	Providence	300	7 Jly 1685	25/223;32/332
Jones, John, brazier:				
Knt	Baron Ridge Addn.	50	1 Aug 1682	25/16
Jones, John:				
Som	Bridgewater	200	2 Feb 1683	24/518
Som	Good Hope	150	15 Jly 1684	25/135;32/279
Som	Reed's Contrivance	100	2 Feb 1683	24/518
Cec	Petton	50	20 Nov 1682	24/482
Tal	Barren Ridge	60	5 Oct 1695	40/9
Tal	Jones's Armour	180	25 Oct 1697	38/30
Jones, John of Mattapony Hundred:				
Som	Worcester	100	3 Jun 1689	27/121
Jones, John of Anne Arundel Co:				
Bal	Push Pin	200	1 Oct 1700	34/285
Bal	Treaven	100	1 May 1700	34/316
Jones, Lewis:				
Dor	Cypress Swamp	250	27 Apr 1682	24/409;29/392
Jones, Moses:				
PG	Hazard	167	1 Apr 1699	34/202;38/142
Cha	Moses' Delight	90	10 Nov 1695	37/196
Cha	Partnership	100	10 Nov 1695	37/215
Jones, Richard Sr:				
Tal	Jones's Addition	50	21 May 1681	24/364;31/331
Tal	Labour in Vain	20	18 May 1682	24/455;31/295
Jones, Richard Jr:				
Tal	Jamaica	100	1 Mar 1687	32/309
Tal	Jones's Park	200	20 May 1681	24/364;31/234
Tal	Adventure	200	21 May 1681	24/339,455;29/406
Jones, Richard:				
Tal	Denby	50	20 Aug 1683	31/123
Tal	Hackett's Addition	150	17 Apr 1679	24/233
Tal	Jones' Hall	200	16 Aug 1680	28/30
Tal	Jones's Fancy	50	18 Aug 1681	24/376;29/326
Tal	Jones's Fortune	100	15 Oct 1682	24/491;30/71

County	*Name of Tract*	*Acreage*	*Date*	*Reference(s)*
al	Shrewsbury	300	10 Apr 1684	25/173;32/463
Tal	Spring Branch	100	26 Oct 1681	24/382;31/108
Cha	Richard's Delight		24 Mar 1688	25/374;32/551
Cha	White Oak Plain	101	5 May 1687	25/309;33/554
Jones, Robert of Somerset Co:				
Transported by James Ambrose before Apr 1681.				28/129
Jones, Robert, Deputy Surveyor for Calvert Co:				
Cec	Piccadilly	1,000	25 May 1683	24/550
Jones, Robert:				
Bal	(Broken?)head's Forest	150	21 Jly 1683	30/23
Jones, Robert of Calvert Co., gent:				
Bal	Jones' Inheritance	1,000	28 Sep 1683	25/79;32/467
Cal	Lower Gronery	440	12 Jly 1682	24/414
Jones, Samuel, planter:				
Som	Jones' Adventure	50	14 Feb 1683	25/81;33/171
Som	Jones's Choice	600	[6 Sep 1675]	24/144
Som	Jones's Meadows	300	10 Nov 1696	38/26
Jones, Solomon of St. Mary's Co:				
Bal	Level	200	19 Jly 1688	25/444;34/4
Jones, Solomon:				
Tal	Widow's Chance	50	10 Jun 1679	24/213;28/478
Jones, Thomas:				
Transported by Christopher Rousby of Calvert Co.				24/22
Jones, Thomas, planter:				
AA	Cadwallader	100	8 Sep 1683	25/46;31/449
AA	Robin Hood's Forest	150	8 Sep 1683	25/46
Jones, Thomas:				
Som	Ape's Hole	200	1 Nov 1698	38/145
Som	Flat Cap	50	10 Nov 1695	40/174
Som	Friendship	500	27 Nov 1685	25/232;30/255
Som	Little Bolton	850	15 Jly 1695	40/42
Tal	Jones' Delight	200	-- Nov 1679	24/221;28/441
Cal	Purchase	100	14 Mar 1681	24/299;29/178
Jones, William:				
Cal	Cuckold's Delight	186	26 Feb 1682	24/395;34/367
Cal	Cuckold's Desire	100	10 Aug 1683	29/358
Dor	Mulgrove	100	4 Apr 1685	25/293;32/498
Tal	Jones's Lot	50	20 Jly 1681	24/339;31/118
Tal	Sandy Bite	50	13 Aug 1680	24/285;28/498
Tal	Widow's Chance	50	10 Jun 1679	24/213;28/478
Jones, William of Cecil Co., administrator of Francis Bellowes of Cecil Co., deceased:				
Knt	Shadshold	650	10 Dec 1681	24/388
Jones, William of Bristol, England, mariner:				
Tal	Jones' Forest	500	16 Aug 1680	28/31
including lands for transportation of ten persons				

County	*Name of Tract*	*Acreage*	*Date*	*Refe*
Jordan, Alexander, planter:				
Tal	Jordan's Folly	160	17 Jly 1680	24/174;28/
Joseph, William Esq. of St. Mary's Co:				
Dor	Forest of Joseph	1,500	6 Jun 1689	27/276;34/
Cha	Hermitage	866	6 Jun 1689	34/1
Jowles, Col. Henry of Calvert Co:				
Cal	Colonel's Brigade	300	7 Mar 1682	24/396;31/22
Tal	Gillingham	400	6 Aug 1684	25/110;33/58
Cha	Grange	500	10 Apr 1685	25/166;33/91
Cha	Grovehurst	500	10 Apr 1685	25/166;32/142
Joyce, Francis:				
Som	Nothing Worth	225	8 Oct 1695	37/112
Joyner, William:				
Knt	Cooper's Hill	100	29 Oct 1680	25/15
Judd, Michael, ship carpenter:				
Bal	Friendship	400	10 Nov 1695	40/529
Bal	Hopewell Marsh	55	6 Jly 1684	25/150
Bal	John's Interest	200	12 May 1682	25/3,288;33/502; 30/53
Bal	Judd's Addition	28	28 Feb 1689	25/439
Bal	Judd's Purchase	100	18 May 1686	25/290;33/408
Bal	Little Marlow	200	27 Sep 1684	25/158;33/141
Bal	Oxford	65	12 Apr 1681	25/14;30/15
Cec	Tuttle Fields	50	11 Apr 1681	25/14;31/511
Bal	Waterton's Neglect	6	1 Aug 1687	25/349;33/706
Jump, William:				
Tal	Horse Pasture	200	19 Feb 1685	25/174;30/167
Tal	Jumpe's Addition	49	3 Jun 1682	24/468;31/214
Tal	Jump's Chance	500	16 May 1689	27/187
Tal	Jump's Choice	100	30 Jly 1681	24/372;29/373
Tal	Jumpe's Lane	100	3 Apr 1682	24/404;29/485
Keare, Thomas:				
Knt	Ash Point	42	29 Aug 1687	25/362;32/544
Keeble, William, son of John Keeble deceased:				
Som	Newtown	450	21 Apr 1683	29/268
Keech—See Keetch.				
Keene, Francis:				
Transported by James Round of Somerset Co. before April 1681.				28/129
Keene, Mr. John:				
Cal		300	24 Oct 1683	25/20;33/483
Keen, John:				
Dor	Keen's Neglect	99	13 Oct 1684	25/152;33/120
Keene, Susannah:				
Cal	Chance	200	13 Feb 1683	24/512;32/22

	Name of Tract	Acreage	Date	Reference(s)
[illegible], William:				
Som	Cheevely	100	22 Sep 1682	25/65
Som	Harrington	200	27 Nov 1688	27/56
Som	Partners' Choice	600	22 Sep 1682	25/66
Som	Wash Water	36	10 Nov 1695	40/146
Keetch [Keech], James:				
Cal	Good Luck	100	5 Jly 1686	32/429
StM	Town Neck	200	10 Aug 1698	38/92
Keete, William:				
StM	Keete's Purchase	50	6 Feb 1683	24/487;29/277
Keiton, Thomas of St. Mary's Co., planter:				
Bal	Keiton's Range	500	26 Aug 1684	25/141;33/29
Kellum, John:				
Som	Kellum's Choice	800	8 Oct 1695	37/138
Kembell, John:				
Dor	Kembell's Increase	50	29 Apr 1682	24/427;29/504
Kemble, Robert, planter:				
Cec	Contrivance	100	3 Jly 1685	25/201;32/397
Cec	Kemble's Addition	300	4 Jly 1685	25/182;32/420
Cec	Wood Land	100	3 Jly 1685	25/201;32/401
Kempe, John, planter:				
AA	Kempe's Addition	100	28 Sep 1683	25/39;31/437
Kempe, Robert:				
Tal		100	1 Aug 1679	24/124
Tal	Kemp's Lot Addition.	52	10 Nov 1695	37/298
Tal	Mable Addition	50	10 Nov 1695	40/122
Tal	Wolf Harbour	62	10 Nov 1695	40/155
Kemp, Rose:				
Transported by Samuel Gibson of Calvert Co.				24/4
Kempe, Thomas:				
Cal	Thomas & Anthony's Chance	250	10 Nov 1679	24/161;28/197
Kendall, Daniel:				
Bal	Kendall's Delight	500	1 May 1701	34/363
Kendell, John:				
AA	Kendell's Purchase	100	26 Mar 1696	40/363
Kendall, Richard:				
Dor	Kendall's Chance	50	27 Feb 1682	29/115
Dor	Stafford	103	16 Apr 1682	24/423;31/356
Dor	Wiltshire	47	19 Apr 1682	24/423;31/355
Kenna, Sarah:				
Transported by Samuel Gibson of Calvert Co.				24/4
Kennett, William:				
Som	Eagle Point	150	9 Oct 1683	25/57
Som	Herring Quarter	300	24 Dec 1682	25/80

County	Name of Tract	Acreage	Date	Reference(s)
Kinnemont, Ambrose:				
Tal	Long Point	42	10 Nov 1695	40/171
Kennimont, John:				
Tal	Dundee	400	16 Aug 1680	28/32
including lands for transporting himself, his wife Ann and children Patrick and John in 1654.				
Tal	Hopewell	80	10 May 1683	24/528;31/523
Kennystone, Thomas:				
Cal	Cade's Landing	72	20 Mar 1696	37/161
Kent, John:				
Cal	Hawk's Nest	73	16 Oct 1694	27/264
Kent, Robert:				
Cal	Kent's Chance	190	6 May 1689	34/26
Cal	Kent's Choice	100	15 Sep 1688	25/429
Kerby [Kirby], Walter:				
Knt	Ashford	100	29 Oct 1680	25/15
Knt	Kerby's Addition	50	10 Jun 1681	25/15
Knt	Kirby's Prevention	50	11 Jly 1694	27/360
Kerby, William, bricklayer:				
StM	Kerby's Choice	272	3 Dec 1680	24/197;28/328
Kerkley, Christopher of St. Mary's Co., joiner:				
Cha	Long Acre	40	5 Dec 1684	25/196;32/379
Kersley, Peter:				
Som	Kersley's Industry	300	4 Jly 1702	35/364
Kethin, Richard:				
Bal	Bold Venture	200	1 Jun 1700	34/250
Kibble, William, Som, orphan son of John Kibble:				
Som	Newtown	450	16 Nov 1679	24/161;28/178
Kidd, William:				
Cal	Island Plain	59	26 Jly 1684	25/106;32/143
Cal	Kidd's Levels	84	20 Jun 1684	25/36;32/9
Kindall, John:				
AA	Kindall's Purchase	100	6 Mar 1697	34/142
King, Elias:				
Knt	Bishford	200	26 Jun 1686	25/226;33/221
Knt	King's Prevention	34	10 May 1695	40/491
Knt	Poplar Farm	400	10 Jun 1682	24/413;31/202
King, Henry:				
Bal	Kingsberry	124	10 Jly 1698	38/88
King, John:				
Transported by John Quigley of Cecil Co. by 1679.				24/93
King, John, planter:				
Tal	Betty's Dowry	150	4 Oct 1687	25/369
Tal	King's Forest	150	10 Nov 1695	40/459

County	*Name of Tract*	*Acreage*	*Date*	*Reference(s)*
Tal	King's Neglect	115	10 Oct 1696	40/457
Tal	King's Plains	158	15 Oct 1687	25/326;30/332
Tal	Swineyard	175	10 Nov 1695	34/85;40/156
King, John:				
Som	Canadee Island	50	5 Jun 16883	25/112;30/189
Som	Coney Warren	125	7 Feb 1680	24/271;28/281
Som	Cow Quarter	50	15 Jun 1683	25/67;30/1
Som	King's Chase	100	15 Jun 1683	25/67
Som	Winter Harbour	80	10 Oct 1695	37/73
King, Richard:				
Bal	Whitehall	100	1 Jly 1701	34/348
Kinnemont—See Kennimont.				
Kirby—See Kerby.				
Kirk, John, planter:				
Som	Dickenson's Folly	200	[30 Aug 1680]	24/249;28/279
Som	Galloway	150	20 Apr 1680	24/333;29/460
Som	Jones's Hole	230	3 Jun 1689	27/100
Som	Middle Ridge	200	11 Jly 1683	29/327
Som	Puzzle	170	3 Jun 1689	27/105
Som	Woover Marsh	150	20 Apr 1680	24/333;29/459
Kirk, John:				
Dor	Adventure	191	[1697]	39/39
Dor	Kirke's Range	50	7 Dec 1681	24/387;31/142
Dor	End of Controversy	404	1 Nov 1701	34/357
Kirkham, William, planter:				
Tal	Kirkham's Discovery	150	24 Oct 1682	24/549;31/525
Tal	Kirkham's Lot	200	26 Jun 1679	24/217;32/320
Tal	Mount Hope	150	8 Aug 1680	24/285;28/412
Dor	Rattlesnake Ridge	150	10 Apr 1683	25/122;32/363
Tal	Wolverton	250	8 May 1683	24/548;31/526
Kirkwood, James:				
Transported by Samuel Gibson of Calvert Co.				24/4
Kirsteed, Joakim:				
Cal	Hazard	42	6 Jly 1694	27/282
Knapp, Robert:				
Tal	Poplar Neck	50	10 Apr 1679	24/211;28/350
Knight, Edward, planter:				
Cha	Find One	150	15 Jun 1683	24/524;30/126
Knighton, Thomas:				
AA	Knighton's Purchase	197	26 Jly 1680	28/37
Knightsworth, Thomas:				
Bal	Knightsworth's Folly	94	2 Jan 1696	40/513
Knowles, Lawrence:				
Transported Peter Vallon bef. Sep 1680.			28/127	
Tal	Discovery	220	10 Nov 1695	37/288

County	*Name of Tract*	*Acreage*	*Date*	*Reference(s)*
Tal	Knowles' Range	500	7 Nov 1685	25/215;32/253
Tal	Partnership	400	10 Nov 1695	34/98;40/236
Kytely, Humphrey:				
Cec	Hopewell	200	16 Mar 1681	25/12
Labett, John:				
Bal	Chinkasian Forest	61	[21 Jun 1694]	37/9
Lacey, Thomas, son & heir of Thomas Lacey:				
Tal	Frankford St. Michael's	616	6 Sep 1682	29/186
Ladd, Capt. Richard:				
Cal	Belfast	200	10 Dec 1680	24/445
Cal	Charles' Gift	616	12 Mar 1688	25/344
Cal	Charles' Gift Addition	200	10 Dec 1680	24/272;29/212
Cal	Ladd's Desire	100	4 Jan 1681	24/363;29/182
Lamb, Pearce, son of Pearce Lamb:				
Cec	Lamb's Meadow	215	2 Nov 1694	27/159
Cec	Lamb's Range	100	15 Jly 1683	25/42
Lambert, Ann:				
AA	Rocky Point	50	8 Jly 1680	28/13
Lampton, Mark:				
Cha	Jesmond	370	22 Mar 1688	25/379
Cha	Lampton	150	-- Jun 1682	24/473;33/34
Cha	Run at a Venture	148	22 Mar 1688	25/379
Lancham, Josias:				
Assignor of lands in Cecil Co. in Dec 1682.				24/450
Lane, Charles:				
StM	Rounton Ramour	100	27 Feb 1685	25/162;33/43
Lane, Dutton of Anne Arundel Co:				
Bal	Triangle	300	10 Nov 1695	38/69
Lane, George:				
Som	Fishing Island	20	12 Oct 1681	24/530
Lane, Jasper of Somerset Co:				
Transported himself bef. Apr 1681.				28/174
Lane, John, planter:				
Tal	Charleville	150	13 Dec 1680	24/285;28/460
Tal	Corke	100	6 Dec 1682	24/493;32/64
Tal	Irish Discovery	350	26 Mar 1687	25/365
Tal	Kingsaile	250	13 Dec 1680	24/285;28/413
Tal	Lane's Folly	100	10 Nov 1696	39/14
Tal	Lane's Ridge	200	10 Nov 1695	37/351
Lane, John:				
Som	Friends' Discovery	500	29 Aug 1688	25/397;32/643
Som	Lane's Addition	150	11 Jun 1689	27/96
assigned from Walter Lane				
Som	Old Head	100	1 Apr 1686	32/275

County	*Name of Tract*	*Acreage*	*Date*	*Reference(s)*
Lane, Timothy:				
Tal	New Town	100	19 Jan 1685	25/269
Lane, Walter:				
Som	Corke	100	5 Jly 1680	24/264;32/280
Som	Davis's Inlet	50	12 Jun 1689	27/87
Som	Friends' Discovery	500	27 Apr 1688	25/396
Som	Jones's Caution	200	29 May 1689	27/58
Som	Londonderry	500	2 May 1688	25/399;32/647
Som	Old Head	100	5 Jly 1680	24/264,25/211
	assigned from John Winder.			
Langford, John:				
Som	Chance	200	17 May 1688	25/421;32/651
Langley, Robert, gent:				
Bal	Langley's Habitation	300	1 Jun 1685	32/106
Bal	Langley's Tents	640	4 Apr 1684	25/100
Bal	Langley's Forest	356	10 Mar 1684	25/29;30/13
Bal	Overton	300	14 May 1684	25/103
Langrell, James:				
Som	Long Lot	50	5 Aug 1695	37/60
Langston, James:				
Som	Boddam	400	15 Jly 1684	25/133
Langton, Edward:				
Transported by Mark Cordea bef. Sep 1680.				28/51
Langworth, William:				
StM	Barbary's Addition	120	4 Mar 1682	24/395;29/121
Cha	Widow's Mite	600	[1 Jly 1685]	30/166
Lanman—See O'Lanman.				
Larkey, Thomas:				
Tal	Lancashire	50	29 Jly 1679	24/85
Tal	Larkey	50	5 Sep 1679	24/85
Larkin, John of Anne Arundel Co., innholder:				
Cec	Clifton	883	5 Jly 1686	32/254
bequeathed to him by will of George Holland				
AA	Eaton	400	11 Dec 1679	24/16
AA	Mill Haven	201	26 Feb 1683	29/145
Cec	New Hall	485	12 May 1681	24/547,25/2
Bal	United Friendship	700	15 Oct 1684	25/287;33/534
Larkin, Mr. Thomas of Anne Arundel Co:				
Cal	Angle	100	14 Jly 1694	27/340;34/122
Cal	Larkin's Forest	400	13 Jly 1694	27/61;34/118
Larramore, Alexander:				
Tal	Bampshire	50	28 Apr 1679	24/212;28/248
Tal	Larramore's Addition	50	20 May 1682	24/456;31/300
Larramore, Thomas:				
Som	Clear of Cannon Shot	100	25 Nov 1685	25/265;33/369
Cal	Goodwill	100	10 Jun 1680	24/193;28/347

County	*Name of Tract*	*Acreage*	*Date*	*Reference(s)*
Law, John:				
Tal	Castletown	100	10 Nov 1695	37/346
Law, William, carpenter:				
Som	New Scotland	400	5 Nov 1685	25/235;33/261
Lawer, William:				
Dor	Lawer's Discovery	258	15 Mar 1696	40/592
Lawrence, Benjamin:				
Cal	Desart	1,048	25 Oct 1682	24/517
Lawrence, Daniel:				
Dor	[unnamed]	100	12 Sep 1683	25/121;30/57
Lawrence, Daniel, tailor:				
Bal	No Name	100	5 Feb 1684	25/85;32/405
Lawrence, Henry:				
Bal		25	24 Jly 1688	25/443
Bal	Lawrence's Chance	10	13 Aug 1688	25/441
Lawrence, John:				
Bal	Canny Hill	25	19 Jly 1688	25/444
Lawrence, Capt. William:				
Knt	Folorn Hope	100	12 Jun 1682	24/413;31/55
Lawter, James:				
Transported by Mark Cordea bef. Sep 1680.				28/51
Layfield, George Esq:				
Som	Bashan	300	15 Jly 1695	40/46
Som	Fruitful Plain	550	15 Jly 1695	40/46
Som	Great Goshen	500	15 Jly 1695	40/46
Som	Little Goshen	300	15 Jly 1695	40/46
Som	Salem	800	15 Jly 1695	40/46
Layton, Henry:				
Som	Layton's Convenience	140	10 Mar 1698	38/117
Layton, William, planter:				
Som	Cuckold's Delight	500	25 May 1688	25/421
Som	Friend's Choice	300	8 Jan 1687	25/317
Som	Layton's Discovery	300	10 Nov 1695	40/574
Leach, Edward of London, merchant:				
Knt	Worth's Folly	1,036	30 Aug 1687	25/334
Leach, John, Deputy Surveyor for Calvert Co:				
Cal	Chance	137	25 Oct 1686	25/259;33/474
Cal	Peehen's Nest	100	3 Feb 1682	24/298;28/447
Leake, Mr. Richard:				
Cec	Addition	180	16 May 1684	25/256
Cec	Fork	300	1 Oct 1683	25/256
New	Greenfield	600	3 Mar 1684	25/253
Cec	Green Forest	200	29 Jly 1679	24/46
New	Green Oak	600	3 Mar 1684	25/253
Cec	Indian Range	500	14 Aug 1683	25/46

County	Name of Tract	Acreage	Date	Reference(s)
Lease, Francis of Anne Arundel Co:				
Bal	Lease's Chance	375	14 Jly 1679	24/75
Cal	Trundle Bed	200	7 Mar 1682	24/396
Lecompte, John:				
Dor	John's Good Luck	50	2 Dec 1683	25/201;32/450
Lecount, John:				
Dor	Indian's Ridge	87	15 Apr 1696	40/585
Dor	Lecount's Delight	50	1 Feb 1682	24/422;29/421
Lydiatt [Ledgeate], Thomas:				
Cal	Parnassus	75	31 Dec 1680	24/287;31/35
Lee, John:				
Dor	Lee's Chance	50	10 Nov 1695	40/595
Lee, Robert of St. Mary's Co:				
Dor	Lowe's Gift	200	27 Aug 1686	25/294;30/252
Lee, William, planter:				
Dor	Lancaster	250	29 May 1683	25/45,118;30/83
Dor	Scotland	50	27 Mar 1682	24/421;30/86
Leepe, Francis of Calvert Co., sawyer:				
Bal	Leep's Junior	252	10 May 1696	37/205
Legg, William:				
Knt	Adventure	50	27 Jly 1680	25/14
Lemaster, Abraham:				
Cha	Lemaster's Delight	200	1 Oct 1700	34/214
Leming, Philip:				
PG	Philip's Folly	106	1 Jun 1699	38/144
Lenham John:				
Cha	Oxmontown	438	10 Dec 1695	37/168
Leniger, John, planter:				
Bal	John's Habitation	200	29 Sep 1683	25/84;31/521
Letchworth, Joseph:				
Cal	Joseph & Mary	1,001	4 Apr 1686	25/333;33/563
Leverett, John:				
Cha	Leverett's Purchase	85	10 Nov 1695	37/257
Levin, Philip:				
Cha	Philip's Addition	92	10 Jan 1687	25/271;33/468
PG	Philip's Folly	106	1 Jan 1699	34/220
Lewellin, Audry, formerly wife of Thomas Cocks deceased:				
Knt	Kindness	500	15 Jly 1695	40/2
Lewellin, James of St. Mary's Co., clerk, gent:				
StM	Gallows Green	4	26 Apr 1681	28/132
StM	Enfield Chace	1,600	4 Oct 1681	24/354;29/334
Knt	Fancy	500	24 Jly 1682	24/475;29/154
Dor	Hab Nab at a Venture	950	13 Nov 1684	25/401;32/659

County	Name of Tract	Acreage	Date	Reference(s)
Knt	Partnership	3,000	24 Nov 1684	25/97
Cec	Piccadilly	1,000	14 Jun 1683	24/550;30/135
Tal	Willenle	1,000	6 Nov 1681	24/448;29/333
Lewis, David:				
StM	Asquith's Folly	100	5 Apr 1682	24/405;29/416
Lewis, Glode & Sarah:				
Dor	Sarah's Lot	50	20 Feb 1684	24/540;30/87
Lewis, Henry:				
StM	Asquith's Folly	100	5 Apr 1682	24/405;29/416
assigned from William Asquith.				
Lewis, Henry, physician:				
AA	Lewis's Addition	325	[19 Jun 1678]	24/159;28/102
Lewis, Richard:				
Som	Stepney	150	28 May 1681	24/321;29/50
Lewis, Thomas:				
Tal	Lewis's Chance	50	25 May 1682	24/458;31/187
Light, Joshua:				
Som	Castle Hills	250	4 Jun 1681	24/325;29/22
Lillingstone, John:				
Tal	Berke's	200	4 Aug 1682	24/490;33/393
Lillingston, John, clerk & Mary his wife:				
Tal	Bridgenorth	150	10 Mar 1686	25/246;30/323
Lillingstone, John, gent:				
Tal	Enjoyment	300	19 Dec 1680	24/341;33/393
Tal	Lillingstone's Addn.	350	19 Dec 1680	24/340;32/49
Tal	Lillingston's Castle	500	29 Oct 1679	24/224;29/253
Tal	Porter's Lodge	300	23 May 1682	24/456;31/286
Lincoln, Jonathan:				
Cec	Lincoln's Inn Field	403	10 Nov 1695	39/33
Lingan, George of Calvert Co., gent:				
Bal	Adventure	1,000	16 Jun 1681	24/498;32/23
Bal	Adventure Addition	300	11 Jly 1683	25/99;33/63
Bal	Back Lingan	525	6 Nov 1682	24/549;32/15
Bal	Back Lingan	450	20 Apr 1696	40/422
Cal	Elizabeth	300	10 Aug 1680	24/192;29/46
Cal	Lingan's Adventure	310	26 Apr 1682	29/45
Cal	Lingan's Purchase	502	10 Nov 1697	37/546
Linham, John:				
AA	Linham's Search	38	11 Mar 1688	25/346;33/718
Linn, John:				
Dor		50	1 Jan 1680	24/197
Lithcoe, John:				
Cec	Eagle's Nest	169	16 Dec 1680	25/12
Littleton, Bowman, son of Col. Southy Littleton:				
Som	Key	100	26 Mar 1680	24/257

County	Name of Tract	Acreage	Date	Reference(s)
Litton, Thomas:				
Bal	Litton's Improvement	40	16 Jan 1697	38/40
Lloyd, Edward:				
Tal	Fortune		4 Aug 1679	24/31
Tal	Guinney		4 Aug 1679	24/31
Tal	Long Neglect	100	10 Nov 1697	39/29
Tal	Moorgate Addition	267	10 Nov 1697	39/29
Tal	Skinner's Fresh		4 Aug 1679	24/31
Tal	Stock Range	400	10 Nov 1695	37/322
Lloyd, Henrietta Maria, widow and administratrix of Philemon Lloyd of Talbot Co:				
Tal	admitted to 517 acres patented by her husband.			25/317
Tal	Adventure	446	10 Nov 1695	40/115
Tal	Bachelor's Plains	216	10 Nov 1695	40/408
Tal	Henrietta M's Discovery	216	4 Feb 1696	40/112
Tal	H'ietta M's Purchase	412	20 May 1696	40/400
Tal	John's Forest	200	10 Nov 1695	40/406
Tal	Outlet	220	10 Mar 1696	40/409
Lloyd, Capt. [later Col.] Philemon:				
Tal	Attorney for Edward Lloyd of Talbot Co. 4 Aug 1679			24/31
Tal		120	8 Jan 1679	24/208
Tal		325	10 Jan 1679	24/208
Tal		1,700	15 Jly 1681	24/304
Tal	Addition	120	16 Dec 1679	24/21
Tal	Cedar Point	48	23 Oct 1684	25/317
Tal	Darland	1,400	25 Oct 1679	24/221;28/426
Tal	Lloyd Costin	500	20 Feb 1680	24/232;32/229
Tal	Lloyd's Meadows	600	[10 Nov 1678]	24/144;28/106
Tal	Lloyd's Town	1,000	16 Mar 1680	24/231;31/513
Tal	Lloyd's Freshes	1,000	20 Feb 1680	24/232
Tal	Lloyd's Insula	1,795	15 Nov 1682	29/88
Tal	Long Neglect	133	15 Aug 1684	25/317
Tal	Meergate Addition	267	10 Aug 1684	25/317
Tal	Refresh	350	26 Oct 1679	24/221;28/497
Locker, Thomas of Prince George's Co:				
Cha	Canton	100	10 Feb 1696	37/243
Cha	Langly	170	10 Feb 1696	37/239
Lockier, George:				
Transported by Christoher Rousby of Calvert Co.				24/22
Lockwood, Robert of Anne Arundel Co:				
Bal	Friendship	1,000	[15 Jun 1679]	24/143;32/89
AA	Little Buxton	29	18 Jun 1686	25/250;30/269
AA	Lockwood's Great Park	33	5 Mar 1688	25/347;33/733
AA	Lockwood's Luck	52	6 Jly 1698	38/1
AA	Lockwood's Park	50	6 Aug 1682	24/462;29/351
AA	Lockwood's Security	50	6 Aug 1682	24/462;31/64
AA	Tear Coat Thicket	108	18 Jun 1686	25/249;30/269
Lomax, Cleborne:				
Cha	Lomax's Addition	98	5 Jly 1687	25/306;33/505

County	Name of Tract	Acreage	Date	Reference(s)
Londey, John:				
Tal	Waterford	200	30 May 1688	25/414;32/676
Tal	Woodhouse	300	30 May 1688	25/413;32/675
London, Maj. Ambrose:				
Som	Flat Lands	50	20 Nov 1685	25/235;33/313
Som	Jericho	100	2 Jun 1688	25/419;32/652
Long, Maj. Thomas:				
Bal	Long Port	111	14 Jun 1683	25/26
Bal	Swede's Folly	23	4 Apr 1682	24/499;30/45
Long, Samuel, planter:				
Som	Long Lot	100	10 Jun 1680	24/311;29/51
Som	Long's Prevention	69	10 Nov 1695	40/290
Long, Thomas:				
Som	Long's Purchase	123	10 Nov 1695	34/66;40/221
Dor	Long's Chance	30	10 Nov 1695	40/601
Bal	Longworth	123	1 Aug 1680	28/35
Longbotham, Reuben:				
Transported by James Round of Somerset Co. before April 1681.				28/129
Longsden, William :				
Transported by Samuel Smith of Virginia by 1680.				24/33
Loockerman, Jacob:				
Dor	Addition	50	16 Mar 1682	29/102
Dor	Taylor's Promise	1,000	10 Dec 1688	25/435;34/159
Dor	Wenman's Rest		29 May 1682	24/459
Loskin, William:				
Bal	Brotherly Love	100	10 Sep 1697	38/20
Love, Robert:				
Bal	Forest of Bucks	200	1 Jun 1700	34/315
Bal	Whitacre's Ridge	150	10 Nov 1696	38/40
Love, Thomas:				
StM	Freestone Point	324	5 Mar 1688	25/350;33/324
StM	Love's Adventure	136	10 Nov 1695	40/125
StM	Love's Enjoyment	311	10 Nov 1695	40/133
StM	Partnership	260	5 Oct 1695	40/63
Loveday, John:				
Transported himself before Aug 1684.				31/496
Lowder, Charles of Kent Co				
Cec	Constantinople	100	1 Oct 1701	34/336
Low, Charles:				
Som	Rawley	300	5 Sep 1695	37/228
Lowe, Mr. Henry:				
Cal	[unnamed]	1,004	1 Apr 1685	32/313
Cal	Golden Grove	1,500	9 Feb 1684	25/90;31/317
Cal	Inclosure	200	16 Aug 1694	27/162
Lowe, Henry, gent:				
Dor	Horn	658	2 Jun 1684	25/152

County	*Name of Tract*	*Acreage*	*Date*	*Reference(s)*
Lowe, John:				
StM	Inclosure	75	1 Jun 1700	34/232
Lowe, Nicholas:				
Tal	Controversy	500	10 Nov 1695	37/348
Tal	Discovery	530	[21 May 1696]	37/515
Tal	Good Luck	180	10 Nov 1697	39/8
Tal	Lowe's Ramble	1,440	31 May 1696	37/452
Lowe, Susan:				
Cec	Castle Green	150	4 Sep 1688	32/593
escheated estate of Ralph Castle who went to England in 1671 having granted his lands to Susan Allome, the rent to be paid by her father Nicholas Allome. Susan Allome married John Darnall of Calvert Co. and, on his death, Henry Lowe.				
Lowe, Col. Vincent, Surveyor-General of Maryland appointed in 1677:				
Cec	[unnamed]		21 Jun 1683	24/553
Tal	Addition	500	18 Feb 1680	24/286;28/253
Tal	Adventure	1,700	18 Feb 1680	24/286
Tal	Beginning	500	13 Sep 1681	28/250
Tal	Chesterfield	500	10 Apr 1680	24/291;28/251
Dor	Cyprus Swamp	40	16 May 1687	25/304;33/403
Tal	Expectation	300	18 May 1687	24/364;29/207;31/505
Dor	Golden Grove	1,500	25 May 1683	24/552
Tal	Hackett's Field	143	4 Dec 1684	25/153
Tal	Lady's Delight	3,000	28 Jun 1683	31/220
Tal	Long Bennington	250	16 Feb 1686	25/245;33/279
Tal	Lowe's Aracadia	1,000	20 Jun 1681	24/368;29/390
Tal	Lowe's Desire	1,500	18 May 16871	24/364;29/292
Cec	Lowe's Lot	500	3 Apr 1683	24/520;29/210
Dor	Lowe's Purchase	1,000	12 Sep 1684	25/181;32/74
Cec	Mount Pleasant	300	[7 Aug 1683]	25/39
Cec	Quigly's Grove	1,000	25 May 1683	24/552
Cec	St. Vincent's	1,000	10 Aug 1684	31/503
Tal	Slaughterton	500	14 Mar 1683	24/522;29/218
Tal	Tawton Field	920	19 Nov 1686	25/365;33/920
Bal	Thurston's Neighbour	1,000	14 Oct 1686	25/257;33/277
Tal	Timber Ridge	2,700	[7 Aug 1683]	25/42;31/500
Bal	Vincent's Castle	500	13 Jly 1683	24/553;31/502
Lowe, William:				
Cha	[unnamed]	100	31 Mar 1682	24/404
Descended to his heir [unnamed] under the guardianship of Adam Butcher.				
Lowry, William:				
	Lowry's Chance	50	26 Nov 1679	24/160
Cal	Lowry's Reserve	340	20 Jly 1688	28/1
Cal	Surplusage	50	20 Apr 1683	29/216
Loyle, William:				
Transported by William Stone Esq. after 1650.				29/149
Lucas, Thomas:				
Som	Lucas's Choice	200	20 Oct 1684	25/175

County	Name of Tract	Acreage	Date	Reference(s)
Luffman, William:				
AA	Luffman's Due	131	5 Sep 1685	25/250
Lumley, Alexander:				
Bal	Convenience	50	4 Mar 1698	38/34
Lundy, John, gent:				
Tal	Bachelor's Plains	216	13 May 1687	25/340
Tal	John's Forest	200	7 Apr 1687	25/340
Tal	Lundy	200	29 Nov 1686	25/297;33/462
Lunn, Edward:				
AA	Lunn's Addition	55	7 Aug 1681	24/351;29/279
Lunn, John:				
Dor	Cabin Quarter	50	26 Apr 1683	29/251
Dor	Short Acre	100	21 Oct 1679	24/159;28/479
Lunn, Thomas—See under Price, Edward.				
Lurkey, John:				
Tal	Lurkey's Mills	100	10 Nov 1695	34/95;40/145
Lurkey, Nicholas:				
Tal	Beggar's Hall	36	10 Nov 1695	37/312
Lyle, William of Calvert Co:				
Cha	Waugh Town	492	4 Aug 1686	25/239;30/280
Lyndsey, Thomas:				
Cec	Level	100	15 Jly 1695	40/17
Lynes, Philip of Charles Co., merchant:				
Cha	unnamed with sketch map	840	25 May 1681	24/366
Cha	"several tracts"	640	25 Mar 1682	24/402
Bal	Lynes' Addition	600	22 Jly 1684	25/93;33/18
Cha	Lynes' Discovery	146	18 Mar 1689	25/432;34/3
Bal	Lynes' Forest	1,000	11 May 1684	25/33;31/518
Dor	Lynes' Part	2,000	9 Aug 1688	25/434;34/3
Lyon, Jane:				
Transported by Samuel Gibson of Calvert Co.				24/4
Lyon, John:				
Som	Lyon's Lot	100	15 Jly 1684	25/138;32/241
Som	Walles	50	15 Jly 1684	25/138;32/239
Som	Whitmarsh	300	20 Mar 1682	24/401
Lytfoot, Thomas of Anne Arundel Co., Deputy Surveyor for Baltimore Co:				
Bal	[unnamed]	500	18 May 1683	25/3;31/471
Bal	Best Endeavour	1,000	27 Nov 1686	25/291
Bal	Best Success	600	29 Oct 1683	25/231
Bal	Paradise	1,000	5 Jun 1683	25/4;31/472
Lytfoot, Thomas, gent:				
Bal	Pleasant Hills	350	17 Nov 1686	25/290;31/473
Bal	Prosperity	140	20 Sep 1684	25/193;33/170
Bal	Senaker Ridge	100	11 Jun 1685	25/286
Bal	Win(dley's) Forest	100	3 Mar 1686	33/54

County	*Name of Tract*	*Acreage*	*Date*	*Reference(s)*
AA	Expectation	1,000	16 Serp 1683	25/26
AA	Range	380	4 Jly 1684	25/98;31/484
AA	Re----'s Delight	320	3 Mar 1686	33/53
Lytfoot, Thomas of Baltimore Co:				
Cec	Land of Delight	600	3 Nov 1683	25/260
Cec	Success	300	3 Nov 1683	25/260
Maccullough, Alexander:				
Som	Inch	200	7 Dec 1686	25/275;33/406
Mackdaniell, Patrick:				
Tal	Patrick's Delight	65	10 Nov 1696	38/11
Macgregar [Macgregory], Hugh:				
Cec	Dunbar	228	31 Aug 1686	25/256;33/367
Cec	Long Land	78	30 Aug 1686	25/253;30/321
Cec	Macgregar's Delight	80	5 Oct 1683	25/255
"stopped by Macgregar, this being the same lane as Long Land."				
Cec	Macgregory's Delight	240	10 Nov 1695	40/472
Mackanney, Joan:				
Transported by Thomas Maisterman before Sep 1680.				28/53
Mackay, Robert, tanner:				
Cec	Biman	200	2 Oct 1682	24/479
Mackeele, Charles:				
Dor	Charles's Delight	75	30 Oct 1682	24/535;30/113
Dor	Charles's Desire	50	26 May 1682	24/440;29/386
Mackeele, James:				
Cal	Makeele's Desire	100	14 Feb 1682	24/392;31/34
Mackeele, John Sr:				
Dor	Stareling	15	11 May 1687	25/303
Mackerelle, James:				
Transported by Samuel Gibson of Calvert Co.				24/4
Mackhollister, Elinor:				
Transported by Samuel Gibson of Calvert Co.				24/4
Macklin, Robert, gent:				
Tal	Ashbury Addition	35	31 May 1696	37/433
Tal	Macklin's Addition	36	10 Nov 1695	34/101;40/136
Tal	Macklin's Beginning	400	14 Dec 1682	24/495;32/66
Tal	Macklin's Fancy	400	14 Dcc 1682	24/496
Tal	Yarmouth	100	14 Dec 1682	24/492
Macleere, Richard, turner:				
Som	Turners' Hall	200	15 Apr 1686	25/283;33/427
Macrah, Owen:				
Som	Addition	100	30 May 1683	25/76;30/175
Som	Middle	100	30 May 1683	25/77;30/214
Som	Pecking's Ridge	250	20 Nov 1681	24/384
Som	Wolf's Den	120	12 Mar 1688	25/357;32/511

County	Name of Tract	Acreage	Date	Reference(s)
Maddox, Thomas:				
AA	Maddox's Adventure	148	4 Jun 1683	31/422
AA	Rachel's Hope	72	4 Jun 1683	29/514
Magee, Edmond:				
Transported by Samuel Gibson of Calvert Co.				24/4
Magelehome, Terlaugh:				
Bal	Terlaugh's Choice	175	30 Mar 1698	38/15
Magruder, Ninian:				
Cal	Beale's Gift	42	10 Nov 1695	40/94
Maisterman, Thomas of Talbot Co:				
Assignor of lands in 1680.				24/173
Makinna, David:				
Cec	Woodbridge	200	17 Mar 1681	25/13
Makitt, John:				
Som	Waterford	450	26 Jun 1679	24/265;28/332
Malden, Francis:				
Cal	Malden's Luck	25	20 Apr 1681	24/298;32/28
Cal	Prevent Danger	250	27 Apr 1681	24/298;28/465
Mallett, William:				
Som	Coopers' Hall	200	27 Nov 1685	25/263;33/364
Mankind, Stephen:				
Cha	Mankind's Adventure	65	24 Mar 1688	25/374;32/588
Manley, JohnDeputy Surveyor for St. Mary's Co:				
StM	Basford Manor	4,000	21 Jly 1679	24/151
Manlove, George, planter:				
Som	George's Marsh	50	29 Jly 1680	24/274
Som	Manlove's Grove	500	29 Jly 1680	24/443;29/470
Manlove, Luke, planter:				
Dor	Penpipe Point	100	9 Sep 1684	25/205;32/455
Som	Cowley	800	28 May 1681	24/317;28/262
Manlove, Mark:				
Som	Pharsalia	600	2 Dec 1679	24/23
Manlove, Thomas:				
Som	Bear Ridge	200	23 Mar 1688	25/358;33/712
Som	Hockley	50	20 Nov 1679	24/246;28/400
Som	Hog Ridge	200	30 May 1683	25/88;32/458
Som	Wanborough	100	[24 Oct 1679]	24/245;28/429
Mann, James of Calvert Co:				
Cha	Fortune	500	2 Apr 1685	25/266
Man, Joseph:				
Tal	Chorley	100	21 Sep 1685	25/224;32/465
Man, Josias:				
Dor	Mann's Chance	28	20 May 1696	37/262

County	Name of Tract	Acreage	Date	Reference(s)
Mannocks, Hugh, John, Margaret, Katharine & Elizabeth:				
Transported by John Robins of Somerset Co. by 1679.				24/126
Mansell, Vincent:				
StM	Chester	100	6 Aug 1683	31/173
StM	Gloster	200	4 Jun 1683	29/303
Mansfield, William:				
Cec	Stoole Head	40	1 Sep 1686	25/328;33/725
Marbury, Francis:				
PG	Marbury's Chance	200	1 Sep 1698	38/66
Marchant, William of Dorchester Co:				
Transported Mary Saunders before Feb 1682.				28/469
Dor	Marchant's Lot	50	13 Jan 1682	28/485
Dor	Mount Silly	108	15 Apr 1696	40/583
Marcombe, Jeremiah:				
Dor	Marcombe's Desire	50	14 May 1679	24/113
Markingbear, Francis of Talbot Co:				
Assignor of lands in May 1679.				24/213
Marks, John:				
Som	Bengill	100	9 Oct 1683	25/24
Tal	Chance	200	26 Jun 1679	24/217;28/483
Som	Vale of Easum	200	18 Dec 1683	25/127;32/236
Marling, Francis:				
Tal	Bachelor's Branch	100	13 Jun 1679	24/214;29/223
Tal	Marling's Chance	50	16 Feb 1679	24/209;33/152
Tal	Marling's Folly	50	15 Feb 1679	24/209;32/350
Marlowe, Edward:				
Cha	Westmorland	198	10 Nov 1695	37/448
Marr, William, commander of the ship *Prosperous*:				
Cec	Camel's Worth More	1,150	17 Jun 1682	24/472;31/248
Marriot, John:				
AA	Cordwell	300	4 Sep 1682	24/463;29/511
Marser, Sarah:				
Transported by John Abington of Calvert Co. before August 1680.				28/34
Marsey, Nicholas:				
Knt	Hazard	90	8 Jly 1702	35/436
Marshall, Thomas of London, mariner:				
Transported himself and his sons William & Thomas before September 1680.				28/79
Tal	[unnamed]	86	1 Oct 1700	34/345
Marsham, Mr. Richard of Calvert Co:				
Cal	[unnamed]	300	6 Jan 1681	24/292
Bal	Adventure	1,000	16 Jun 1681	24/498
PG	Barren Points	50	20 Jan 1697	38/14

County	*Name of Tract*	*Acreage*	*Date*	*Reference(s)*
Cal	Black Walnut Thicket	300	27 Sep 1680	28/56
Cal	Content	300	26 Jan 1682	28/457
Cal	His Lordship's Favour	150	2 Apr 1681	24/300;29/165
Cal	Ware	300	4 May 1681	24/301;28/453
Martin, Ann, widow:				
StM	Widow (bounds of)	100		24/549;
StM	St. James's	100	20 Oct 1682	25/201;32/191
Martin [Martyn], Francis:				
Som		100	10 Jan 1680	24/56
Som	Cherry Hinton	150	4 Jun 1681	24/325;29/78
Som	Frustration	40	10 Mar 1696	37/216
Som	Parker's Peace	130	29 May 1689	27/77
Som	Troublesome	130	9 May 1695	37/109
Martin, Lodowick:				
Cec	Martin's Nest	100	24 Oct 1680	25/10
Bal	Martin's Rest	196	15 Jly 1688	25/440
Martin, William:				
Cal	Martin's Chance	130	6 Feb 1683	24/452;32/21
Martindale, John of St. Mary's Co:				
Tal	Little Minories	200	19 Nov 1686	25/259;30/322
Mase, Josias & Nicholas:				
Dor	Outlet	110	10 Oct 1695	40/580
Mash, John:				
AA	Mash's Forest	60	10 Nov 1696	38/11
Mason, Hugh:				
Knt	Buck Hill	150	19 Sep 1682	24/478
Mason, Robert of St. Mary's Co., gent:				
StM	Ambersley	65	3 Jan 1682	24/392
Bal	Paradise	190	10 Nov 1695	40/465
StM	Pounds	21	4 Jun 1687	25/305;33/416
Cha	Salom	300	22 Sep 1685	25/267;33/267
Mason, William:				
Som	Mason's Adventure	100	15 Feb 1688	25/356
Massey, Nicholas:				
Dor	Nicholas's Point	50	8 May 1679	24/125
Masson, Philip:				
Cha	Leads Addition	60	15 Dec 1686	25/272;33/544
Mathena, Daniel, planter:				
Cha	Mathena's Folly	100	[15 Dec 1680]	24/253;29/85
Matson, Andrew, planter:				
Bal	Andrew's Conquest	780	10 Sep 1683	25/36
Matson, Andrew of Cecil Co., carpenter:				
Bal	Matson's Lot	10	3 Apr 1682	24/499;31/515
Bal	Sister's Dowry	120	[31 Jly 1683]	25/45;30/21

County	Name of Tract	Acreage	Date	Reference(s)
Mattenly, Thomas:				
StM	Mattenly's Hope	200	28 Sep 1680	28/74
StM	Mount Misery	100	28 Sep 1680	28/71
Mathews, Ignatius:				
Cha	Mathews' Purchase	460	26 Apr 1687	25/321;33/616
Matthews, William:				
Som	Matthews' Adventure	135	25 Nov 1696	38/104
Som	Meadows' Ground	50	8 Apr 1695	37/68
Som	Worthless	100	10 Oct 1695	37/76
Matthias, Mary:				
Completed her time of service before Oct 1678.				29/479
Mattox, Lazarus, planter:				
Som	Mattox's Adventure	150	30 Aug 1679	24/261;29/5
Som	Mattox's Enclosure	100	13 Jun 1680	24/313;29/80
Som	Mattox's Enclosure	250	10 Mar 1696	37/512
Maudlin, Francis of Talbot Co:				
Assignor of lands in July 1679.				24/218
Mawnter, Alexander:				
Tal	Sutton Grange	645	7 Apr 1684	25/109
Maxwell, Maj. James:				
Bal	James's Chance	47	10 Nov 1695	40/107
Bal	Major's Choice	553	10 Nov 1695	40/106
Bal	Narrows	77	10 Nov 1695	40/522
May, Daniel, son & heir of Richard May deceased:				
StM	Vineyard	343	6 Jun 1681	28/168
assigned by George White of Runwell, Essex, England, brother & heir of Jerome White Esq. deceased.				
Mayle, Anthony:				
Tal	Goose Neck	50	8 Mar 1679	24/210;29/224
Tal	Wyatt's Fortune	50	4 Mar 1679	24/210;29/229
McAlaster, John:				
Som	Sweetwood Hall	400	10 Nov 1696	38/117
McClane [Maclane], Hector:				
Bal	Hector's Fancy	100	10 Mar 1696	40/549
Bal	Hector's Hopyard	300	9 Nov 1695	34/109;40/69
McLaney, Wooney:				
Som	Belfast	300	4 May 1688	27/110
McNemara [Macknamarrah], Timothy:				
Dor	Bachelor's Fancy	50	18 Mar 1680	24/204;28/283
Dor	Galloway	100	2 Jly 1702	35/370
Dor	Timothy's Prevention	57	16 Mar 1681	24/198,259;28/308
Dor	Turkey Range	50	10 Oct 1695	37/282
Dor	Turkey Ridge	50	10 Nov 1695	37/283
Dor	West Chester	200	1 Apr 1680	24/254;29/99

County	Name of Tract	Acreage	Date	Reference(s)
McWilliams, James:				
Som	Aghen Lowe	100	10 Nov 1696	38/37
Meade, Francis:				
AA	Bear Neck	225	24 Sep 1680	28/63;28/152
Meakin, William:				
StM	St. William's	50	16 Apr 1683	25/2
StM	Wolverhampton	150	3 May 1681	24/515
Meares, John:				
Som	Durham	150	2 Jly 1683	25/21
Mechary, Richard:				
Cec	New Coroborough	200	28 Oct 1683	25/254;30/318
Mechell, John:				
Tal	Mechell's Hermitage	100	10 Nov 1695	37/317
Meckay [Mecay], Alexander:				
Cec	Meckay's Purchase	150	16 Jly 1683	25/40
Cec	Philip's Neglect	400	15 Apr 1696	40/499
Medcalfe—See Metcalfe.				
Medford, Thomas of St. Mary's Co:				
Cec	Range	100	15 Jly 1695	40/20
Medsley, James:				
Dor	Medsley's Addition	100	1 Jan 1695	37/20
Meeke, Guy:				
AA	Meeke's Rest	350	1 Oct 1681	24/353
AA	Weston	30	1 Oct 1681	24/353;31/101
Meekins, Mr. Richard:				
Dor	Meekins' Hope	779	24 Dec 1679	24/179;28/298
Dor	Plain Dealing	50	5 Jun 1700	34/195;38/159
Dor	Porter's Point	100	24 Dec 1679	24/179;28/323
Dor	Rumney Marsh	50	1 Jan 1682	24/417;31/251
Mellifont, Nicholas, planter:				
Dor	Milland	100	18 Apr 1682	24/407;31/384
Mellson, John of Accomack Co., Virginia:				
Som	Gore	200	6 Jan 1686	25/360
Melton, William:				
Cal	Huckleberry Quarter	46	20 Jun 1687	25/305;33/578
Cal	Roasted Pig	52	30 Nov 1686	25/292;33/459
Cal	Wm's [Melton's] Lot	110	17 Nov 1682	24/481;31/10
Menteship, Robert of Talbot Co., gent:				
Transported himself, his wife Elizabeth and Roger Menteship Sr. before November 1680.				28/111
Mercer, John of Anne Arundel Co:				
Bal	Mill Haven	100	20 May 1696	37/487

County	Name of Tract	Acreage	Date	Reference(s)
Merchant, William:				
Dor	Mount Silly	60	2 May 1682	24/429;29/503
Meredith, John:				
Dor	Meredith's Chance	100	29 May 1682	24/441;31/148
Dor	Tewksbury	50	28 May 1682	24/440;31/423
Meredith, Lewis:				
Knt	Adventure	50	22 Jan 1683	25/14
Merrikin, Hugh:				
AA	Point Look Out	40	10 Nov 1695	40/116
Merrill [Merrell], William:				
Som	Gilly's Adventure	100	7 May 1700	38/150
Som	Merrell's Adventure	95	10 Aug 1688	27/37
Merriman [Mereman], Charles:				
Bal	Addition	120	10 Nov 1695	37/419
Bal	Merriman's Lot	210	29 Jun 1688	25/437;34/369
Merriton, John of Anne Arundel Co., gent:				
AA	Merriton's Fancy	500	15 Oct 1685	25/251;30/268
Bal	Merriton's Lot	500	18 Oct 1684	25/109
Meryday [Meriday], John, planter:				
Dor	Stubbs' Desire	50	28 May 1683	25/120;32/462
Dor	Valley of Misery	100	29 May 1683	25/43;30/82
Mesech, Julian:				
Som	Nantz		8 Oct 1681	24/510;33/82
Meshue, William				
Dor	Paradise	50	23 Jly 1681	28/356
Mester, Marmaduke:				
Som	Bachelor's Contrivance	150	15 Jun 1683	25/62
Som	Bachelor's Delight	250	15 Jun 1683	25/60;32/132
Som	Bachelor's Invention	250	15 Jun 1683	25/61
Som	Tilbury	150	8 Jun 1683	30/4
Metcalfe [Medcalfe], John:				
AA	Bachelor's Hall	180	26 Mar 1696	40/298
AA	Medcalfe's Chance	80	30 Sep 1681	24/353;31/104
AA	Middle Mount	70	21 Jun 1683	25/96;32/174
Metcalf, Thomas:				
Transported by Thomas Maisterman before Sep 1680.				28/53
Michai, Robert:				
Cec	Biman	200	10 Sep 1683	29/323
Michell—See Mitchell.				
Mickes, Walter:				
Cec	Forest of Dane	300	20 Sep 1682	25/143
Middleton, Robert:				
Cha	Appledore	607	27 Mar 1688	25/378;32/589
Cha	Apple Hill	552	21 Mar 1688	25/371

County	Name of Tract	Acreage	Date	Reference(s)
Cha	Aspinall's Choice	160	18 Apr 1680	24/258
Cha	Carrickfergus	181	22 Dec 1687	25/373
Cha	Dalkeith	183	19 Mar 1688	25/372
Cha	Garden	155	28 Mar 1688	25/373
Cha	Hard Shift	160	18 Apr 1683	29/238
Cha	Indian Neck	500	5 Jly 1686	32/432
Cha	Middleton's Lot	96	28 Mar 1688	25/374
Cha	Saturday Work	500	12 Jun 1686	25/227
Cha	Saugwhar	350	19 Mar 1688	25/372
Cha	Wickham	112	14 Jly 1679	24/143;28/86
Middleton, William:				
Cha	Godfather's Gift	123	22 Mar 1688	25/379;32/577
Miles, Francis:				
StM	Back Acres	100	[7 Jan 1682]	24/357;31/25
Miles, Henry, planter:				
Som	Trouble	50	30 Aug 1679	24/261;28/543
Miles [Myles], John:				
Bal	Addition	200	10 Jan 1696	40/434
Bal	Hope	200	10 May 1685	33/142
Bal	Miles's Forest	200	1 Jun 1700	34/325
Bal	Stepney	200	3 Oct 1683	25/111
Millburn, Nicholas:				
Tal	Lobb's Corner	60	10 Jun 1696	37/476
Millburne, Ralph:				
Som	Forest Grove	400	17 Oct 1701	34/298
Miller, John, carpenter:				
Som	Brent Marsh	400	2 Apr 1686	25/266;30/259
Som	Partners' Contentment	500	2 Apr 1686	25/278;33/441
Miller, John:				
Tal	Hobson's Choice	100	8 Aug 1681	24/374;29/499
Tal	Miller's Purchase	100	9 May 1681	24/363;29/500
Tal	Miller's Hope	132	8 Apr 1684	25/97;32/187
Miller, Michael of Kent Co., gent:				
Knt	Arcadia	1,500	18 May 1680	24/187;28/524
Knt	Chedle	50	10 Jun 1681	28/159
Cec	Covent Garden	500	25 Sep 1683	25/142;32/127
Cec	Miller's Satisfaction	78	4 Sep 1694	27/60
Knt	Mother's Gift	300	6 Aug 1682	24/496;31/477
Knt	Neglect	320	10 Nov 1695	40/492
Knt	Slydle	50	26 May 1680	24/187
Millington, Samuel:				
Dor	Millington's Adventure	100	26 Feb 1680	24/267;29/267
Dor	Millington's Folly	50	10 Oct 1695	37/279
Dor	Millington's Lot	50	12 Sep 1679	24/90
Dor	West Chester	200	1 Apr 1680	24/254;29/99

County	*Name of Tract*	*Acreage*	*Date*	*Reference(s)*
Millny?, Christopher & Elizabeth his wife:				
AA	Millny's Purchase	120	3 Apr 1698	39/17
Mills, Humphrey:				
Completed his time of service before Aug 1684.				31/496
Mills, William:				
Dor	Fortune	30	28 Feb 1687	25/292;33/415
Minges, Edward, planter:				
Cha	Minges' Chance	150	15 Mar 1683	24/504;33/19
Mishen, William:				
Dor	Godstone	40	30 Jly 1688	25/407;32/699
Mitchell, Geffery:				
Som	Haphazard	100	10 Dec 1697	38/67
Mi(t)chell, John:				
StM	Michell's Choice	47	7 Jly 1686	25/242;32/501
Mitchell, John, planter:				
Tal	Mitchell's Lot	100	7 Dec 1682	24/493;32/46
Mitchell, Randall, planter:				
Som	Mitchell's Lot	400	8 Nov 1679	24/269;28/293
Mitchell, Richard, planter:				
Tal	Colne	500	7 Dec 1681	24/387;31/323
Mitchell, Thomas, planter:				
Dor	Hog Quarter	100	12 Aug 1683	25/121;33/237
Michell, William, planter:				
AA	Michell's Chance	205	29 May 1684	25/105;32/209
Mitford, Thomas of St. Mary's Co:				
Cec	Range	118	2 Apr 1685	25/186
Mold—See Mould.				
Moody, Edmond:				
Cha	Ralph's Folly	98	10 Sep 1695	37/241
Moore, Alexander:				
Tal	Moorfields	94	10 May 1687	25/314;33/594
Tal	Moorfields Addition	30	15 Oct 1687	25/324;33/624
Moore [More], James of Calvert Co., carpenter:				
Cal	Beale Hunting Quarter	300	8 Mar 1681	24/300;29/169
Cal	Child's Portion	227	11 Sep 1694	27/242
Cal	Defence	150	7 Mar 1682	24/397;31/20
Cal	Four Hills	400	5 Jly 1686	33/165
Cal	Horse Race	300	6 Mar 1682	24/396;32/146
Cal	Leith	500	22 Feb 1682	24/393;38/57
Cal	Moore's Addition	231	10 Nov 1695	37/160
Cal	Moore's Little Worth	40	30 Aug 1694	27/144
Cal	Morefields	150	23 Sep 1680	28/87
Cal	Potterne Wake	203	2 Jly 1685	25/169;32/156

County	Name of Tract	Acreage	Date	Reference(s)
Moore, John:				
Transported by John Abington of Calvert Co. before August 1680.				28/34
Moore, Mordecai of Anne Arundel Co:				
Cal	Beale's Reserve	455	10 Nov 1695	40/85
AA	Moore's Morning Choice	1,368	10 Nov 1695	40/179
Moore, William:				
Transported by John Abington of Calvert Co. before August 1680.				28/34
Moorewood, Ann:				
Transported by Thomas Clipsham before Sep 1680.				28/44
Morecroft, John—See under Squire, Jonathan.				
Morgan, Abraham:				
Tal	L---ey's Fortune	16	25 Mar 1697	38/3
Morgan, Harbert:				
Tal	Morgan's Enlargement	260	1 Jun 1700	38/158;30/354
Morgan, Henry:				
Som	Morgan's Choice	251	2 May 1688	25/396;34/44
Som	Rochester	500	31 Aug 1688	25/395;34/46
Som	Sandy Wharf	400	26 Nov 1679	24/41
Morgan, John:				
Tal	Morgan's Neglect	150	10 Mar 1696	37/327
Morgan, William:				
Cec	[unnamed]	50	11 Sep 1679	24/43
Cec	Walles	50	28 May 1683	25/5;32/423
Morgan, William of Anne Arundel Co:				
Bal	Morgan's Lot	200	25 May 1687	25/311;33/514
Morley, John:				
Tal	Hawk Hill Addition	100	6 Jun 1679	24/213
Morris, John:				
Cec	Bachelor's Folly	100	21 Jun 1684	25/343
Morris, Manasses, cooper:				
Som	Elizabeth's Choice	200	23 Mar 1688	25/357;33/682
Som	Morris's Lot	300	15 Jun 1683	25/87,423;32/268
Som	Tower Hill	150	23 Mar 1688	25/357
Som	Turkey Cock Hill	150	15 Jun 1683	25/60;31/537
Morris, Thomas, surgeon:				
Som	Northfleet	200	16 Dec 1683	25/131;30/204
Som	Southfleet	200	11 Dec 1683	25/180;33/216
Morris, William:				
Som	Middlesex	450	28 Apr 1680	24/308;28/389
Som	Suffolk	1,000	20 Jun 1679	24/144;28/108
Mosely, James:				
Dor	Mosely's Outlet	100	14 May 1679	24/38

County	*Name of Tract*	*Acreage*	*Date*	*Reference(s)*
Moses, Richard:				
Assignor of lands in Talbot Co. in 1679.				24/224
Moss, Richard:				
AA	Moss's Pasture	32	24 Apr 1685	25/250;33/535
Mould [Mold], Humphrey, planter:				
Dor	Creek's End	50	20 May 1682	24/436;31/345
Dor	Knivar Heath	120	2 Mar 1684	24/540;30/88
Mould, John:				
Bal	Mould's Lot	15	10 Jun 1681	24/547;31/468
Bal	Mould's Success	400	10 Jun 1681	25/1;31/467
Moure, William, gent:				
Transported himself and Elizabeth his wife before September 1680.				28/56
Moxon, Adam of Transquaking, carpenter:				
Dor	Middleton Grange	50	10 Aug 1683	31/367
Dor	Middleton in Oaks	100	7 Jun 1683	25/145;32/407
Dor	Moxon's Adventure	86	12 Oct 1681	24/379;29/397
Moy, Daniel, son & heir of Richard Moy:				
StM	Fowle's Discovery	100	7 Apr 1682	29/19
Mudd, Thomas, gent:				
StM	Jarvis	120	13 Apr 1681	24/278;28/425
StM	Mudd's Rest	200	12 Jly 1686	25/242;33/349
Mulliken, Daniel:				
Tal	Mulliken's Delight	150	31 May 1696	37/410
Mullican, James:				
PG	Level	300	24 Oct 1683	38/101
Mullican, John, planter:				
Tal	Mullican's Choice	170	2 May 1696	40/563
Mullikin, Patrick:				
Tal	Patrick's Plain	300	5 Jly 1686	32/316
Mulraine, Cornelius of Talbot Co., planter:				
Tal	Cornelius's Garden	50	12 Apr 1683	29/213
Dor	Mulrain	150	20 Sep 1683	25/124;32/212
Tal	Quillen	50	21 Jan 1679	24/209;29/220
Tal	Ware Point	50	20 Jan 1679	24/209
Munford, Edward:				
Bal	Hart's Green	35	1 Apr 1682	24/502;30/59
Bal	Hopewell	15	1 Mar 1682	24/499;30/33
Murah, Auguste:				
Dor	Murah's Land	100	19 Mar 1682	24/421
Murphew, John, tanner:				
Som	Kilkenny	400	31 Mar 1686	25/237;33/309
Murph(e)y, Capt. James, merchant:				
Tal	Barnes' Neck	100	25 Aug 1680	24/171
Tal	Barnes' Neck Addn.	100	4 Jly 1681	28/408

County	Name of Tract	Acreage	Date	Reference(s)
Tal	Level Ridge	1,000	17 Aug 1683	25/46;32/44
Tal	Mount Hope	500	16 Aug 1683	25/44;33/73
Dor	Murphey's Addition	480	26 Oct 1684	25/206;30/162
Cec	Skelton	500	13 Sep 1682	24/517;29/162
Tal	Snelling's Delight	150	4 Aug 1684	25/271;30/328
Murph(e)y, Patrick:				
Bal	Cuckold Maker's Palace	100	1 Jun 1700	34/258;38/153
Bal	Luck	15	10 Nov 1695	40/510
AA	Murphey's Choice	125	19 Jly 1684	25/143;32/194
Cec	Murphy's Forest	1,000	1 Sep 1696	38/60
Murray, Anguish:				
Dor	Marsh Land	100	30 Jan 1682	30/97
Murray [Murrey], James:				
Bal	Athol	617	10 Nov 1695	34/103;40/77
Bal	Morgan's Delight	500	10 Nov 1695	40/531
Bal	Murray's Addition	89	10 Nov 1695	40/532
Bal	Murrey's Point	68	16 Oct 1698	38/125
Mustard, John:				
Transported by Samuel Gibson of Calvert Co.				24/4
Myles—See Miles.				
Nailer, George:				
PG	Nailer's Purchase	36	1 May 1698	38/69
PG	Nailer's Range	164	1 May 1698	38/68
Nash, Richard:				
Cec	High Park	200	24 Jun 1683	31/274
including land for transporting himself according to a grant of 1658.				
Nash, Richard & Ann—See under Wheeler, Ann.				
Neale, Mr. Anthony, son of Capt. James Neale deceased:				
Cha	[unnamed]	494	10 Oct 1695	40/300
Cha	Neale's Gift	500	1 Aug 1682	25/91
Neale, Francis, planter:				
Tal	Shadwell	100	26 May 1686	25/416;32/679
Tal	Shadwell Addition	300	31 Jan 1689	27/201;34/82
Tal	Fairfield	200	26 Jun 1679	24/217
Neale, Capt. James:				
Cha	Neale's Desire	125	17 Jly 1683	25/1
Neale, Jonathan:				
AA	Neale's Purchase	198	28 Jun 1694	27/324
Nelson, John:				
PG	Dumfrese	336	20 Jly 1696	37/485
Cha	Gilliard's Beginning	277	10 Nov 1695	34/115;40/231
Nelson, Richard:				
Cha	Coal	330	10 Nov 1695	37/531
Nelson, Thomas:				
Cal	Nelson's Reserve	135	10 Mar 1683	24/511;32/29

County	*Name of Tract*	*Acreage*	*Date*	*Reference(s)*
Neaves, Robert:				
Knt	Rushmore	100	4 Dec 1682	24/554,25/17
Nevett, John:				
StM	Nevett's Beginning	100	22 Oct 1681	24/348;31/13
Nevill, James:				
Som	Nevill's Folly	200	19 Jun 1689	27/117
New, Richard, planter:				
Cha	Rowley	200	[17 Dec 1680]	24/255;29/109
Newman, Henry, carpenter:				
Tal	Leeke Hill	179	[28 Mar 1683]	24/545;33/80
Tal	Willingham	50	10 Apr 1683	24/545
Newman, John:				
Tal	Bedworth	200	16 Jun 1681	24/367;31/128
Tal	Newingham	100	11 Oct 1683	25/25
Tal	Newman's Addition	50	18 Jun 1681	24/337;31/341
Newman, Roger of Anne Arundel Co:				
Bal	Newman's Delight	450	10 Nov 1695	40/257
Newman, William:				
StM	Monmouth	87	15 Jun 1687	25/309;33/524
Newnam—See Nunam.				
Newson, Thomas:				
Bal	Miles Hill	100	10 Nov 1695	40/544
Newsum, Thomas:				
Bal	Newsum's Adventure	230	1 Jun 1700	34/259;35/391
Newton, Edward:				
Dor	Angle	6	30 Mar 1681	24/269
Dor	Mazarine's Hall	10	24 Oct 1681	24/381;31/152
Dor	Partnership	1,000	20 Apr 1681	24/282;34/173
Newton, John:				
Dor	Westminster	100	10 Mar 1682	24/399;31/378
Nicholes, John of Dorchester Co:				
Assignor of lands in Jan 1680.				24/267
Nicholls, Francis:				
Transported by Jeremiah Hooke of Somerset Co. by Feb 1682				28/402
Nicholls, John:				
His time of service completed before Aug 1684.				31/496
Cha	Nicholls' Hope	135	17 Mar 1688	25/381;32/576
Nicholls, Thomas:				
Cec	Londonderry	200	10 Dec 1695	37/2
Nicholls, Thomas & Elizabeth:				
Cec	Mulberry Dock	205	15 Apr 1696	37/1
in the right of Elizabeth Nicholls by the will of her late husband Thomas Yerbury				

County	Name of Tract	Acreage	Date	Reference(s)
Nicholls, William:				
Cal	Nicholls' Chance	210	10 Mar 1683	24/512;32/13
Nicholson, John of Anne Arundel Co., plasterer:				
AA	Nicholson's Addition	36	16 Jan 1695	25/144;27/333;33/167
Bal	Plasterers' Hall	100	7 Jly 1683	25/92;33/109
Nicholson, Richard:				
Som	Nicholson's Lot	100	23 Mar 1688	25/357;33/681
Nicholson, Symon of Calvert Co:				
Cha	Blackash	146	4 Aug 1686	25/238;33/362
Noble, Isaac:				
Som	Noble's Lot	73	6 Mar 1686	25/281
Som	Winterbourne	100	10 Jly 1683	29/450
Noble, John:				
StM	Noble's Victory	50	17 Aug 1682	24/477;31/57
Noble, Robert:				
Tal	Noble's Addition	150	12 Mar 1680	24/231;31/253
Tal	Noble's Meadow	150	24 Oct 1681	24/381
Tal	Noble Range	200	1 Jly 1679	24/218
Noble, William:				
Som	Cherry Garden	86	10 Nov 1695	34/63;40/216
Som	Timber Grove	150	15 Jun 1683	25/285;33/384
Noe, John:				
Cha	Timber Swamp	45	1 Jun 1698	38/136
Noland, Darby:				
Cec	Bandon Bridge	60	3 May 1687	25/351;32/535
Noland, Peirce:				
Cec	Feddard	300	30 Oct 1686	25/328;32/540
Norris [Norrest], Robert, carpenter:				
Tal	Clarkson Hill	150	13 Jan 1682	24/390;29/332
Tal	Clarkson Hill Addition	80	22 Jun 1686	25/342;33/636
Tal	Long Run	100	21 Feb 1685	25/170;33/164
Tal	Mount Malicke	150	30 Nov 1684	25/222;32/336
Tal	Norrest's Addition	120	22 Jun 1686	25/342
Norrest, Robert:				
Cec	Norrest's Desire	18	29 Jun 1694	27/220
Cec	Philip's Neglect	400	15 Apr 1696	40/499
Norris, Thomas:				
Bal	Envell Chace	230	1 Jun 1696	40/550
Knt	Norris's Forest	100	14 Mar 1680	24/233;29/111
Norwood, Andrew:				
AA	Norwood's Angles	103	22 Jun 1683	25/55;31/447
AA	Norwood's Recovery	104	6 Jun 1686	25/219;30/229
Nott, John of Calvert Co., planter:				
Cal	Holland's Purchase	300	15 May 1683	30/242

County	Name of Tract	Acreage	Date	Reference(s)
Nowell, James:				
Dor	Margaret's Fancy	100	20 Mar 1697	38/2
Dor	Nowell's Pockety	150	28 Nov 1681	24/386;31/136
Nowell, Mr. William:				
Cec	[blank]	300	5 May 1684	25/343
Cec	Nowell's Adventure	80	8 Jly 1687	25/331
Nowland, Moses:				
Transported by John Quigley of Cecil Co. by 1679				24/93
Nugent, Christopher:				
Som	Come by Chance	150	22 Sep 1682	25/66
Nugent, Edmond:				
StM	St. Katharine's	180	5 Oct 1695	40/28
Nunam [Newnam], John, planter:				
Tal	Bobshill	10	16 Jun 1681	24/356;31/297
Tal	Coventry	300	22 Feb 1680	24/231;31/322
Tal	Good Chance	50	10 Feb 1685	25/391
Tal	Nunam	50	16 May 1679	24/213;29/222
Tal	Nunam's Folly	50	20 Mar 1696	37/404
Tal	Jacob & John's Pasture	340	15 Jly 1687	25/300;32/477
Tal	Newnam's Range	100	18 Jun 1681	24/337;32/506
Tal	Nunam's Thicket	50	16 Aug 1687	25/300;32/479
Nuthead, William of St. Mary's, printer:				
Tal	Nuthead's Choice	300	19 Nov 1686	25/295
Nutter, Christopher, planter:				
Som	[marsh land unnamed]	50	18 Nov 1685	25/279
Som	Attowattocoquin	1,200	22 Feb 1683	24/508;31/330
Som	Nutter's Rest	450	21 Apr 1684	25/361
Som	Rich Ridge	239	22 Feb 1683	24/507;31/325
Som	Tossewondoke	134	22 Feb 1683	24/507;31/320
Nutwell, Elias:				
Tal	Nutwell's Chance	300	9 Oct 1687	25/366;33/655
O'Dwyre, Mr. Edmund:				
Cec	Crossayle	575	29 Nov 1683	25/161;32/199
O'Dwyre, Mr. Edmund & others:				
Cec	New Munster	6,000	29 Aug 1683	25/36;32/201
O'Higgerty, Dennis:				
Som	Hopewell	350	24 May 1688	27/113
O'Keene, Roger, planter:				
Som	Old Town	100	[20 Nov 1677]	24/104,158
O'Lanman [Lanman], Dunham:				
Som	Dublin	125	15 Jun 1683	25/87;33/228
Som	Pemminie	50	20 May 1682	24/448;29/453
O'Norton, William:				
Som	O'Norton's Lot	300	9 May 1687	25/335;32/707

County	*Name of Tract*	*Acreage*	*Date*	*Reference(s)*
Ocklen, Margaret:				
Tal	Brigling	100	23 Jun 1679	24/216;31/200
Offett, William:				
Cal	Offett's Delight	101	12 Sep 1694	27/195
Offley, John, gent:				
Assignor of lands in Dorchester Co. in 1678/9.				24/99,156
Oglesby, George, planter:				
Bal	Frogmorton	53	10 May 1687	25/310;33/550
Bal	Ogilsby's Chance	200	5 Aug 1684	25/99;33/133
Bal	Oglesby's Mount	45	28 Jly 1688	25/441
Oldfield, George:				
Cec	Bristol	150	30 Oct 1683	25/264
Cec	Gloster	750	30 Oct 1683	25/264
Cec	Oldfield's Lot	100	16 Mar 1681	25/13
Oldfield, George Jr:				
Cec	George's Friendship	100	16 Mar 1681	25/13
Omealy, Brian of Talbot Co:				
Cec	Adventure	510	10 Aug 1684	32/50
Cec	Angel's Lot	1,200	21 Jun 1683	24/525
Cec	Angel's Rest	1,200	21 Jun 1683	24/525;32/41
Tal	Bachelor's Range Add*	500	4 Sep 1681	24/377;31/228
Cec	Bryan's Lot	400	20 Apr 1683	24/524
Tal	Bryan's Lot	50	10 Apr 1679	24/211;28/346;31/530
Tal	Omealy's Grange	200	8 Nov 1680	24/196
Tal	Omealy's Range	200	10 Sep 1681	24/340;28/351
Tal	Poplar Level	100	21 Dec 1679	24/221
Oram, Valentine:				
Transported by John Edmondson before Nov 1680.				28/57
Orem, Andrew:				
Tal	Fox's Den	56	10 Nov 1695	37/513
Orworke, James:				
AA	Orworke's Fancy	150	14 May 1683	25/7;31/464
Osborne, Edward:				
Transported by John Richens bef. Oct 1680.				28/97
Osbourn, Henry, Rebecca & Sarah of Calvert Co:—See under Dawson, Anthony.				
Osbo(u)rne, Capt. John:				
Som	Choice	1,200	5 Nov 1685	25/237;30/254
Som	Conveniency	1,200	15 Dec 1681	25/15;29/523
Osburne, William, planter:				
Bal	Osburne's Lot	500	15 Jly 1684	25/93;32/94
Oulson, John:				
Knt	Oulson's Pasture	20	5 Oct 1695	40/12
Knt	Oulson's Relief	100	5 Oct 1695	40/36

County	***Name of Tract***	***Acreage***	***Date***	***Reference(s)***
Oulton, John:				
Bal	Bold Venture	161	20 Mar 1696	37/443
Bal	Darby Hall	300	10 Nov 1696	38/45
Bal	Fellowship	200	10 Jly 1696	34/123;40/392
Bal	Oulton's Garrison	240	1 Jun 1696	40/516
Outon, John:				
Som	Outen's Addition	150	10 Dec 1695	37/94
Overton, Thomas:				
Bal	Overton's Care	70	7 --- 1679	24/151
See also under Langley, Robert.				
Owen [Owing], Richard:				
AA	Long Acre	225	10 Nov 1695	37/540
AA	Lowest Thickets	384	10 May 1688	25/406;32/631
Bal	Owing's Adventure	400	10 Oct 1694	27/322
Owens, Ann, relict of Richard Owens, merchant, deceased:				
AA	Smith's Neck	315	8 May 1684	25/69
Owens, Richard:				
AA	Owens' Range	162	26 Mar 1696	40/359
Owlles, Robert:				
Bal	Worram	37	10 Oct 1695	40/543
Oxford, Thomas, planter:				
Som	Oldberry	200	22 Dec 1683	25/127;30/201
Som	Seylly	100	18 Dec 1683	25/128;30/186
Som	Thornbury	400	21 Dec 1683	25/126;30/199
Paddeson, John:				
Tal	Judeth Garden	193	10 Nov 1695	37/307
Pade, Timothy:				
Som	Pargum	200	8 Aug 1679	24/53
Page, Robert:				
Tal	Ulthorpe	100	10 Jun 1683	29/393
Pagett, John:				
Transported by John Abington of Calvert Co. before August 1680.				28/34
Paggett, Thomas:				
Cal	[unnamed]	400	10 Jan 1696	27/357
Paine, Thomas:				
Transported by John Abington of Calvert Co. before August 1680.				28/34
Painter, Nicholas of St. Mary's Co:				
Cec	Bristol	150	17 Jly 1683	25/142,255;32/211
Cec	Friendship	1,400	18 Feb 1680	24/271;28/139
Cec	Gloster	750	17 Jly 1683	25/129;32/86
Painter, Nicholas of Anne Arundel Co:				
AA	Chance	200	20 Jun 1680	29/197
AA	Dining Room	500	25 Jun 1680	29/194
AA	Greeniston	700	22 May 1683	31/353

County	Name of Tract	Acreage	Date	Reference(s)
Tal	Kindness	400	6 Nov 1678	24/282;28/140
AA	Vianen	300	25 Jun 1680	29/195
Palmer, Daniel:				
Deputy Surveyor for Baltimore Co. in 1697				
Pam-----, Rebecca:				
Transported by John Bodden of Somerset Co. before April 1681.				28/129
Pant(h)er, John:				
Som	Gladstones	170	18 Jun 1689	27/85
AA	Greeniston		7 Apr 1863	24/513
Som	Hanslope	150	25 Jly 1679	24/291;28/270
Som	Little Worth	50	3 Aug 1681	24/372;29/440
Som	Newport Pannell	50	10 Mar 1681	24/289
Som	Roudie	200	4 Jun 1688	25/386;32/645
Pardoe, John:				
Cal	Fox's Walk	70	10 Nov 1695	37/212
Cal	Toby's Quarter	100	12 May 1682	29/29/42
Pardoe, Walter:				
Transported by Christopher Rousby of Calvert Co.				24/22
Parish, Edward of Anne Arundel Co:				
Bal	Parish's Range	2,000	15 Apr 1696	40/418
Parrish, John:				
AA	Parrish's Purchase	50	18 Aug 1699	30/402
Parker, Charles of Accomack Co., Virginia:				
Som	Armenia	400	25 Aug 1698	38/103
Parker, George of Accomack Co., Virginia:				
Som	Brotherhood	340	18 May 1689	27/92
Parker, George of Calvert Co., gent:				
Bal	Parker's Chance	500	15 Jun 1683	25/4;31/480
Parker, Henry, Deputy Surveyor for Talbot & Kent Cos.				
Tal	Bromley	200	30 May 1681	24/345;31/47
Tal	Dun's Range	200	20 Oct 1681	24/380
Tal	Dunn's Range Addn.	200	10 Aug 1683	29/389
Tal	Fork	250	10 Dec 1685	25/298
Tal	Freshes	200	15 May 1681	24/344;31/235
Tal	Huntington's Addition	150	27 May 1681	24/344;31/124
Tal	Neglect	100	27 May 1681	24/344;31/46
Tal	Nineveh's Addn.	200	16 Aug 1680	28/26
Tal	Parker's Farm	450	28 May 1681	24/344;29/404
Tal	Parker's Freshes	300	28 May 1681	24/344;31/215
Tal	Parker's Thicket	100	27 May 1681	24/344;29/487
Tal	Salisbury	300	12 Aug 1681	24/346;31/233
Tal	Timber Neck	100	24 May 1682	24/457
Tal	Warwick	400	28 May 1681	24/344;31/45
Tal	Winchester	200	7 Jly 1681	24/346;31/127

County	Name of Tract	Acreage	Date	Reference(s)
Parker, John of Accomack Co., Virginia:				
Som	Armenia	400	15 Aug 1698	38/103
Som	Brotherhood	340	18 May 1689	27/92
Parker, John:				
Som	Cambridge	300	24 May 1688	25/422;34/41
Som	Harman	350	8 Feb 1684	25/21;30/153
Som	Wickenhoe's Neck	40	10 Nov 1695	37/525
Bal	Parker's Choice	224	1 Sep 1698	38/87
Bal	Parker's Folly	214	10 Nov 1695	40/534
Bal	Parker's Lot	176	10 Nov 1695	40/536
Parker, Peter, planter:				
Som	Margaret's Rest	300	5 Apr 1686	25/278
Parker, Philip of Accomack Co., Virginia:				
Som	Brotherhood	340	18 May 1689	27/92
Parker, Robert:				
Bal	Parker's Adventure	207	20 Jun 1696	37/482
Bal	Parker's Palace	500	10 Dec 1695	40/271
Parker, Thomas:				
Transported by James Round of Somerset Co. by Apr 1681.				28/129
Parker, William:				
Transported by John Abington of Calvert Co. before August 1680.				28/34
Parker, William of Anne Arundel Co:				
Cal	Godwell	805	13 Oct 1679	24/67
Parker, William:				
Cal	Second	200	5 Jan 1681	24/267
Cal	Stroud	200	13 Jan 1681	24/301;29/144
Bal	Parker's Choice	224	1 Sep 1698	38/87
Parkinson, Elizabeth:				
Transported by Samuel Gibson of Calvert Co.				24/4
Parmin, Francis:				
Transported by William Peerie of Cecil Co. before November 1681.				24/383
Parramore, John:				
Som	Chance	300	12 Jun 1683	25/73;30/246
Parrett—See Parrott.				
Parrish—See Parish.				
Parrott, Benjamin, planter:				
Tal	Parrott's Lot	82	17 Jly 1686	25/248;33/304
Tal	Parrot's Reserve	200	25 Oct 1683	25/22;32/52
Parrott [Parrett], George:				
Tal	Eagle Neck	100	16 Nov 1679	24/225;29/257
Tal	Poplar Level	116	22 Apr 1686	25/416;32/677
Parret, Henry:				
Tal	Buck Range	50	18 Apr 1683	29/233
Tal	----- Oak	100	24 Nov 1678	24/193

County	*Name of Tract*	*Acreage*	*Date*	*Reference(s)*
Parrot, William of Talbot Co., planter:				
Dor	Brotherly Kindness	250	8 May 1683	25/122
Parrett, William:				
Tal	Strawberry Fields	100	[25 Sep 1678]	24/140;28/110; 32/219
Tal	Strawberry Hills Addition	50	10 Oct 1682	24/490;32/59;33/76
Parsons, John:				
StM	[unnamed]	150	1 Sep 1687	33/428
including lands for transporting himself, his wife & children [unnamed].				
StM	Barnscott	50	1 Sep 1687	33/530
Parsons, John:				
Knt	Beaver Dams	1,000	4 Mar 1687	25/334;32/536
Knt	Charles' Lot	300	5 Jun 1686	25/223;33/207
Knt	Parsons' Addition	28	5 Jun 1686	25/220;33/206
Knt	Well Meaning	830	8 Jun 1686	25/220;33/204
Som	Bears' Quarter	100	10 Nov 1695	34/69;40/224
Parsons, John of Talbot Co:				
Tal	Drumfield	400	27 Apr 1688	25/415;32/665
Knt	Plain Dealing	250	18 Oct 1683	25/38;33/56
Knt	Quake's Lot	98	18 Oct 1683	25/142;32/149
Parsons, Peter, planter:				
Som	Bacon Quarter	200	13 Nov 1685	25/233;33/269
Patey, Richard:				
Som	Patey's Folly	200	20 Sep 1687	25/352;33/680
Pattison, Jacob:				
Dor	Jacob's Lot	31	16 May 1682	24/435;31/138
Pattison, James, planter:				
Dor	Barbados	50	27 Apr 1682	24/425
Dor	Buckland	150	25 May 1682	24/437
Dor	Bull Point	71	2 May 1682	24/430
Dor	Charleton	200	20 May 1682	24/436
Dor	Cross Manor	1,200	29 Sep 1681	28/202
formerly lands of Walter Hall who died testate in 1678 and whose relict Margaret Hall married Pattison				
Dor	Dover	150	18 Jly 1681	28/260
Dor	Racoon's Lodge	50	30 Apr 1682	24/428
Dor	Ransom Point	50	20 Jly 1681	24/342
Dor	Regionle?	150	20 May 1682	24/437;31/164
Dor	Rochester	400	4 Jan 1682	24/418
Dor	Rye	100	26 May 1682	24/439;31/67
Dor	Sandish	50	2 May 1682	24/430
Pattison, Joan, daughter of Thomas Pattison:				
Dor	Smithson's Recreation	200	5 Nov 1680	24/201
Dor	Surveyor's Point	50	9 Dec 1680	24/203;28/322
Pattison, Thomas, Deputy Surveyor for Dorchester Co.				
Dor	---- Swamp	100	10 Sep 1683	31/80

County	*Name of Tract*	*Acreage*	*Date*	*Reference(s)*
Dor	Barbados	50	17 May 1682	24/425;31/78
Dor	Biggin	50	20 Feb 1681	24/343;29/241
Dor	Buckland	150	25 May 1682	24/437;31/76
Dor	Bull Point	71	19 May 1682	24/430;33/105
Dor	Cabin Quarterly	50	[8 Dec 1679]	24/253
Dor	Charleton	200	30 May 1682	24/436;31/79
Dor	Pad(r)e Arme	81	1 Jun 1685	33/103
Dor	Racoon Point	50	13 Apr 1683	29/215
Dor	Racoon's Ridge	50	7 May 1682	24/428;31/352
Dor	Ransone's Quarter	100	[20 Apr 1678]	24/166
Dor	Regionle(?)	150	30 May 1682	24/437
Dor	Rochester	400	19 Mar 1682	24/419;31/75
Dor	Sandish	50	12 May 1682	24/430
Pattison, Thomas, son of Thomas Pattison:				
Dor	Lover	150	20 Feb 1680	24/181
Dor	Pattison's Delight	300	29 Nov 1679	24/178;28/183
Pauley, William:				
Bal	Paying Debts	400	1 Oct 1701	34/303
Paxton, Hugh:				
Tal	Emery Paxton	372	4 May 1687	25/313;33/581
Tal	Paxton's Lot	100	5 Dec 1682	24/492
Tal	Range	200	12 May 1685	25/224;32/327
Peacock, John:				
Cal	Poppy Gay	40	27 May 1682	24/412;31/31
Peacock, Richard, Deputy Surveyor for St. Mary's Co:				
Tal	Anderby's Addition	100	3 Nov 1682	24/518;29/157
Tal	Sarah's Jointure	600	13 Sep 1682	24/516;29/159
Tal	Toas' Purchase	400	4 Dec 1682	24/513;29/158
Pead, Timothy:				
Som	Layes	150	28 Feb 1680	24/257;28/386
	including lands for transporting himself, Elizabeth his wife and daughter Jane.			
Som	West Ridge	150	20 May 1680	25/81;30/218
Som	Wotten Under Edge	150	4 Jun 1681	24/324;29/29
Peaker, Aquilla:				
Bal	Aquilla	74	2 Jun 1698	35/408
Peakes, Richard, planter:				
Som	Amity	50	18 Nov 1685	25/265;33/363
Pearce [Pierce], John, orphan son of Francis Pierce:				
Tal	Pierce Land	200	25 Jly 1686	25/247;30/279
Pearce, Robert:				
AA		300	[20 Dec 1677]	24/140
Pearse, Richard:				
Dor	Anything	84	10 Oct 1695	40/587
Pearce, Thomas:				
Cec	Middle Grounds	200	10 Oct 1695	40/470

County	Name of Tract	Acreage	Date	Reference(s)
Pearce [Peirce], Capt. William of Cecil Co:				
Cec	Addition	422	14 Jun 1684	25/343
Knt	Benjamin's Lot	350	10 Nov 1683	25/171
Cec	Duck Pye	100	27 Feb 1680	24/142
Cec	Fork	200	14 Nov 1681	24/383;31/255
including lands for transportation of 7 persons.				
Cec	Hangman's Folly	300	7 Dec 1682	25/17;31/511
Cec	Hopeful Unity	150	12 May 1682	24/454;29/517
Cec	St. Andrew's Cross	350	10 Nov 1683	25/26;30/132
Pearch, Simon:				
StM	Hard Adventure	276	20 Feb 1695	37/494
Peasly, George:				
AA	Peasly's Inheritance	100	1 Jly 1680	28/38
Peasley, John:				
AA	Peasley's Lot	109	20 Jly 1684	25/116
Peck, Benjamin:				
Tal	Limbrick	70	1 Feb 1696	37/331
Pedder, Richard of Kent Co:				
Tal	Forest of Windsor	250	4 Sep 1679	24/222;29/120
Peert, James:				
Cha	Truman's Lodge	200	10 Dec 1679	24/97
Peirie, John of Calvert Co:				
Cha	Jamaica	500	23 Sep 1685	25/267;33/310
Cha	Port Royal	500	23 Sep 1685	25/267;33/330
Pelkey [Pelkee], John:				
Som	Locust Hummock	50	15 Sep 1682	25/79;30/212
Som	Locust Hummock	75	1 Nov 1697	38/73
Pemberton, John:				
Tal	Boston	300	23 Jun 1679	24/215;29/221
Tal	Boston Addition	150	13 Dec 1680	24/281;28/468
Pemberton, Thomas, merchant:				
Som	Fairfield	900	20 Feb 1683	24/532
Som	Kellam's Folly	550	30 May 1682	24/412
Som	Pemberton	900	29 Sep 1682	24/531
Som	Rhodee	350	1 Feb 1683	24/530
Som	Somerfield	500	1 Feb 1683	24/531;30/155
Pencott, James:				
Cha	Pencott's Invention	239	10 Jun 1687	25/306;33/465
Penerell, Daniel:				
Bal	Daniel's Lot	454	16 Jun 1688	25/444
Penn, Edward of Anne Arundel Co:				
Bal	Planter's Pleasure	100	1 Jun 1700	34/233
Penneck, Richard:				
Som	Weaver's Portion	125	1 Jun 1698	34/248;38/144

County	*Name of Tract*	*Acreage*	*Date*	*Reference(s)*
Pennington, Mr. Francis:				
Cha	St. Thomas's Manor	3,337	16 Nov 1685	25/206
Pennington, Henry:				
Cec	Pennyworth	71	14 Oct 1680	24/342,25/10
Cec	Sylvan's Folly	100	1 Oct 1680	24/354,25/10
Cec	Sylvane's Folly	100	14 May 1695	40/21
Pennington, Thomas:				
AA	Foothold	135	7 Sep 1682	24/464;31/105
Pennington, William:				
AA	Pennington's Search	100	6 Mar 1697	34/138;40/366
Pepper, Richard:				
Som	Cartwheel	150	2 Oct 1683	25/89
Pepper [Peper], Tobias, planter:				
Som	Millbury Heath	200	22 Dec 1683	25/131
Som	St. Leonard's	200	22 Sep 1683	25/63
Percon, Edward:				
Transported by John Bodden of Somerset Co. bef. Apr 1681.				28/129
Percy, Thomas—See under Hardy, Henry.				
Perke, Robert of Kent Co:				
His time of service completed by 1679				24/106
Perkin, Francis:				
Tal	Demenis Recovered	136	10 Nov 1695	37/507
Perkins, John:				
Som	Winter Harbour	150	9 Aug 1688	27/19
Perkins, Richard:				
Bal	Brotherly Love	100	10 Sep 1697	38/20
Perkins, Richard, cooper:				
Bal	Perkington	100	16 Sep 1683	25/111;30/165
Perrie, Mr. Robert:				
Som	Glascoe	500	1 Oct 1687	25/400
Som	Penny Street	200	10 Nov 1695	40/281
Peterkin, James:				
Dor	Partnership	1,000	20 Apr 1681	24/282;34/173
Peters, Samuel:				
Cal	Harford	130	10 Jan 1696	37/152
Petite, Thomas—See under Brandt, Randolph.				
Petticoate, William:				
AA	Petticoate's Rest	100	9 Sep 1679	24/98
Phelps [Felps], Cuthbert:				
Tal	Cudlington's Addition	50	16 Aug 1681	24/376;29/247; 31/213
Phelps, Walter:				
AA	Phelps' Choice	200	12 Oct 1684	25/144;33/97

County	*Name of Tract*	*Acreage*	*Date*	*Reference(s)*
AA	Phelps' Increase	300	30 Jun 1680	24/175;28/214
AA	Phelps' Luck	83	27 Feb 1685	25/274;33/397
AA	Phelps' Luck	238	10 Dec 1695	40/326
Philkes, Edward:				
AA	Philkes' Rest	316	23 Sep 1680	28/63
Phillips, James, gent:				
Bal		150	5 Sep 1683	25/155
Bal	Aron's Spring	100	4 Oct 1683	25/48;30/40
Bal	Contrivance	200	23 Aug 1683	25/100
Bal	Fork	150	14 Oct 1683	25/39;30/27
Bal	James's Addition	630	[1697]	39/36
Bal	James's Park	1,175	23 Apr 1681	24/497
Bal	Phillip's Purchase	2,000	15 Jly 1683	25/4,85;30/12
Bal	Plum Point	100	27 Jun 1680	28/7,23
Bal	Polecat Ridge	150	28 Jun 1680	28/7
Bal	Sedgley	200	4 Oct 1683	25/86;32/168
Phillips, John Sr.:				
Dor	Bacon Quarter	200	5 Jly 1681	28/199
Phillips, John, son of John Phillips:				
Dor	Bacon Quarter	200	6 Mar 1680	24/178;28/199
Dor	Orphan's Increase	50	18 Jly 1681	24/182;28/226
Dor	Phillips' Pasture	166	6 May 1682	24/432;29/361
Dor	Phillips' Range	50	2 Jan 1682	24/418;29/490
Phillips, Mary:				
Transported by Thomas Clipsham bef. Sep 1680.				28/44
Philips, Michael of Talbot Co:				
His time of service completed by 1679.				24/119
Phillips, Robert:				
AA	Truswell	30	14 May 1683	25/7;31/438
Phillips, Roger:				
Som	Phillips' Addition	25	9 Oct 1695	37/124
Som	Roxborough	210	10 Jun 1695	37/223
Phillips, Thomas, planter:				
Dor	Williams' Goodwill	50	22 Apr 1683	24/539;30/107
Philpott [Fillpott], Edward:				
Cha	Fillpotts' Chance	108	10 Nov 1695	34/114;40/237
Pierce—See Pearce.				
Pierpoint, Amos:				
AA	Peirpoint's Chance	418	28 Jun 1688	25/404;32/630
assigned to him by Mary Pierpoint.				
Pierpoint, Jabez:				
AA	Pierpoint's Range	45	10 Nov 1695	34/136;40/311
Pierson, Robert:				
Tal	Bishoprick	100	10 Mar 1696	40/454

County	Name of Tract	Acreage	Date	Reference(s)
Pierson, Simon:				
Bal	Pierson's Park	300	3 Sep 1698	38/130
Pile, Joseph of St. Mary's Co., son of John Pile deceased:				
StM	Baltimore's Bounty	1,150	20 Nov 1680	28/133
survey made on behalf of the said Joseph Pile, his brother John Pile & his mother Sarah Pile, widow.				
Cha	Baltimore's Gift	110	22 Nov 1681	24/385;29/248
StM	Ferne	100	11 Apr 1683	29/209
Pile, Capt. Joseph:				
StM	Salisbury	191	2 Jly 1688	25/383;33/704
Pile, Joseph, gent:				
StM	Sarum	2,600	[12 Nov 1680]	24/203
	See also under Poore, Mary.			
Pinder, Edward, gent:				
Dor	Desborough	150	10 Oct 1683	25/122;33/315
Tal	Pindar's Garden	10	2 Apr 1684	25/158
Dor	Pinder's Lodge	300	27 Mar 1689	25/435
Piner, Thomas:				
Knt	Lyons Hall	100	2 May 1687	25/335
Knt	Penrose	50	2 May 1687	25/335;32/543
Knt	Piner's Addition	152	10 Nov 1695	40/137
Pinkstone, Peter:				
AA	Pinkstone's Delight	200	26 Mar 1696	40/348
AA	Pinkston's Folly	180	1 Oct 1700	34/238
Pitt, John:				
Tal	John's Hill	400	[10 Aug 1678]	24/140;29/86
Pitt, Philip:				
Dor	Strawberry Garden Addn.	50	27 Jly 1687	25/408;32/700
Plane, David:				
Dor	Rogues Beguiled	100	7 Jly 1702	35/434
Planner, William:				
Som	Alexander's Desire	200	13 Nov 1696	39/21
Som	Boston Town	500	30 Mar 1682	24/452;31/304
Som	Cheap Price	225	10 Nov 1696	38/138
Som	Double Purchase	150	30 Aug 1680	24/243;28/366
Plater, George of Calvert Co:				
Tal	Pochiccory Ridge	1,000	10 Nov 1695	37/211
Plunkett, Thomas:				
PG	Chance	87	17 Jan 1700	38/155;30/341
Pointer, Capt. Thomas:				
Som	Head of St. Lawrence Neck	361	10 Nov 1697	37/545
Som	St. Lawrence Neck	366	29 Aug 1684	25/261;29/34
Polke, Robert:				
Som	Polke's Folly	100	7 Mar 1688	25/356
Som	Polke's Lot	50	7 Mar 1688	25/356

County	Name of Tract	Acreage	Date	Reference(s)
Poalk, Robert Jr:				
Som	Ballyhack	200	6 Apr 1702	35/404
Pollack, Ephraim:				
Som	Clonmell	100	6 Apr 1702	35/420
Pollard, John, gent:				
Dor	Good Luck Point	30	18 Feb 1682	24/420;31/154
Dor	Gore	37	25 May 1683	25/119;33/235
Dor	Goshen	63	25 May 1683	25/119;32/384
Dor	Hallowing Point	100	24 Mar 1683	29/196
Dor	Herring Point	100	13 Apr 1682	29/124
Dor	Island	25	23 Mar 1687	25/294;33/423
Dor	John's Desire	50	13 Apr 1682	29/105
Dor	Obscurity	50	29 Aug 1683	29/340
Dor	Pig Point	50	13 Apr 1682	29/101
Dor	Race	20	16 Feb 1682	24/420
Dor	Range Point	50	13 Apr 1682	29/123
Dor	Wolf Trap Ridge	50	6 Sep 1684	25/203;32/406
Pollett, Thomas:				
Som	Prestune	220	8 Jly 1695	37/119
Ponder, John:				
Tal	Ponderfield	200	6 Mar 1689	32/691
Pooly, John, planter:				
Tal	Pooly's Discovery	168	20 Oct 1687	25/369;33/635
Poore, Mary, daughter & heir of Capt. Joseph Pile who died testate:				
StM	Pyle's Discovery	245	10 Nov 1695	40/560
Pope, John:				
Som	Long Island	400	6 Oct 1687	25/391
Som	Middle Moor	120	4 Oct 1687	25/397;32/640
Tal	Rome	156	10 Nov 1696	40/570
Som	Room	500	18 May 1683	25/68;30/244
Som	Shaftesbury	200	15 Jly 1684	25/133;30/174
Pope, Mary of Charles Co:				
Transported herself before Sep 1680.				28/48
Cha	Clipsham's Mount	68	[17 Apr 1678]	24/141
Cha	St. Marie	68	10 Jun 1683	29/369
Pope, Mathew:				
Cec	Hermitage	300	18 Jun 1686	25/223
Cec	Pope's Forest	300	2 Jly 1687	25/332;32/534
Pope, Robert:				
Dor	Waterford	80	26 Dec 1679	24/160
Popplewell, John:				
Som	Bosworth	150	9 Oct 1683	25/57
Porter, Hugh:				
Som	Coventry	450	10 Nov 1695	40/430
Som	Porter's Discovery	232	26 Mar 1688	25/359;33/675

County	*Name of Tract*	*Acreage*	*Date*	*Reference(s)*
Porter, William:				
Tal	Belfast	100	22 Apr 1679	24/212;28/306
Posey, John, carpenter:				
	Middle Branch	75	29 Apr 1682	24/410;29/313
Potter, Thomas:				
Som	Mitchell's Choice	180	6 Jly 1695	37/105
Poullan, Thomas:				
Transported by William Thomas of Charles Co. before September 1680.				28/121
Poulson, Andrew:				
Cec	Long Point	100	16 Mar 1681	25/13
Powell, Charles:				
Dor	Whitefriars	77	15 Jan 1696	40/448
Powell, John:				
Dor	Powell's Lot	100	14 May 1687	25/303;33/588
Cal	Addition	50	10 Nov 1695	40/87
Powell, John & Mary his wife:				
AA	Jacob's Point	21	30 May 1686	33/93
Powell, John & James:				
AA	Powell's Inheritance	125	9 Sep 1682	24/464;30/236
Powell, Walter, planter:				
Som	Friend's Gift	150	30 Aug 1679	24/242;28/235
Som	Hilliard's Discovery	150	30 Aug 1679	24/240;28/313
Som	Oliver's Portion	150	30 Aug 1679	24/241;28/236
Som	Powell's Addition	50	22 Sep 1683	25/89;33/287
Som	Powell's Inclusion	256	2 May 1686	25/284
Som	Powell's Lot	443	2 May 1687	25/387;37/285
Som	Powell's Recovery	112	10 Nov 1695	37/511
Som	Winter Quarter	200	30 Aug 1679	24/240;28/238
Power, John:				
Tal	[unnamed]	400	22 Jun 1683	24/528
Prather, Jonathan:				
Cal		100	17 May 1684	25/32
land formerly occupied by his mother Jone Prather.				
Pratt, Thomas:				
AA	Pratt's Security	150	7 Aug 1682	24/461;31/416
Presley, Francis:				
Cha	Virgin Garden	185	10 Nov 1695	37/255
Preston, Thomas:				
Bal	Bradwell Hill	288	10 Nov 1695	40/554
Bal	Everly Hill	395	10 Nov 1695	40/515
Bal	Hog Point	40	17 Jly 1680	28/12
Bal	Hopewell	65	17 Jly 1680	28/12
Bal	Lodwick's Refuse	50	10 Jly 1680	28/12
Bal	Pitchcraft	112	10 Nov 1695	34/135;40/268
Bal	Preston's Luck	50	6 Oct 1682	24/504;30/34

County	Name of Tract	Acreage	Date	Reference(s)
Bal	Thompson's Neglect	126	10 Nov 1695	38/86
Bal	Wittly	172	1 Jly 1697	38/25
Price, Alexander:				
Som	Newberry	300	27 Nov 1688	27/119
Som	Price's Purchase	100	10 Aug 1695	37/82
Price, Andrew:				
Tal	Brecknock	100	2 Nov 1679	24/225;29/206
Tal	Good Hap	126	1 Feb 1698	38/51
Tal	Good Increase	200	29 Oct 1679	24/223
Tal	Keep Out	100	14 Jun 1683	24/527;33/391
Tal	Liberty	100	14 Jun 1683	25/44
Tal	Margaret's Hill	200	16 Jly 1679	24/218;28/492
Price, Edward:				
Som	Price's Conclusion	500	10 Mar 1696	37/522
Price, Edward & Elizabeth his wife, daughter of Thomas Lunn deceased:				
AA	Holloway	147	17 May 1700	34/183
AA	Oliver's Neck	147	17 May 1700	38/151
Price, Henry:				
Tal	Copartnership	373	1 Feb 1698	38/63
Price, James:				
Som	Agreement	100	15 Jun 1683	25/72;33/187
Som	Mickle Meadow	300	15 Jun 1683	25/72;30/217
Price, John:				
Tal	Hobson's Choice	100	8 Aug 1681	24/374;29/337
Cha	Lichfield	100	24 Jun 1680	28/18
Cal	Price's Lot	164	18 Jly 1682	24/414
Cal	Refuge	50	18 Jly 1682	24/415;29/356
Dor	Herriford	100	2 Jly 1702	35/423
Som	Refuge	160	18 Oct 1684	25/361
Price, Roger, planter:				
Tal	Battlefield	100	20 Mar 1682	24/399;31/285
Tal	Lee Hall	150	27 Sep 1680	24/200;28/333
Tal	Price's Neck	200	22 Sep 1681	28/292
Price, Thomas:				
Tal	Sallop	200	23 Oct 1683	25/37;30/72
Price, William, planter:				
Cec	Price's Forest	150	14 Nov 1685	25/244;33/334
Prindevall, John:				
Bal	Jackson's Venture	350	10 Nov 1695	40/159
Pritchard, John:				
Dor	Little Goshen	50	25 Apr 1683	24/541;30/112
Dor	Ringwood	50	14 Nov 1681	28/373
Prichard, Obadiah:				
Bal	Prichard's Park	200	1 Nov 1701	34/339

County	*Name of Tract*	*Acreage*	*Date*	*Reference(s)*
Pritchard, Thomas:				
Dor	Ringwood	50	20 Feb 1681	24/283
Pritchett, John:				
Dor	Hope	75	[1 Apr 1679]	24/158
Proctor [Procter], Robert, innholder:				
AA	Bear Neck	146	8 Feb 1683	25/8;31/456
AA	Green Spring	250	7 Feb 1683	25/9;31/445
AA	Millford	717	17 Jly 1683	25/86;32/82
AA	Mill Land	100	16 Oct 1683	25/105;33/111
AA	Poplar Ridge	500	7 Feb 1683	25/9;31/454
AA	Proctor's Chance	30	28 Jun 1680	28/13
AA	Procter's Park	518	14 May 1682	24/454;29/309
AA	Timber Neck	463	8 Feb 1683	25/7;31/439
Prophett [Profitt], Thomas:				
Som	Brickhill	200	13 Dec 1683	25/139;30/200
Som	Key	100	26 Mar 1680	24/257
Prosser, James of Talbot Co., planter:				
Dor	James' Park	200	10 Apr 1683	25/47,123
Prout, John, planter:				
Dor	Prout's Meadows	150	31 May 1683	25/145;32/383
Pullen, Richard:				
Cec	Hopeful Unity	150	12 May 1682	24/454;29/517
Cec	Pullen's Refuge	500	20 Jun 1681	24/500
Purdue, William:				
Som		70	before 1679	24/27
Purnell [Purnall], Richard:				
Tal	Partnership	500	27 Oct 1683	25/23;31/527
Tal	Purnell's Addition	300	27 Apr 1688	25/415;32/692
AA	Purnall's Angle	140	30 May 1683	31/102
Purnell [Purnall], Thomas:				
Som	Chance	360	10 Nov 1695	37/509
Som	Cold Harbour	325	15 Dec 1683	25/115;30/203
Som	Fairfield	400	29 Dec 1683	25/126;32/387
Som	Farne Lull	130	10 Nov 1685	25/262
Som	Key	100	26 Mar 1680	24/257
Som	Mattapony Marsh	275	27 Dec 1683	25/126;32/224
Som	New Timber Quarter	250	10 Nov 1695	34/75;40/226
Som	Timber Quarter	200	10 Dec 1679	24/64
Purnell, William:				
Tal	Partnership	500	27 Oct 1683	25/23;31/527
Tal	Purnell's Addition	300	27 Apr 1688	25/415;32/692
Tal	Purnell's Chance	100	27 Oct 1683	25/22;32/34
Tal	Purnell's Forest	500	4 Jly 1683	25/167;32/112
Pursell, Edmond:				
Transported by Thomas Maisterman before Sep 1680.				28/53

County	Name of Tract	Acreage	Date	Reference(s)
Purvis, John & Elizabeth:				
Transported by Christopher Rousby of Calvert Co.				24/22
Pye, Mme Anne:				
Cal	Pye Anne's Grove	1,001	2 Oct 1686	25/258
Queeny, Sutton [Sutthin]:				
Cec	Bachelor's Choice	80	7 Jly 1687	25/331;32/536
Cec	Hermitage	300	18 Jun 1686	25/223
Quigley, Charles of St. Mary's Co:				
Cec	Mount Quigley	300	22 Sep 1686	25/327;33/705
Cec	Quigley's Lodge	108	22 Sep 1686	25/327;33/603
Quigley, John:				
Assignor of lands in Cecil Co in 1679.				24/93
Quillam, Daniel:				
Som	Limbrick	150	4 Jun 1681	24/319;28/533
Quinton, Walter, planter:				
Tal	Cross Haze	50	8 Dec 1682	24/494;30/75
Tal	Tatturnhurst	38	12 Sep 1697	38/43
Tal	Timothy's Lot	25	10 Nov 1695	34/99;40/121
Rackliffe—See Ratcliffe.				
Raddon, Henry:				
Dor	Raddon True Dealing	600	2 May 1686	25/294;33/464
Ralph, Thomas:				
Som	Contention	95	15 Aug 1688	25/402;32/644
Som	Ralph's Prevention	9	23 May 1688	25/420;32/654
Ramsay, Andrew:				
Dor	Rachel's Chance	79	1 Oct 1700	34/306
Ramsay, Charles:				
Cec	Adventure	100	1 May 1701	34/341
Ramsey, William of Anne Arundel Co., planter:				
Bal	William the Conqueror	200	24 May 1685	25/182;30/226
Randall, Benjamin, gent:				
Knt	Battersey	250	1 Jun 1694	24/453,27/148
Knt	Benjamin's Choice	200	1 Jun 1680	24/187;28/417
Randall, Christopher:				
AA	Randall's Purchase	102	26 Sep 1680	28/65
AA	Randall's Range	100	7 Jly 1681	28/150
Randall, Robert, planter:				
Cec	Issue Adam	150	7 Dec 1681	24/449;31/263
Ratcliffe [Rackliffe], Capt. Charles:				
Som	Genesar	2,200	10 Jan 1680	24/101
Som	Mount Pleasant	450	3 Dec 1679	24/126
Som	Ortney	80	18 Dec 1683	25/126;32/389
Som	Rackliffe's Discovery	320	17 Dec 1683	25/125;30/206
Som	Scanderoone	150	10 Mar 1696	37/500

County	*Name of Tract*	*Acreage*	*Date*	*Reference(s)*
Ratliffe, Emanuel:				
Cha	Pencott's Folly	100	22 Mar 1688	25/398;34/15
Ratcliff, Nathaniel of Accomack Co., Virginia:				
Som	Ratcliff	200	1 May 1696	37/533
Raven, Luke:				
Bal	Luke's Adventure	317	30 May 1687	25/309;33/516
Rawles, William:				
Knt	Oyer Moyne	200	27 Sep 1680	28/76
Rawles, William, innholder:				
Knt	Town Relief	320	30 Jun 1680	24/186;29/87
Rawley, James:				
Som	Keep Poor Hall	100	10 Apr 1695	37/72
Rawlins, Aron of Anne Arundel Co:				
Bal	Young's Lot	300	10 Apr 1699	38/50
formerly granted to Theodorus Young.				
Rawlings, John:				
Dor	Content	100	13 Mar 1677	25/117
Dor	Inheritance	300	10 Sep 1679	24/48
Dor	Partnership	1,000	2 Mar 1681	24/282
Rawlings, Mary:				
Transported by William Peirce of Cecil Co. before November 1681.				24/383
Rawlings, Richard:				
AA	Rawlings' Purchase	50	14 Aug 1680	24/256;29/146
Rawth, James:				
Knt	Town Relief	800	6 Mar 1682	24/396
Ray, Alexander:				
Tal	Bachelor's Branch Addn.	100	24 Jun 1689	27/344
Ray, John:				
AA	Ray's Chance	115	27 Mar 1687	25/312;33/412
Reanerger, Charles of Anne Arundel Co:				
Bal	Reanerger's Range	200	18 May 1687	25/300;33/598
Read [Reed], Abraham:				
StM	Dunsmore Heath	40	22 Jun 1681	24/280;28/467
Reed, Matthew, planter:				
Tal	[unnamed]	377	18 Mar 1680	24/305,343
Reed, Walter of Somerset Co:				
Transported himself & 3 others.				30/156
Som	Bridgewater	200	16 Dec 1682	24/518
Som	Eannton	100	13 Mar 1689	27/51
Som	Reed's Contrivance	100	23 Nov 1682	24/518;38/119
Som	Watchett	90	20 May 1689	27/79
Read, William:				
Dor	Bugby's Hole	50	[2 Feb 1680]	24/194;29/234

County	Name of Tract	Acreage	Date	Reference(s)
Reeve, Richard of Calvert Co.:				
Assignor of lands in Somerset Co. in Nov 1680				24/336
Reeves, Edward, planter:				
Bal	Coblar's Neglect	50	9 Sep 1679	24/96
Bal	Hog Neck	50	15 Dec 1684	25/244;33/316
Reeves, Roger:				
Bal	Roger's Rode	100	10 Mar 1696	40/445
Regester, Robert:				
Tal	Durham	73	10 Nov 1695	37/302
Reley, Hugh:				
Cal	Reley's Folly	128	1 May 1688	25/399
Cal	Reley's Horse Pasture	330	5 May 1688	25/393
Rendall, Daniel:				
Bal	Rendall's Delight	500	1 May 1701	34/363
Renshaw, John:				
Som	Adventure	200	9 Oct 1688	27/31
Revell, Randell:				
Assignor of lands in Somerset Co. in 1682.				25/58
Reynes, John:				
Cha	Wellford	100	12 Oct 1684	25/273;33/447
Reynolds, Christopher:				
Som	Farne Hill	215	17 Jly 1685	25/361
Reynolds, John:				
Tal	Chesterton	150	1 May 1684	25/96;33/162
Reynolds, Thomas:				
StM	Fox's Den	100	6 Sep 1686	25/270;33/329
Rich, William:				
Tal	Rich Park	569	10 Nov 1695	34/89;40/217
Richards, John, planter				
Som	Betty's Choice	200	4 Jan 1680	24/78
Dor	Noble Quarter	150	26 Apr 1682	24/408;29/492
Som	Wesson	100	4 Jun 1681	24/318;29/79
Som	Would Have Had More	50	29 Apr 1680	24/308;28/389
Richardson, Angell:				
Som	Sandown	300	1 Mar 1689	27/24
Richardson, John of Transquaking:				
Dor	Addition	200	[1 Oct 1674]	24/159
Dor	Falsham Rushes	200	20 May 1680	24/284;31/377
Dor	Helensborough	982	2 Nov 1680	28/104
Dor	Middle Plantation	200	19 Nov 1679	24/142
Dor	Richardson's Choice	532	[22 Nov 1678]	24/142;28/103
Dor	Richardson's Lot	215	7 Oct 1684	25/205;33/222
Dor	Well Middle Plant.	200	2 Nov 1680	28/115
Dor	Willenbrough	980	14 Nov 1679	24/142;29/91

County	Name of Tract	Acreage	Date	Reference(s)
Richardson, John:				
New	Northampton		[27 Nov 1680]	24/445;29/93
New	Willingbrooke		11 Oct 1680	24/444
Bal	Bushy Neck	200	20 Mar 1696	37/421
Bal	Come by Chance	282	10 Nov 1695	38/84
Bal	Horse Range	200	10 Nov 1695	37/542
Bal	Richardson's -----	?	10 Nov 1696	39/20
Richardson, Lawrence, planter:				
Bal	Lawrence's Pasture	150	28 Sep 1683	25/103;30/223
Richardson, Mark:				
AA	Burgess's Delight	200	10 Nov 1696	38/4
Richardson, Mark, planter:				
Bal	Poplar Neck	1,000	20 Sep 1683	25/48;30/28
Richardson, Mary:				
Bal	Maiden's Choice	218	10 Nov 1695	37/407
Richardson, Robert, gent:				
Som	Husborne Tarrant	400	[12 Nov 1678]	24/139;29/27
Som	Richardson's Ridge	150	16 Jly 1683	29/429
Richardson, Samuel:				
Bal	Richardson's Forest	226	10 Nov 1695	39/11
Richardson, Thomas, Deputy Surveyor for Baltimore Co. in 1695–1698:				
Bal	Gates' Close	30	5 Jun 1684	25/110;33/130
AA	Huckleberry Forest	611	6 Jun 1687	25/315
Bal	Long Point	150	4 Sep 1681	24/501;30/19
AA	Pound	68	6 Jun 1687	25/315
Bal	Providence	169	26 Apr 1684	25/93
Bal	Richardson's Forest	226	12 Mar 1686	25/299
Bal	Richardson's Outland	808	10 Nov 1695	39/19
Bal	Richardson's Plaint	100	22 Sep 1683	25/42
Bal	Richardson's Prospect	100	7 Oct 1683	25/111,130;33/138
Bal	Richardson's Reserve	214	5 Jun 1684	25/34;30/42
Bal	Richardson's Thicket	808	12 Mar 1686	25/299
Richens [Richins], John:				
Transported himself & 4 others before Oct 1680.				28/97
Som	Hope	100	31 May 1682	24/486
Som	Peace	200	12 Nov 1688	27/82
Som	Oxford	100	31 May 1682	24/486
Som	Richin's Addition	100	31 May 1682	24/486;29/456
Som	Troublesome	200	10 Nov 1688	27/43
Ricketts, John:				
Som	Cross	150	10 Nov 1695	40/288
Ricketts, William:				
Som	Ricketts' Chance	360	10 Nov 1695	40/182
Ridgely, Henry Sr. of Anne Arundel Co:				
AA	Huntington Quarter	259	1 May 1696	40/380
PG	Ridgley's Addition	100	1 Nov 1701	34/364
AA	Ridgely's Forest	264	3 Jun 1686	25/219;40/338

County	Name of Tract	Acreage	Date	Reference(s)
Ridgely, Henry Jr:				
AA	Huntington Quarter	259	1 May 1696	40/380
AA	Ridgely's Lot	273	8 Dec 1694	27/311
AA	Ridgely's Beginning	282	4 Oct 1694	27/298
Ridgely, James, planter:				
Tal	Ridgely's Chance	200	6 Jly 1685	25/296
Ridgely, Robert of St. Mary's Co:				
Som	Lott	200	13 Apr 1681	24/306
Som	Western Fields	1,400	4 Apr 1680	24/194;28/91;29/134
Ridgely, Thomas:				
StM		1	9 Jun 1678	24/154
Ridgely, William:				
AA	Ridgely's Chance	305	[1696]	40/411
Ridley, James:				
Tal	Broad Layne	153	1 Dec 1697	38/54
Rigby, James of Anne Arundel Co:				
Bal	Rigby	300	10 May 1679	24/140
Rigge, Thomas:				
Cha	Nonsuch	87	22 May 1686	25/225;32/444
Riggen, Teague:				
Som	Riggen's Mine	100	15 Jun 1683	25/60;30/8
Riley [Ryly], Hugh:				
Cal	Beginning	231	10 Nov 1695	37/180
Cal	Hugh's Labour	112	10 Aug 1695	37/177
PG	Riley's Discovery	561	15 Jly 1700	34/331
Cal	Ryly's Lot	310	20 Mar 1696	37/182
PG	Riley's Purchase	242	1 Jun 1700	34/282
Cal	Ryley's Range	800	19 Feb 1695	27/238
Ringold, Thomas:				
Knt	Ringold's Chance	200	15 Apr 1696	40/497
Rixon, John:				
	Dowgate	400	10 Jan 1680	24/20
Roach, John:				
Som	Bald Ridge	200	28 May 1681	24/326;29/26
Som	Cabin Swamp	150	28 May 1681	24/326;29/2
Som	Exchange	200	12 Sep 1679	24/117
Som	Mead Land	64	1 Dec 1697	38/75
Som	Roach's Privilege	57	10 Nov 1695	34/73;40/242
Som	Vale of Misery	88	3 May 1695	37/115
Robeard, John:				
Bal	Robeard's Choice	464	10 Nov 1695	37/423
Roberts, Andrew:				
AA	Triangle	100	1 Sep 1681	28/224

County	*Name of Tract*	*Acreage*	*Date*	*Reference(s)*
Roberts, Francis:				
Som	Jashimon	150	15 Sep 1682	25/78;32/244
Som	Newfoundland	125	10 Oct 1700	34/253
Som	Roberts' Recovery	100	15 Sep 1682	25/78;30/215
Roberts, Thomas:				
Som	Kelsey Hill	400	30 May 1683	25/71;30/190
Bal	Roberts' Choice	153	27 Mar 1688	25/349;33/713
Bal	Roberts' Park	200	10 Nov 1695	34/119;40/75
Robertson, Richard:				
Bal	Robertson's Addition	38	10 Nov 1695	40/426
Robins, George:				
Tal	Buckingham	300	25 Jun 1679	24/216;28/446
Tal	Goldsbrough	400	24 Dec 1679	24/225
Tal	Hilsdon	200	26 Jun 1679	24/216;28/448
Tal	Jamaica	450	26 Dec 1680	24/281
Tal	Lambert	500	26 Jun 1679	24/217;28/456
Tal	Robin's Range	300	21 Dec 1679	24/226;32/271
Robins, George, gent:				
Dor	Robin's Grange	200	24 Nov 1679	24/184;28/296
Robbins, Henry:				
PG	Mud Hole	173	1 Jun 1700	34/191;38/157
Cha	Robbins' Delight	120	5 Oct 1695	34/110;40/35
Robins, John of Virginia, cordwainer:				
Transported himself, his wife Katharine, Mary & Sarah Robins & five other persons to Somerset Co. by 1679				24/126
Robins, Capt. John:				
Som	Key	100	26 Mar 1680	24/257
Som	Late Discovery	600	28 Nov 1679	24/157;28/535
Robinson, John:				
Tal	Chestnut Meadow	200	6 Dec 1682	24/493
Tal	Content	200	10 Aug 1681	24/375;31/107
Tal	Jamaico's Addition	50	17 Jan 1682	24/391
Tal	Providence	600	24 May 1681	24/365
Tal	Robinson's Addn.	200	10 Aug 1683	31/232
Tal	Robinson's Adventure	200	24 May 1682	24/457;31/110
Robinson, Mr. Joseph of Accomack Co., Virginia:				
Som	Brotherhood	340	18 May 1689	27/92
Robinson, Richard:				
Transported by William Stone Esq. after 1650.				29/149
Robinson, Thomas:				
Cha	Robinson's Purchase	214	1 Feb 1682	28/410
Robinson, Thomas of London, merchant:				
Bal	Turkey Point	1,000	19 Jun 1699	34/156

County	*Name of Tract*	*Acreage*	*Date*	*Reference(s)*
Robinson, William:				
Som	Cow Pasture	50	15 Aug 1688	25/421;32/656
Som	Spring Quarter	500	1 Dec 1688	27/126
Robinson, William Jr:				
Dor	Hazard	85	1 May 1701	34/308
Rob(b)ison, John:				
Completed his time of service by January 1680.				24/20
Robbison, Thomas, planter:				
Cha	Robbison's Purchase	214	7 Jun 1681	24/302
Robotham, George, gent:				
Tal		200	25 Sep 1680	24/206
Tal	Company	350	15 Jun 1682	24/472;29/343
Tal	Epsom	100	28 Oct 1680	24/206;28/58
Tal	Kingsale Addition	100	10 May 1683	25/195;30/251
Tal	Robotham's Park	500	1 Jly 1685	25/224;33/213
Tal	Vineyard	700	18 Feb 1685	25/171;32/165
Tal	Wrench's Farm	100	28 Oct 1680	24/284,348; 28/407
Robson, Charles:				
Dor	Robson's Range	100	27 Sep 1680	28/79
Robson, John:				
Dor	Robson's Folly	27	10 Nov 1700	34/332
Robson, Rowland of Talbot Co., planter:				
Dor	Rowland's Plain	140	12 Sep 1683	25/124;32/176
Robson, William:				
Dor	Fardingworth	100	9 May 1682	24/433;31/343
Dor	Robson's Chance	100	12 Feb 1682	24/419
Dor	Robson's Delight	150	12 Jan 1680	24/85
Dor	Robson's Desire	50	1 Jan 1682	24/417;31/406
Dor	Robson's Lot	300	27 Sep 1680	28/72
Dor	Robson's Range	100	28 Sep 1680	28/83
Rockho(u)ld, John, gent:				
AA	Rockhold's Purchase	243	10 Apr 1696	34/124;40/398
AA	Rockhould's Range	200	22 May 1683	25/9;31/454
AA	Rockhold's Search	180	10 Nov 1696	34/140;40/394
Roe, Thomas:				
Assignor of lands in Somerset Co. in Oct 1679.				24/263
Rogers, Abraham:				
StM		100	21 Mar 1684	25/42
Rogers, David, planter:				
Tal	Chance	160	10 Sep 1685	25/296;33/477
Tal	Mary's Dower	200	10 Nov 1695	37/406
Tal	Moorfields Addition	65	26 Mar 1687	25/314;33/566
Rogers, Henry, planter:				
Som	Shrewsbury	150	17 Dec 1683	25/132;30/221

County	*Name of Tract*	*Acreage*	*Date*	*Reference(s)*
Rogers, Robert of Anne Arundel Co:				
Bal	Robin's Camp	100	24 Apr 1701	34/352
Rookwood, Edward:				
Cha	Rookwood's Chance	144	19 Mar 1688	25/377;32/553
Rooles, Christopher:				
AA	Rooles' Chance	11	9 Aug 1681	24/352
Roper, Philip:				
Bal	Philip's Rest	150	10 Oct 1695	40/524
Roper, William:				
AA	Roper Gray	480	4 Aug 1681	24/350;31/410
Rosewell, Mr. William:				
StM	Clarken Addition	75	2 Dec 1680	24/257;29/140
StM	Green Meadow	200	17 Apr 1682	24/511;30/143
StM	St. Barbara's Addition	120	28 Dec 1680	24/266
Ross, James, surgeon:				
Tal	Bangor	300	10 Nov 1695	37/353
Ross, John:				
Dor	Ross's Range	200	22 Dec 1681	24/416;29/318
Dor	Fishing P-----	15	[20 Nov 1678]	24/141
Dor	Ross's Chance	84	[11 Jun 1677]	24/138;29/122
Round, James, merchant:				
Som	Bletchinghurst	500	[25 Feb 1681]	24/249;28/131
Som	Collick Moor	500	27 Apr 1681	28/129
Som	Fair Meadow	334	28 Apr 1685	25/274;33/439
Som	Good Success	300	2 May 1685	25/179;30/239
Som	Mill Angle	25	20 Dec 1683	25/115;32/276
Som	Morehouse	200	18 Dec 1683	25/175;30/238
Som	North Benfleet	400	13 Sep 1684	25/175;40/260
Som	Redland	300	17 Dec 1683	30/237
Som	South Benfleet	500	13 Sep 1684	25/176;30/241
Som	Taylor's Choice	200	7 Apr 1686	25/264
Round, William, merchant:				
Som	Convenience	150	10 Oct 1701	34/294
Som	Conveniency	500	1 Apr 1686	25/233;33/270
Rounds, Benjamin:				
Cec	Deprived Mischief	100	13 Oct 1695	40/489
Rousby, Christopher, gent:				
StM		1	9 Jun 1678	24/154
Cal	Rousby	500	16 Dec 1679	24/22
Rousby, John, gent:				
Tal	Morgan's Point	50	6 Sep 1679	24/222;28/161
Cal	Sledar	800	17 Dec 1679	24/4
Rousby, Mr. William of London, gent:				
Cal	Crane		12 Jan 1693	37/425
formerly lands of Christopher Rousby.				

County	Name of Tract	Acreage	Date	Reference(s)
Rousell, John:				
Som	Little Derry	200	3 Aug 1684	25/178;32/333
Som	Providence	200	3 Aug 1684	25/179;32/335
Rowell, John:				
Som	Shoemaker's Meadow	109	6 May 1685	25/177
Rowland, Lawrence:				
Cal	Long Green	91	10 Sep 1685	25/185;32/430
Royston, Richard:				
Tal	Claye's Addition	50	8 Apr 1679	24/210,211
Tal	Cumberland	200	10 Aug 1681	24/338;29/166
Tal	Royston's Purchase	500	18 Aug 1683	25/46
Rozer, Benjamin:				
Cha		1,000	21 Jan 1680	24/138
Ruley, Anthony:				
AA	Ruley's Search	74	6 Aug 1696	37/486
Rumsey, Mr. James:				
Cal	Land Over		11 Jan 1684	25/17;31/476
Rumsey, Thomas:				
Cec	King's Aime	500	29 Nov 1679	24/169;28/158
Russell, George:				
Som	Mill Branch	400	15 Jun 1683	25/54;30/151
Russell, John:				
Dor	Lidney	100	1 Nov 1701	34/337
Dor	Lucky Chance	100	1 Nov 1701	34/353
Russell, Michael Jr:				
Tal	Addition	80	29 Apr 1683	24/526;34/137;40/344
Russell, Michael Sr. & Jr:				
Tal	Huntington	510	10 Apr 1696	40/396
Rust, John:				
Som	Staynes	850	28 May 1681	24/330
Som	West Chester	200	28 May 1681	24/330;29/168
Rutter, John:				
Som	Tower Hill	150	23 Mar 1688	25/357;33/670
Ruxton, Nicholas:				
Bal	Ruxton's Range	100	10 Sep 1679	24/79
Ryley—See Riley.				
Sadler, Robert:				
Som	Cuckold's Delight	500	24 Apr 1689	34/43
Safford, William of Fox Creek, Dorchester Co:				
Dor	Betty's Lot	100	[20 Oct 1678]	24/145;28/97
Dor	Safford	428	15 May 1682	24/435;31/221
Dor	Safford's Desire	50	8 May 1682	24/433;31/223
Dor	Safford's Hermitage	50	30 May 1683	25/145;32/472

County	Name of Tract	Acreage	Date	Reference(s)
Salisbury, John of Transquaking, Dorchester Co:				
Tal	Bradford's Addition	100	22 Aug 1681	24/377;31/121
Dor	Salisbury Plain	100	[11 Jun 1678]	24/199;32/412
Salisbury, Pettigrew, son of John:				
Dor	Pettigrew's Lot	38	14 Apr 1683	24/534;30/98
Salisbury, William:				
Cec	Have At All	100	19 Jun 1683	31/271
Salter, John:				
Knt	Fair Dealing	300	4 Sep 1688	25/436;34/36
Knt	Fair Dealing Addition	42	8 Jun 1686	25/222;32/470
Knt	Honest Dealing	400	10 Sep 1685	25/211;32/456
Knt	Jericho	200	2 Sep 1687	25/362
Knt	Well Meaning	830	8 Jun 1686	25/220;33/204
Sam(p)son, Richard:				
Bal	Addition	101	19 Jly 1688	25/439;34/289
Bal	Sampson's Addition	50	13 Oct 1698	38/129
Samuell, Richard:				
Som	Fair Ridge	100	6 Jun 1683	29/477
Som	Samuell's Lot	200	10 Nov 1696	38/66
Sanders, James, gent:				
AA	Equality	140	30 Jun 1684	25/94;33/139
Sanders [Saunders], Mary:				
Transported by William Marchant of Dorchester Co. before February 1682.				28/469
Sanders, Mathew:				
Cha	Sanders' Folly	84	19 Mar 1688	25/377;32/554
Cha	Sanders' Pleasure	164	16 Mar 1689	25/433;34/11
Sanders, Robert:				
Cec	Hopeful Unity	150	12 May 1682	24/454;29/517
Sanders, William, planter:				
Cec	Sanders' Addition	100	18 Dec 1685	25/218
San(d)ford, James:				
Tal	Sandford's Folly	45	14 Jan 1696	37/490
Sanford, James:				
Tal	Sanford's Hermitage	250	20 Mar 1696	37/413
Sands, Robert:				
Tal	Chance	50	10 Nov 1695	40/161
Tal	Sands' Lot	153	10 Nov 1695	40/153
Sanen, Elizabeth:				
Transported by Thomas Browning of Cecil Co. by 1680.				24/105
Sangster, James:				
Som	Aberdeen	300	22 Apr 1689	27/15
Som	Boddam	400	3 Jly 1683	30/198
Som	Cannon's Lot	100	8 Sep 1681	24/509

County	Name of Tract	Acreage	Date	Reference(s)
Som	Handy's Meadow		9 Sep 1681	24/510
Som	Nantz		8 Sep 1681	24/510
Som	New Machir	200	30 Jly 1683	25/59;30/9
Santee, Christopher:				
Tal	Christopher's Lot	200	22 Oct 1679	24/223;28/475
Tal	Knave Stand Off	50	19 Apr 1684	25/113;33/145
Sargent [Serjant], Seth of St. Mary's Co., gent:				
Bal	Sargeant's Chance	500	27 Oct 1684	25/153
Bal	Serjant's Hall	500	19 Sep 1684	25/101
Sargeant, William:				
Cha	Sargeant's Mount	93	10 Nov 1695	34/120;40/176
Cha	William's Purchase	195	10 Nov 1695	34/117;40/118
Sasarson, Isaac:				
Tal	Abraham's Inheritage	160	12 Jun 1696	37/462
Saugher, George:				
AA	Content	150	4 Aug 1682	24/415;31/470
Saunders—See Sanders.				
Savin, William:				
Cec	Savin's Lot	50	[31 Oct 1680]	24/137;28/95
Sawcer [Sawser], Benjamin:				
Som	Addition	50	5 Jun 1688	25/399;32/714
Som	Sawser's Folly	100	6 Jly 1679	24/246;28/534
Som	Sawser's Lot	50	1 Oct 1681	24/379;29/378
Saxon, John:				
StM	Fowle's Discovery	100	16 Oct 1680	24/185
Sayer, John:				
Cec	Horsell Manor	1,000	1 Jun 1585	33/51
Sayer, Capt. (later Maj.) Peter:				
Tal	Branfield	800	15 Aug 1681	28/247
Tal	Gore	175	9 Oct 1687	25/418
Tal	Sayer's Addition	200	3 Aug 1681	24/373;31/63
Tal	Sayer's Forest	2,250	9 Oct 1687	25/417
Tal	Sayer's Range	300	2 Aug 1681	24/372;29/352
Tal	Sayer's Range Addn.	500	4 Jun 1685	25/172;32/70
Cec	Worsell Manor	1,000	10 Oct 1683	25/92
Scarbrough, Mr. Matthew:				
Som	Durham	200	5 Oct 1681	24/446
Som	Islington	109	8 Jan 1684	25/260
Som	Locke	250	16 Dec 1680	24/444
Som	Middlesex	500	3 May 1687	25/354;33/677
Som	North Petherton	500	27 May 1688	25/392;32/634
Som	Nunn's Green	350	5 Oct 1681	24/447
Som	Pemminie	50	7 Oct 1681	24/448
Som	Piney Purchase	200	10 Sep 1683	29/434
Som	Ravenstone	400	28 May 1681	24/327;28/539
Som	Reserve	250	6 Oct 1681	24/446

County	Name of Tract	Acreage	Date	Reference(s)
Som	Scarbrough's Adventure	500	3 May 1687	25/354;33/678
Som	South Petherton	430	10 Nov 1695	40/286
Som	Timber Quarter	250	5 Oct 1681	24/446;29/364
Scott, Cuthbert, gent:				
StM	Hopton's Park	1,680	27 Feb 1682	28/377
Scott, Cuthbert & Elizabeth his wife:				
StM	Hopton Park	2,100	14 May 1681	28/137
Scott, Daniel:				
Bal	Scott Hopewell	500	10 Nov 1696	38/41
Bal	Scott's Grove	500	15 Jan 1696	40/432
Scott, Edward:				
Bal	Scott's Folly	200	20 Mar 1696	40/509
Scott, James:				
Transported by Thomas Marshall bef. September 1680.				28/79
Scott, James, planter:				
Tal	Scotland	50	18 Dec 1682	24/496;30/79
Tal	Timberland	400	10 Nov 1682	24/491;32/61
Tal	Triangle	100	[2 Aug 1680]	24/136;28/98
Scott, John of Calvert Co., gent:				
Bal	Dunkell	340	23 Feb 1682	24/394,25/83; 31/2;33/72
Scott, John, mariner:				
Cha	Strabane	500	15 Feb 1686	25/211;33/181
Scott, Thomas:				
Tal	Piney Point	50	19 Apr 1682	24/407;31/147
Scott, William:				
Cec	Howard's Gift	300	12 Jun 1682	24/471;31/281
Tal	Leith	40	28 Jun 1688	25/410;32/678
Som	Rugland	150	30 May 1683	25/59
Som	Scotland	300	12 Jly 1683	31/204
Som	Scott's Folly	50	30 May 1683	25/77;30/181
Scotton, Thomas:				
Knt	Scotton's Addition	60	1 Dec 1700	34/324
Screwton, Mary:				
Transported by John Quigley of Cecil Co. by 1679.				24/93
Scudamore, Thomas, gent:				
Bal	Scudamore's Last	130	13 Aug 1687	25/345
Bal	Westwood	200	11 Nov 1686	25/287;30/329
Scutt, John:				
Bal	Morning Chance	400	10 May 1696	40/275
Bal	Scutt's Addition	100	1 --- 1700	38/160;30/345
Seaman, Thomas:				
Dor	Clark's Neck Addn.	13	4 Jly 1683	31/402

County	Name of Tract	Acreage	Date	Reference(s)
Sears, Daniel:				
Dor	Cooker's Plantation	30	10 Nov 1695	40/600
Seawall—See Sewall.				
Seaward—See Seward				
Sedgwick, James of Talbot Co:				
Tal	Camberwell	500	25 Jun 1681	24/338,25/74
Knt	Chance	500	20 Sep 1683	25/382;32/549
Tal	Hackney Marsh	300	24 Jun 1684	25/100;32/99
Tal	Stepney	300	4 Jan 1688	25/366;33/631
Sedgwick [Sedwicks], Thomas:				
Cal	Neighbourhood	250	13 Dec 1679	24/93
Cal	Whore's Range	100	7 Jun 1680	24/191
Selby, Daniel:				
Som	Ashankin	70	1 Oct 1689	27/230
Som	Bastable	150	15 Jly 1679	24/136;28/93
Som	Cade's Contrivance	150	10 Nov 1695	37/504
Som	Carragensicke	390	2 Jan 1683	24/509
Som	Doublin	300	13 Sep 1684	25/176
Som	Key	100	26 Mar 1680	24/257
Som	Kilkenny	284	1 Sep 1687	25/352;33/673
Selby, Edward Jr:				
AA	Selby's Stop	201	14 Mar 1688	25/348;33/730
Selby, John of Anne Arundel Co:				
Bal	Knavery Prevented	400	10 Apr 1702	35/388
Selby, William of Calvert Co., planter:				
PG	Leith	500	30 Oct 1698	38/58
Sely—See Cely.				
Semans, Henry:				
Dor	Little Britain	50	24 Mar 1686	25/190
Sergent/Serjant—See Sargeant.				
Sergeson, William:				
StM	Sergeson's Folly	50	18 Dec 1680	24/255
Sertcleife, William:				
StM	St. William's	90	3 Jun 1685	25/192;32/457
Seth, Jacob:				
Tal	Addition	40	15 Apr 1696	37/320
Settle, William of Baltimore Co:				
Assignor of lands in Anne Arundel Co. in May 1688.				25/406
Sewall, Henry, gent:				
AA	Henry's Increase	43	1 Jly 1680	28/41
AA	Sewall's Increase	500	23 Sep 1680	28/75
Sewall [Sewell], John:				
Cal	[unnamed]	450	23 Nov 1681	24/358

County	Name of Tract	Acreage	Date	Reference(s)
Cal	Cuthbert's Fortune	100	7 Nov 1694	27/169
Cal	Cuthbert's Fortune Addn.	100	10 Nov 1695	40/83
Sewall, Maj. Nicholas of Calvert Co:				
Bal		2,000	27 Sep 1683	25/41
Cal	Partnership	1,500	9 Nov 1680	24/196;34/148
StM	Partnership	1,878	13 Dec 1697	38/96
Tal	Poplar Ridge	500	24 Sep 1683	25/26,94;32/2
Tal	Sewall Manor	4,000	29 Apr 1684	25/110
Cal	Sewall's Addition	210	18 Oct 1687	25/318;32/515
Bal	Sewell's Fancy	1,000	28 Sep 1680	28/69
Tal	Sewall's Fork	1,000	24 Sep 1683	25/26;32/1
Seawall, Peter:				
Cal	Seawall's Purchase	30	25 Jly 1681	24/191;28/242
assigned to him by John Sewall of Calvert Co.				
Sewell, Thomas:				
Som	Holwell	100	[30 Aug 1680]	24/243;28/369
Se(a)ward, John:				
Dor	Padre Arme(?)	81	21 Apr 1675	25/161
Seaward, Jonas:				
Som	Kinsale	150	12 Oct 1677	24/234
Seaward, Josias:				
Som	Chance	50	1 Oct 1683	25/28
Som	Harper's Increase	100	1 Oct 1683	25/27
Som	Venture	100	[2 Sep 1679]	24/243;28/239
Se(a)ward, Thomas:				
Tal	Molden	283	7 Jly 1686	25/338;33/652
Knt	Seaward's Hope	300	20 May 1686	25/227;32/443
Sexton, Mr. Patrick:				
New	Corneckestown	265	3 Jun 1684	25/111;32/222
Shadwell, Christopher:				
Transported by Thomas Clipsham bef. Sep 1680				28/44
Shanke, Thomas:				
Som	Norwich	100	1 Apr 1681	24/306;28/397
Shanklyn, William:				
Som	Parker's Adventure	300	2 Jly 1688	27/116
Share, William:				
Transported by Christopher Rousby of Calvert Co.				24/22
Sharpe, John:				
Tal	Haukes Hill	100	17 Jly 1680	24/174
Tal	Hawk Hill Addition	100	6 Jun 1679	24/213
Tal	Haukes Hill Hope	100	6 Jly 1681	28/170
Sharp, Peter:				
Tal	son of William			24/1

County	*Name of Tract*	*Acreage*	*Date*	*Reference(s)*
Sharp, William:				
Tal	Head Fresh Spring	400	10 Jan 1680	24/1
Tal	Inclosure	300	10 Nov 1695	37/329
Tal	Sharpe's Addition	24	10 Nov 1695	37/508
Tal	Sharp's Chance	300	10 Jan 1680	24/2
Tal	Sharpe's Fortune	100	10 Jan 1680	24/1
Sharpe, William:				
Tal	Walles	100	1 Jun 1687	32/481
escheated lands of James Forbus surveyed for him in 1663: he died over 19 years ago leaving a duaghter Elizabeth Forbus who died 16 months ago at full age but without heirs leaving the lands in possession of her guardian Robert Blankhorn.				
Shaw, Christopher:				
Bal	Shaw's Delight	97	15 Jun 1688	25/440
Bal	Shaw's Fancy	100	10 Aug 1682	24/497;30/47
Shaw, Ralph, planter:				
Cha	Mobberly	90	27 May 1681	24/292
Shaw, Thomas:				
Som	Mamsbury	200	1 Jun 1700	39/13
Sheele, Capt:				
Transported bef. Aug 1680 by William Jones of Bristol				28/31
Shellito, Thomas:				
Som	Lougtown	150	29 Sep 1683	29/368
Shepherd [Shepard], Charles:				
Cha	Bear Ferrys	105	3 Jan 1689	25/434;34/14
Shepheard [Sheppard], Francis, planter:				
Tal	Ashford	200	5 Jun 1685	25/185,195;32/318
Tal	Barefield	200	28 Oct 1679	24/224;29/259
Tal	Hennifield	200	3 Aug 1684	25/260;33/339
Tal	Molden	283	7 Jly 1686	25/338;33/652
Tal	Partnership	1,000	20 Mar 1680	24/231
Tal	Ramsey's Folly	200	5 Jun 1685	25/196;32/300
Tal	Shaver	200	21 May 1688	25/414;32/672
Tal	Sheppard's Discovery	400	19 Dec 1682	24/496
Tal	Sheppard's Folds	400	4 Feb 1687	25/368;32/671;33/665
Tal	Sheppard's Forest	200	3 Aug 1684	25/157;32/324
Tal	Shepherd's Fortune	500	20 Nov 1681	24/385;29/339
Tal	Sheppard's Redoubt	300	6 Apr 1687	25/340;33/663
Tal	Shepherd's Hook	200	29 Jun 1681	24/357;31/246
Shepheard, John:				
StM	Akar	125	12 Mar 1683	24/488;31/50,161
Shepheard, Nicholas:				
AA	Shepheard's Choice	240	12 Jun 1686	25/249;33/482
AA	Shepheard's Grove	120	12 May 1683	25/8;31/461
Shepley [Shipley], Adam:				
AA	Adam the First	500	8 Apr 1687	25/313;33/571
AA	Shepley's Choice	200	30 Mar 1681	24/295;28/463

County	Name of Tract	Acreage	Date	Reference(s)
Sheridan, Jeremiah:				
Assignor of lands in Calvert Co. in Sep 1694.				27/216
Sherwood, Hugh:				
Tal	Crooked Intention	130	13 Aug 1680	24/173;28/194
Tal	Sherwood's Island	20	13 Aug 1680	24/173;28/171
Shewell, Samuel:				
Som	Shewell's Addition	176	19 Sep 1687	25/390;34/42
Som	Shewell's Discovery	420	14 May 1689	27/102
Shewell, Thomas:				
Som	Cropton	800	25 Nov 1679	24/108
Shiels, Thomas:				
Som	Whitty's Contrivance	100	28 May 1681	24/325;29/53
Shiley, John:				
Som	Shiley's Meadows	60	4 Jly 1702	35/393
Shingleton, John:				
Som	Rhodee	350	26 Jun 1683	24/530
Shinton, William, planter:				
Dor	Shinton's Neglect	100	[2 May 1682]	24/459
Dor	Shinton's Point	50	28 May 1683	25/47,119;30/100
Shipley—See Shepley				
Shippie, Richard:				
StM	Shippie's Rest	100	9 May 1681	24/514;31/519
Shipway, John, planter:				
Som	Shipway's Choice	250	10 Jun 1680	24/310;29/74
Shockley, Richard:				
Som	Shockley's Purchase	400	18 May 1683	30/197
Shores, Thomas:				
StM	Shores' Delight	75	19 Jan 1681	24/255
Shortline, Roger:				
Som	Tilbury	100	15 Jun 1683	25/51;30/4
Shuttleworth, Thomas, planter:				
Cha	New Street	50	[19 Dec 1680]	24/254
See also under Harrison, Joseph.				
Sicklemore, Samuel, planter:				
Bal	Neighbour's Affinity	500	1 Jun 1700	34/288
Bal	Rayma	100	28 Apr 1687	25/311;33/525
Bal	Samuel's Delight	150	18 Sep 1683	25/92;33/125
Bal	Turkey Hill	262	10 Mar 1696	40/443
Bal	Wolf Harbour	318	10 Nov 1695	40/503
Sickmore (*sic*), Samuel:				
Bal	Arthur's Delay	10	21 Jly 1688	25/441
Sidbery, Edward:				
Som	Turkey Cock Hill	120	29 Sep 1683	25/112;30/216

County	Name of Tract	Acreage	Date	Reference(s)
Silvester [Sylvester], James:				
Tal	Bear Garden	353	4 Jly 1688	25/411;32/680
Tal	Golden Lyon	200	5 Aug 1679	24/219
Tal	Mischief	100	2 Mar 1680	24/230
Tal	Silvester's Addition	214	14 May 1689	27/207;34/96
Tal	Silvester's Forest	250	3 Aug 1682	24/475;29/316
Tal	Woodland	100	14 May 1689	27/211;34/111
Simcocks, Alexander:				
Transported by Job Chandler, gent, bef. 1651.				29/149
Simmons, Thomas:				
Cal	Born Again	50	15 Jan 1687	25/291;33/593
Simms, Alexander:				
Cec	Hopewell	270	13 Jun 1682	24/472;29/407
Cec	Simms' Farm	150	13 Jun 1682	24/472;31/268
Cec	Simm's Prime Choice	80	13 Jun 1682	24/471;31/276
Simms, Marmaduke of St. Mary's Co:				
Cec	Simms' Forest	400	14 Nov 1685	25/245;33/282
Simpson, Jeremiah:				
Cal	Round Pond Plain	50	[Apr 1682]	24/134;29/104
Simson, Richard:				
Bal	Simson's Choice	53	15 Jly 1688	25/441
Sincott, Thomas:				
Transported by John Abington of Calvert Co. before August 1680.				28/34
Sinister, Thomas:				
Transported by Thomas Browning of Cecil Co. by 1680.				24/105
Skellington, Thomas:				
Tal	Hambleton's Neck	256	3 Apr 1684	25/108
Skelton, Israel:				
Bal	Holland's Gift	127	29 May 1683	29/307
Skidmore, Nicholas:				
Cha	Aldgate	40	10 Jly 1683	29/314
Cha	Hillport	110	5 Dec 1684	25/241;33/298
Cha	Skidmore's Adventure	37	16 Oct 1679	24/135
Cha	Skidmore's Hope		15 Sep 1679	24/135;28/68
Cha	Skidmore's Rest	80	19 Aug 1681	24/376,512; 29/315
Skinn, Clarke:				
Cal	Skinn's Chance	120	1 Jun 1700	34/271
Skinner, Andrew:				
Tal	Roadway	50	12 Apr 1683	29/214
Tal	Skinner's Outlet	50	13 Apr 1683	29/239
Skinner, Richard, Deputy Surveyor of Talbot Co:				
Tal	Skinner's Addition	150	14 Oct 1687	25/370;33/631
Tal	Skinner's Borders	100	15 Oct 1687	25/369;33/643
Tal	Skinner's Expectation	480	10 Nov 1686	38/23
Tal	Skinner's Vineyard	75	10 Nov 1695	37/516;40/232

County	Name of Tract	Acreage	Date	Reference(s)
Skinner, Mr. Robert:				
Cal	Border	50	27 Sep 1680	28/81
Cal	Island Neck	190	13 May 1684	25/30
Cal	Island Neck Addition	30	17 Sep 1686	25/253;30/274
Cal	Scrap	100	27 Sep 1680	28/67
Skinner, William, son of Thomas Skinner deceased:				
Dor	Beckwith's Addition	50	7 Nov 1680	24/302,355; 30/105;31/386
Dor	Skinner's Neglect	50	28 Nov 1680	24/302;30/102
Tal	Skinner's Point	50	20 Mar 1696	37/429
Skrine, Roger:				
Assignor of lands in Dorchester Co. in Sep 1680.				24/201
Slade, Edward:				
Completed his time of service before Aug 1681.				28/305
Slade, William:				
Bal	Slade's Addition	112	10 Nov 1695	34/116;40/73
Bal	Slade's Camp	188	10 May 1696	34/139;40/384
Slye, Capt. Gerard:				
StM	Bastard Berry's	829	[1679]	24/135
Smallwood, James:				
Cha	Bachelor's Hope	184	10 Nov 1695	40/166
Cha	Eltham	75	10 Jun 1681	24/293;40/201
Cha	Porke Hall	110	15 Mar 1689	25/433;34/14
Smallwood, Matthew:				
Cha	Bachelors' Delight	235	10 Nov 1695	40/130
Smallwood, Thomas:				
Cha	Bachelors' Delight	235	10 Nov 1695	40/130
Cha	Bayne	100	10 Nov 1696	38/3
Smith, Anthony:				
AA	Anthony's Purchase	325	16 Jan 1700	34/241;38/132
Smith, Daniel:				
StM	Buck Branch	50	10 Jan 1687	25/270;30/310
Cec	Gibson's Green	100	15 Nov 1680	25/11
StM	Smith's Rest	35	8 Aug 1694	27/206
Smith, Edward:				
Som	Fladbury	250	[8 May 1678]	24/155;32/242
Som	Ripley	500	2 Feb 1680	24/154;28/192
Smith, Edward of Baltimore Co:				
AA	Smith's Desire	250	12 May 1685	25/184;30/161
Bal	Smith's Addition	45	10 Nov 1695	40/309
Bal	Smith's Forest	212	10 Nov 1695	38/124
Smith, Capt. Henry:				
Som	Corporal's Ridge	50	6 Aug 1681	24/373;29/458
Som	Good Success	300	4 Feb 1687	25/282;32/491
Som	Hartlebury	150	30 May 1684	25/136;32/294

County	Name of Tract	Acreage	Date	Reference(s)
Som	High Meadow	500	11 Feb 1687	25/284;32/502
Som	Ilchester	900	25 May 1683	25/31
Som	Pleasant Meadow	500	7 Feb 1687	25/282;33/386
Som	Smith's Hope	100	25 May 1683	25/32
Som	Smith's Recovery	700	2 Dec 1679	24/157;31/310
Som	Smith's Resolve	350	30 May 1683	25/44
StM	Smith's Rest	100	5 Oct 1695	40/31
Som	William's Hope	1,002	11 May 1688	25/402
Smith, Henry Esq:				
Som		70	9 Dec 1679	24/27
Som	Moorefields	500	5 Apr 1682	24/452
Som	Pitchraft	1,000	24 Dec 1679	24/236,278;29/180
Smith, James of South River, Anne Arundel Co:				
AA	Jacob's Point	21	10 Nov 1676	24/280
Smith, James, planter:				
Tal	Smithfield	200	19 Feb 1685	25/193;32/322
Tal	Smith's Addition	106	5 May 1686	25/369;33/633
Tal	Smith's Beginning	200	13 Dec 1682	24/495
Tal	Smith's Delight	300	13 Dec 1682	24/495;31/499
Smith, John:				
Transported by John Abington of Calvert Co. before August 1680.				28/34
Smith, John of Calvert Co., planter:				
Cal	Orphan's Gift	500	22 Aug 1688	25/427;34/28
Cha	Smith's Chance	144	5 May 1686	25/225;32/359
Cal	Smith's Pasture	150	10 Nov 1695	37/147
Cal	Smith's Greens	50	10 Nov 1695	37/145
Cal	Turrull Green	170	13 Jan 1696	37/142
Smith, John:				
Som	Ferry Hall	100	[20 Feb 1680]	24/245;28/278
Smith, Joseph:				
Dor	Smith's Point	298	18 Feb 1687	25/152,293
Smith, Mark:				
Cal	Island Marsh	19	22 Feb 1686	25/214;30/194
Smith, Marmaduke:				
Assignor of lands in Talbot Co. in 1677.				24/166
Smith, Matthew:				
Cec	New Intersection	159	1 Jly 1701	34/344
Cec	Cedar Branch Neck	841	1 May 1701	34/340
Smith, Nathan:				
AA	Lord's Bounty	200	11 Jan 1683	24/451;29/95
PG	Moore's Plain	105	20 Oct 1701	34/314
Smith, Maj. Nicholas of Calvert Co:				
Bal		1,000	[1679]	24/135
Smith, Oliver:				
Dor	Wadsdowne	50	18 May 1682	24/435;31/162

County	Name of Tract	Acreage	Date	Reference(s)
Smith, Philemon:				
AA	Smith's Forest	200	6 Mar 1695	27/326;34/113
Smith, Ralph:				
Cha	Smith's Adventure	200	3 Aug 1686	25/239;30/277
Cha	Smith's Fortune	25	22 Sep 1680	28/82
Smith, Capt. Richard of Calvert Co., Surveyor-General:				
StM	[unnamed]	95	10 Oct 1701	34/292
Cal	Free Gift 1st Part	2,000	10 Sep 1694	27/166
Cal	Industry	153	15 Oct 1698	38/97
Cal	Smith's Conveniency	186	25 Sep 1694	27/212
Cal	Smith's Forest	2,000	10 May 1695	37/200
Cec	Smith's Fort	500	20 Jun 1685	25/218;33/331
Cal	Smith's Hog Pen	319	18 Sep 1694	27/151
Cal	Smith's Purchase	408	1 Jly 1696	37/334
Smith, Richard Jr. of Calvert Co:				
Bal	Vale of Jehosophat	2,500	27 Sep 1683	25/43;32/25
Bal	Jehosophat Enlargement	500	10 Nov 1695	37/210
Cal	Small Reward	111	10 Nov 1688	25/428;34/29
Smith, Robert Esq:				
Tal	Adventure	160	31 May 1696	37/437
Tal	Adventure	200	7 May 1679	24/35
Tal	Astrak	300	11 Oct 1686	25/307
Tal	Bachelor's Plain	300	18 Dec 1676	24/543
Tal	Bradburne's Delight	200	20 Aug 1676*	24/544
Tal	Chance	200	19 Jly 1681	24/369
Tal	Condover	326	13 May 1687	25/339;33/646
Tal	Contention	100	31 May 1696	37/434
Tal	Double Kill	160	26 Mar 1695	37/30
Tal	Emery Fortune Addn.	270	26 Apr 1695	37/27
Tal	Fishingham	200	7 May 1679	24/29
Tal	Folorn Hope	935	10 Nov 1695	37/395
Tal	Golden Grove	116	6 Feb 1683	24/488;29/304
Tal	Jamaica	100	[1679]	24/133
Tal	Lampton	135	10 Oct 1686	25/297
Tal	Malton	389	26 Jly 1686	25/364
Tal	Manton	300	12 Oct 1686	25/307
Tal	Milland	60	10 Oct 1686	25/308
Tal	Neglect	100	7 May 1679	24/24
Tal	Out Range	400	7 Jun 1688	25/413;32/693
Tal	Pell Takers Loss	100	7 May 1679	24/35
Tal	Plains	105	14 Nov 1685	25/296;33/489
Tal	Pleasant Spring	300	29 Oct 1679	24/221;28/442
Tal	Powell's Fancy	300	25 Oct 1679	24/223;28/444
Tal	Reason?	340	10 May 1695	37/28
Tal	Smithfield	200	27 Feb 1680	24/232;31/288
Tal	Smith's Addition	300	27 Oct 1679	24/223;28/476
Tal	Smith's Chance	50	15 Jun 1685	25/294;33/453
Tal	Smith's Forest	300	25 Jun 1681	24/341;29/175
Tal	Smith's Inlet	200	20 Jly 1681	24/369;31/327
Tal	Smith's Polygon	400	28 Mar 1686	25/298;33/479

County	Name of Tract	Acreage	Date	Reference(s)
Tal	Smith's Range	300	28 Jun 1681	24/339;29/174
Tal	Smith's Range Addition	290	31 May 1696	37/435
Tal	Smith's Reserve	84	21 Feb 1683	24/543
Tal	Smith's Reserve	250	3 Nov 1684	25/295;33/481
Tal	Triangle	100	30 Jun 1681	24/340;29/176
Som	Worton	200	[16 Jun 1679]	24/244;28/406
Smith, Samuel of Virginia:				
Dor	Second Choice	300	10 Jan 1680	24/33
Smith, Thomas:				
Cal	Chance	72	22 Jun 1694	27/259
Cal	Smith's Lot	110	1 Jun 1702	35/365
Tal	Lambeth's Addn.	150	20 Mar 1696	37/389
Tal	Long Acre	150	4 Jun 1682	24/469
Tal	Smith's Park	250	2 Dec 1682	24/482
Bal	Smith's Beginning	100	10 May 1695	40/546
Smith, Capt. Walter:				
Cal	Addition	113	10 Jly 1694	27/271
Cal	Bear Neck	500	10 Nov 1695	40/72
Cal	Hall's Croft	1,672	1 May 1696	37/11
Smith, William:				
Cha	several tracts		30 Jly 1683	25/2
lands escheated for want of heirs to David Thomas.				
Cha	Millford	100	1 Jun 1685	33/48
Cha	Smith's Purchase	300	1 Jun 1685	33/46
Smith, William:				
Cal	Thomas Town	200	10 May 1685	33/43
Smithson, Thomas of Dorchester Co:				
Dor	Camber	100	2 May 1683	25/156
Dor	Sectar	769	21 May 1684	25/154
Dor	Endeavour	500	25 May 1688	25/434
Dor	Kipling	150	1 Jan 1682	24/390;31/359
Smithson, Thomas, Jr:				
Dor	Horton Green	500	27 Oct 1684	25/155;32/409
Dor	Smithson's Trial	500	28 Oct 1684	25/156;33/243
Smithson, Col. Thomas of Talbot Co., (merchant):				
Tal	Arcadia	200	15 Sep 1680	24/201;29/225
Tal	Brafferton	100	26 Apr 1689	27/200
Tal	Brian's Blank	32	10 Aug 1680	24/172;28/186
Tal	Chamber Lake	100	7 May 1700	34/222
Tal	Cumberland	100	15 May 1682	24/455;31/308
Tal	Gaterly Moor	120	26 Aug 1681	24/377;34/256
Tal	Hazard	70	28 Sep 1687	25/367;33/623
Tal	Holden's Range	73	2 May 1683	25/41
Tal	Long Acre	150	10 Sep 1683	29/371
Tal	Micklemire	480	10 Oct 1687	25/325;33/621
Tal	Mill Road Addition	150	4 Jly 1679	24/220;28/502
Tal	Mill Road Addition	300	[1695]	37/543

County	*Name of Tract*	*Acreage*	*Date*	*Reference(s)*
Tal	Reviving Springs	500	2 Mar 1688	25/339;33/629
Tal	Sectar	769	1 Oct 1698	38/89
Dor	Surveyor's Forest	650	1 Apr 1683	25/18
Tal	Sydenburg	100	11 Oct 1683	25/25
Smithson, William:				
Dor		200	10 Nov 1679	24/207
Dor	Yorke	200	1 Jan 1682	24/389;29/363
Smock, John:				
Som	Ainee Down		20 Jly 1679	24/44
Som	Conveniency	200	15 Jun 1683	25/53
Som	Creedwell	500	1 Dec 1679	24/128
Som	St. Martin's Ridge	200	15 Jun 1683	25/54
Smoote, Thomas:				
Cha	Smoote's Chance	160	15 Apr 1687	25/320;33/617
Smullion, William:				
Assignor of lands in Somerset Co. in Oct 1688.				27/136
Snead, Sarah:				
Transported by John Abington of Calvert Co. before August 1680.				28/34
Snowden, Henry, planter:				
Tal	Shoreditch	150	7 May 1687	25/314;33/589
Sno(w)den, Richard:				
AA	Robin Hood's Forest	1,976	5 Jun 1686	25/228;30/230
AA	Turkey Neck	200	10 Sep 1698	38/122
Southerne, Richard:				
Cal	Little Worth	25	17 Jun 1680	28/11
Cal	Southerne's Desire	125	28 Dec 1680	24/287;31/4
Cal	Southerne's Hills	50	17 Jun 1680	28/11
Southern, Valentine:				
Knt	Southern's Addition	84	5 Oct 1695	40/24
Southy, John, planter:				
Dor	Turkey Point	350	29 Mar 1686	25/294;33/476
Dor	Wolverton	50	26 May 1682	24/459
Spalding, Thomas:				
StM	William's Hermitage	109	21 Sep 1688	25/402
Spann, John of Virginia, gent:				
Som	West Loe Neck	533	9 Dec 1676	24/234;28/314
Sparkes, William, planter:				
Tal	Sparkes' Outlet	114	22 Oct 1687	25/370;33/625
Tal	Sparkes' Own	100	21 Jun 1683	24/527;31/567
Sparrow, Solomon:				
AA	Sparrow's Addition	100	1 Jun 1700	34/268
AA	Solomon's Purchase	150	16 Jan 1700	34/274;38/132
Speake, John:				
Cha	Speake's Inclosure	288	23 Mar 1688	25/377;32/557

County	Name of Tract	Acreage	Date	Reference(s)
Speere, Andrew:				
Som	Donnigall	200	10 Nov 1696	38/32
Spence, Adam:				
Som	Londonderry	200	10 Jun 1695	37/222
Spence, John & James, sons of David Spence deceased:				
Som	Hereafter	200	10 Oct 1679	24/263;29/6
Spencer, George of City of York, England, merchant:				
Cec	Danby	500	13 Sep 1682	24/517;29/161
Spencer, John:				
AA	Spencer's Search	17	-- May 1683	31/91
Sperman, Francis:				
Knt	Damme	188	1 Jly 1700	34/322
Sperne?, Nicholas:				
Cec	Tuskarora Plains	961	10 May 1696	40/385
Spernon, Joseph planter:				
Cec	Browning's Neglect	482	28 Mar 1685	25/254
Cec	Friendship	200	[5 Nov 1678]	24/146;28/107
Cec	Manchester	245	13 Oct 1682	24/505;31/475
Spicer, John, planter:				
Dor		50	[25 Dec 1679]	24/204
Dor	Colchester	340	28 Oct 1682	24/537;32/416
Dor	Doe Park	50	24 Jly 1682	24/415;31/374
Dor	Haverill	50	25 May 1682	24/438;29/385
Dor	Helens Bumstead	700	30 Dec 1679	24/195
Dor	Helions Bumstead	50	25 Jly 1681	28/312
Dor	Irish Hope	50	15 Jan 1681	24/442
Dor	Roundhead Proprietor	50	[25 Feb 1680]	24/199
Dor	Saffron Walden	50	23 Mar 1681	24/272;28/484
Dor	Steeple Bumstead	50	29 Dec 1679	24/202;28/345
Dor	Waxford	50	[27 Sep 1680]	24/131;28/118
Spicer, Margaret, wife of John:				
Her time of service completed by 1679.				24/106
Spinke, Henry:				
StM	Linstead's Addition	100	31 May 1682	24/412
StM	St. William Hermitage	170	21 Apr 1684	25/114
Spinkes, Roger:				
Bal	Speedwell	27	11 Jun 1688	25/440
Spottswood, Alexander:				
Transported by William Stone Esq. after 1650.				29/149
Sprigg, Mr. Thomas:				
Cal	Kettering	325	8 Sep 1685	25/179;32/342
PG	Sprigg's Request	500	1 Aug 1698	39/46
Spring, Rose:				
Transported by Job Chandler, gent, before 1651.				29/149

County	Name of Tract	Acreage	Date	Reference(s)
Sprouse, George:				
Dor	Sprouse's Mount	50	9 May 1687	25/303;33/433
Spry, Christopher, planter:				
Tal	Spryley	200	2 May 1687	25/314;33/568
Squire, Jonathan, nephew & heir of John Morecroft of St. Mary's City, gent. deceased:				
Cal	Moffett's Mount	200	30 May 1681	28/154
Squires, John:				
Dor	Killingsworth	50	20 May 1683	31/333
Tal	Squires' Chance	500	20 Aug 1679	24/136;28/88
Tal	Warwick Point	100	7 Sep 1679	24/120
Staley, Thomas:				
Bal	Moorfields	164	22 Feb 1689	25/439;30/356
Standever, William:				
Bal	Hopewell	204	14 Jun 1687	25/311;33/542
Standley, John:				
Tal	Chance	100	-- Jun 1679	24/214
Standford, Augustine, planter:				
Som	Folorn Hope	100	12 Jun 1683	25/75;30/247
Stanford, Joseph:				
Som	Long Ridge	125	10 Oct 1695	37/99
Stanley, Albert:				
Cal	Stanley's Marsh	100	7 May 1681	24/358
Stanley, Christopher:				
Som	Trubridge	700	4 Jun 1681	24/324;29/12
Stanley, John: Deputy Surveyor for Talbot Co:				
Tal	Arcadia	200	15 Sep 1680	24/201,253,363 29/225
Tal	Chayne	200	17 Sep 1683	25/48;31/528
Tal	Timber Neck	300	27 Sep 1683	25/48,325;33/74
Tal	Timber Neck Addn	139	15 Sep 1687	30/335
Stanley, Robert:				
Cal	Stanley's Marsh	100	10 Aug 1683	29/338
Stannaway, Joseph:				
Dor	Fox Point	10	24 Oct 1679	24/136;28/89
Dor	Stannaway's Forest	50	29 Dec 1679	24/180;28/287
Dor	Stannaway's Lot	90	24 Oct 1679	24/136;28/90
Dor	Stanway's Lucky Chance	69	30 Mar 1685	25/188;33/219
Dor	Wadle's Desire	50	[16 Oct 1680]	24/250;29/191
Stansby, Mary, widow of Capt. George Stansby:				
Bal	Island Point	100	[15 Nov 1683]	25/35;30/16
Stapleford, George:				
Dor	Stapleford's Chance	50	10 Jun 1696	37/472
Dor	Stapleford's Outlet	50	10 Nov 1695	40/593

County	Name of Tract	Acreage	Date	Reference(s)
Stapleford, Raymond, gent:				
Dor	Division	100	12 Jly 1679	24/134;28/77
Dor	Stapleford's Adventure	40	13 May 1682	24/467;31/375
Dor	Stapleford's Lot	100	10 Jly 1679	24/134;28/66
Dor	Stapleford's Road	50	4 Jun 1682	24/468;31/87
Staples, Henry, gent:				
Knt	Arundell Grove	550	21 Jun 1680	24/186;29/47
Knt	Kelly Longford	200	3 Jun 1686	25/226;33/246
Knt	Little Grove	220	19 May 1686	25/221;33/233
Knt	Staples' Choice	110	3 Jun 1686	25/328
Knt	Staples' Warren	100	13 Aug 1686	25/328
Staples, Dr. Henry:				
Cec	Staples' Choice	200	9 Aug 1684	25/343
Starky, John, planter:				
Tal	Randon	100	21 Oct 1687	25/325;30/333
Starnbero, Tobias:				
Bal	Huntington	135	29 Jun 1688	25/440
Stavely, James, gent:				
Cec	Suffolk	742	31 Mar 1681	24/295,25/13
Stears, Richard:				
AA	Stear's Park	100	10 Nov 1695	34/120;40/304
Stelle, James:				
Transported by Mark Cordea before Sep 1680.				28/51
Stephens—See Stevens.				
Sterling, John, cooper:				
Som	Sterling's Choice	50	1 Dec 1679	24/60
Sterling, Thomas:				
Cal	Major's Choice Addition	39	20 Aug 1694	27/257
Sterling, Thomas of Calvert Co., gent:				
Bal	Nova Scotia	1,500	9 Jun 1684	25/92;33/64
Cal	Sterling's Chance	40	21 Feb 1683	24/512;31/531
Cal	Sterling's Perch	300	15 Jun 1681	28/196
Sternbrow, Tobias:				
Bal	Strife	185	10 Jly 1695	40/539
Sterrey, John:				
Som	Forest of Dean	200	2 Sep 1687	25/353;32/525
Stevens, Charles:				
AA	Hickory Ridge	262	1 Nov 1694	27/319
AA	Timber Neck	303	10 Nov 1695	34/142;40/312
AA	What You Please	72	10 Nov 1695	40/302
Stephens, Charles:				
Tal	Stephens' Lot	19	20 Dec 1688	27/182;34/88
Stephens, Edward:				
Dor	Cheltenham	39	10 Nov 1695	40/449

County	Name of Tract	Acreage	Date	Reference(s)
Stevens, Francis:				
Knt	Jones's Plot	90	5 Oct 1695	40/15
Knt	Stevens' Adventure	255	10 Nov 1695	40/142
Stevens, John, gent:				
Dor	Chance	50	2 Jun 1682	24/467;31/239
Dor	London & Content	3,180	12 Jun 1682	24/470;29/507
Dor	Nothing Worth	86	30 May 1679	24/112
Stevens, Richard:				
Som	Goddard's Folly	800	9 Jly 1683	29/284
Cha	Stevens' Hope	95	10 Nov 1695	37/274
Stephens, Simon:				
Tal	Addition	75	12 Jly 1683	25/44;33/79
Tal	Stevens' Plain	200	22 Oct 1679	24/222;28/472
Stevens, Col. William:				
Som	Adventure	450	2 Nov 1679	24/270;28/520
Som	Attowattocoquin	1,200	2 Jun 1682	24/508
Som	Basing	1,050	4 Mar 1680	24/270;28/266
Som	Carmell	2,000	11 Dec 1679	24/25
Som	Chance	100	22 Mar 1681	24/320;28/513
Som	Caldicott	1,500	8 May 1684	31/347
Som	Camp	300	2 Jly 1682	29/171
Som	Convenience	1,300	15 Mar 1682	28/514
Som	Cow Pasture	500	14 Apr 1686	25/281;30/264
Som	Fair Meadow	500	8 Apr 1686	25/361
Som	Fishing Harbour	100	23 Mar 1681	24/296;28/367
Som	Flint	50	28 Nov 1679	24/28
Som	Haw Tree Point	100	2 Jly 1683	25/82;32/296
Som	Herring Quarter	300	24 Feb 1683	25/80;33/177
Som	Hilliard's Mistake	200	22 Mar 1681	24/320;28/512
Som	Hollyhead	100	7 Jly 1683	25/23
Som	Howard's Desire	500	13 Apr 1686	25/305;30/263
Som	Key	100	26 Mar 1680	24/257;28/516
Som	Ledbourn	350	2 Nov 1679	24/270;28/254
Som	Little	160	3 Apr 1683	25/196
Som	Manlove's Grove	500	5 Apr 1680	24/443
Som	Mentmore	441	4 May 1686	25/277;30/261
Som	Merrill Hall	200	8 Oct 1683	25/56;33/183
Som	Middlesex	150	4 Oct 1683	25/114
Som	Mulberry Grove	1,000	26 Sep 1680	24/444;29/297
Som	Pemberton	900	29 Sep 1682	24/531
Som	Reek Ridge	239	3 Jun 1682	24/507
Som	Stanes	850	2 Jly 1682	29/173
Som	Supply	300	23 Mar 1681	24/314;28/510
Som	Tonn	200	3 Apr 1683	25/196
Som	Toss Woodcocks	134	2 Jun 1682	24/507
Som	Vernum Dean	350	22 Mar 1681	24/320;28/511
Som	White Oak	250	30 Jly 1683	25/50
Som	Winter Pasture	500	6 May 1686	25/286;30/265

County	Name of Tract	Acreage	Date	Reference(s)
Stevens [Stephens], William, gent:				
Som	Buckingham	1,500	22 Jly 1679	24/137
Som	Little Monmouth	100	[27 Aug 1679]	24/206
Som	Newport Pannell	700	22 Jly 1679	24/137
Som	Hog's Down	150	1 Mar 1684	25/77;32/292
Som	Stevens' Meadow	188	6 Jly 1702	35/432
Dor	Bachelor's Chance	60	10 Nov 1696	38/37
Dor	Cliffe	234	27 Oct 1681	24/484
Dor	Hicke's Place	8	28 May 1682	24/441;31/391
Dor	Laybrooke	26	27 May 1682	24/440;29/298
Dor	Outlet	104	24 Dec 1694	37/19
Dor	Paul's	50	13 Aug 1680	28/29
Dor	Presbury	16	12 Nov 1680	24/284;28/428
Dor	Stevens' Chance	34	28 Oct 1681	24/484;31/145
Dor	Tanton	551	1 May 1698	39/50
Stevenson, Ann:				
Tal	Ann's Chance	50	8 Jun 1679	24/213;33/161
Stevenson, Edward:				
Tal	Stevenson's Range	300	18 Jly 1679	24/220;28/415
Stevenson, William of Talbot Co:				
Knt	Steventon	400	5 May 1684	25/108;32/129
Steward, Josias:				
Som	Linsey's Green		15 Dec 1679	24/6
Stinson, John:				
AA	Stinson's Choice	618	20 Feb 1685	25/190;30/227
Stockes, Peter:				
Dor	Peter's Adventure	34	29 Jly 1687	25/408;32/701
Stockett, Thomas of Anne Arundel Co:				
Bal	Hoppit	118	30 Sep 1679	24/130
Stoddard, James:				
Cha	Yarro Head	506	10 Nov 1695	37/194
Stokes, Peter:				
Dor	Head Range	100	12 Nov 1680	24/253;29/117
Stone, Hugh:				
Cal	Digbeth	100	19 Dec 1679	24/153;28/187
Cal	Stone's Lot	50	19 Nov 1679	24/159;29/217
Stone, John:				
Cal	Stone Hill	50	11 Dec 1679	24/153;29/226
Stone, Thomas:				
Bal	Stone's Range	194	10 Nov 1695	40/535
Stoop, John:				
Cec	Stoop's Folly	100	10 Nov 1695	40/82
Storey, John:				
Tal	Storey's Park	100	18 May 1688	27/172;34/100

County	*Name of Tract*	*Acreage*	*Date*	*Reference(s)*
Storey, Walter:				
Cha	Brant's Discovery	170	10 Nov 1696	38/6
Stratton, John:				
	Transported himself by 1679.			24/90
Strawbridge, Joseph:				
Bal	Westwood Addition	100	2 Jan 1696	40/547
Strut, Thomas:				
Transported by John Abington of Calvert Co. bef. Aug 1680				28/34
Styles, John:				
StM	Styles' Chance	200	12 Jun 1685	25/184;30/191
Snellin, William, boatwright & planter:				
Tal	Endeavour	50	17 Feb 1685	25/172;32/228
Sullivant, Florence:				
Tal	Dungannon	300	12 Aug 1687	25/365;33/664
Summerland, John:				
AA	Summerland's Lot	60	3 Aug 1681	24/350;31/419
Summers, Benjamin:				
Som	Musketter Hummock	200	9 Oct 1683	25/25
Summers, Thomas:				
Dor	Little Britain	50	20 Sep 1684	25/206;32/447
Dor	Tewksbury	50	[14 Aug 1678]	24/156;29/199
Sunell, Lancelot, planter:				
Cal	Yarmouth	70	21 Sep 1686	25/268,317
Sunly, William:				
Cha	Hatton Locoris	70	22 Mar 1688	25/375;32/584
Cha	Locoris	55	22 Mar 1688	25/375;32/583
Sutton, Thomas of Anne Arundel Co:				
AA	Sutton's Addition	20	28 May 1688	25/404;32/621
AA	Sutton's Choice	307	30 Jan 1681	24/175,301;28/216
Cec	Sutton's Forest	100	2 Apr 1685	25/186
Swaine, John of Talbot Co., carpenter:				
Knt	Dallington	500	16 Aug 1680	28/29
Swanson, Francis, son & heir of Francis Swanson deceased:				
Cal	Swanson's Lot	1,303	3 Aug 1683	25/19;32/259
Sweatnam, Edward:				
Knt	Hanham	70	[1 Dec 1681]	24/400;29/502
Knt	Sweatnam's Addition	100	10 Nov 1695	40/102
Knt	Sweatnam's Insula	38	[1 Dec 1681]	24/401;29/497
Sweetnam, Richard:				
Tal	Sweetnam's Hope	120	3 Jly 1683	25/45;32/37,683
Swift, Mark:				
Bal	Swift's Addition	22	10 Nov 1697	39/32

County	Name of Tract	Acreage	Date	Reference(s)
Swindell, Daniel:				
Bal	Daniel's Plains	100	10 Dec 1695	37/276
Swiney, Briant & Mary:				
Transported before August 1680 by William Jones of Bristol, England.				28/31
Swinfen, Francis:				
Cal	Free School Farm	250	8 Mar 1682	24/398;31/27
Swyt, John:				
Tal	Swyt's Chance	80	20 Mar 1696	37/397
Sylvester—See Silvester.				
Talbot, Edward:				
AA	Talbot's Angles	157	6 Jun 1686	25/229;30/231
Talbot, George. Surveyor-General of Maryland & Commissioner for disposal of lands in territory named New Ireland:				
Talbott, George Esq:				
Cec	Bellaconell	2,000	26 Apr 1683	29/271
	Susquehannah River Manor	32,000	22Mar 1683	31/230
Cec	Kildare	700	22 Jan 1681	24/237;29/270
Cec	Ormond	600	22 Jan 1681	24/237;29/269
Talbot, Col. George:				
StM	Cold Wells	331	21 Jly 1680	25/15;31/517
	Izembergh in Delaware	200	9 Jun 1687	25/270
Bal	Mellow Land	200	3 Nov 1687	25/327
Bal	Middleton	300	4 Nov 1687	25/327
	Netherland	1,100	9 Jun 1687	25/270;33/252
Talbott, William:				
Bal	Credentia	311	1 Nov 1701	34/350
Bal	Hurd's Camp	100	1 Nov 1700	34/231
Talley, Thomas:				
AA	New Worster	103	1 Oct 1679	24/154
Taney, John:				
Cal	Tany's Addition	132	20 Sep 1688	25/430;34/30
Taney, Michael:				
Cal	Long Point	100	26 Nov 1681	24/361;31/19
Cal	Wooden Point	25	26 Nov 1681	24/361;31/18
Taneyhill, Andrew of Calvert Co:				
Cha	Headache	300	3 Aug 1686	25/240;33/274
Taneyhill, William of Calvert Co:				
Cha	Ekenhead	500	2 Apr 1685	25/165;32/145
Tanner, Samuel:				
Tal	Rogue Keep Off	50	10 Nov 1695	40/151
Taper, James, executor of will of John Bowles of Charles Co., who died before Sep 1680.				28/82

County	*Name of Tract*	*Acreage*	*Date*	*Reference(s)*
Taplow, William:				
Dor	Taplow's Chance	50	5 May 1682	24/432;31/208
Tarr, John:				
Som	Tinterdale	350	10 Mar 1696	37/503
Tasker, Thomas:				
His time of service completed by 1679.				24/119
Tasker, Thomas of Calvert Co., gent:				
Cal	Kingsbury Marsh	130	19 Jun 1682	24/414
Bal	Tasker's Camp	500	17 May 1684	25/33;31/532
Tatnell, Hannah:				
Transported by Christopher Rousby of Calvert Co.				24/22
Taunt, John:				
StM	Taunton Deane	40	14 Dec 1863	25/44
StM	Taunt's Mark	160	14 Dec 1683	25/38
Taylard, William of St. Mary's Co:				
Tal	Taylerton	800	15 Jly 1695	40/13
Taylor [Tailer], Arthur, planter				
Bal	Arthur's Choice	300	20 Aug 1683	25/191;30/164
Tayler, Edward, planter:				
Dor	Persimmon Point Addition	50	13 Apr 1683	24/535;30/94
Taylor, Edward, innholder:				
Dor	Westward	100	2 Jan 1682	24/418;31/361
Taylor, Frances:				
StM	Fortune	50	19 Oct 1684	25/188;32/189
Taylor, George:				
Tal	Taylor Jane's Discovery	100	20 Mar 1696	37/366
Taylor, Hope:				
Som	Weaver's Choice	300	29 Feb 1688	25/399;32/646
Taylor, John:				
Dor	Balia	200	8 Sep 1684	30/146
Dor	Cyprus Swamp	62	16 Nov 1686	25/302
Dor	Cyprus Thicket	37	16 Nov 1686	25/302;33/553
Dor	Deale	50	30 Apr 1682	24/428;29/375
Dor	Fairfields	396	24 Oct 1684	25/204
Dor	Hog Yard	1,500	10 Oct 1687	25/409;32/667
Dor	Taylor's Adventure	500	27 Oct 1684	25/149;30/119
Dor	Timber Swamp	100	15 Jun 1682	24/441
Taylor, John, tailor:				
Som	Killglass	200	20 Jly 1688	27/22
Taylor, John, planter:				
Som	Sand Ridge	100	20 Nov 1688	27/36
Som	Taylor's Choice	200	10 Apr 1686	25/264
Taylor, Lawrence, planter:				
Bal	God Speed	200	28 Sep 1685	25/258;30/312

County	Name of Tract	Acreage	Date	Reference(s)
Tayler, Richard of Anne Arundel Co:				
Bal	Denton	600	15 Aug 1687	25/286;30/262
Taylor, Richard:				
StM	St. Teresia	100	24 Jan 1683	24/486;31/44
Taylor, Robert:				
AA	Chance	32	3 Sep 1684	25/117;33/114
Taylor, Samuel:				
Cal	Taylor's Coast	150	8 Feb 1682	24/362;32/10
Cal	Taylor's Marsh	25	9 Feb 1682	24/362;31/491
Taylor, Thomas, Deputy Surveyor for Dorchester & Newcastle Cos:				
Taylor, Thomas of Anne Arundel Co:				
Bal	Land of Promise	2,000	4 May 1684	25/35;31/506
Taylor, Thomas of Baltimore Co:				
AA	Tayler's Search	18	19 Jun 1688	25/403;32/620
Taylor, Thomas of Charles Co., gent:				
Assigned lands to his brother Thomas Bonner in 1684.				25/61
Cha	Bachelor's Delight	492	[28 Jly 1679]	24/250;29/152
Bal	Jenifer's Delight	250	18 Oct 1681	24/502
Taylor, Maj. (later Col.) Thomas:				
Transported 41 persons [unnamed] before Nov 1680.				28/115
Dor	Bath Addition	622	10 Nov 1695	37/267
Dor	Bridge Neck	300	19 Mar 1681	25/118
Dor	Dogwood Ridge	100	9 May 1688	25/436;34/210
Dor	Hazard	286	10 Nov 1695	37/269
Dor	Jericho	400	18 Nov 1679	24/533;30/114
Dor	Lot	235	10 Jly 1695	37/362
Dor	Maiden Forest	1,000	18 Mar 1681	24/296;28/470
Dor	Promise	100	10 Oct 1695	37/271
Dor	Samson's Discovery	1,000	30 Jly 1688	25/407;32/666
Dor	Taylor's Kindness	559	20 May 1688	25/436;34/209
Dor	Taylor's Hermitage	490	2 Jly 1688	30/358
Dor	Timber Ridge	150	10 Oct 1695	37/270
Dor	Welshman's Kindness	400	10 Oct 1694	37/272
Taylor, Thomas of Dorchester Co.,, gent:				
Dor	Bristol	300	12 Oct 1679	24/200
Dor	Hog Yard	1,500	27 Sep 1687	25/409
Dor	Kent	400	16 Sep 1679	24/95
Dor	Performance	200	10 Nov 1695	37/360
Dor	Sandwich	100	18 Apr 1682	24/407;31/139
Dor	Taylor's Armitage	490	2 Jly 1688	25/436
Dor	Taylor's Hap	50	2 May 1682	24/428;29/381
Dor	Taylor's Neglect	1,000	16 Sep 1679	24/103
Taylor, Thomas of Kent Co:				
Dor	Taylor's Fords	110	9 Apr 1683	25/18,123;30/94
Taylor, Thomas of Talbot Co:				
Tal	Addition	172	10 Nov 1695	40/131

County	*Name of Tract*	*Acreage*	*Date*	*Reference(s)*
Tal	Kingsbury's Addition	100	27 Mar 1683	29/202
Tal	King's Creek Marsh	50	2 Mar 1680	24/230;29/189
Tal	Partnership	36	10 Nov 1695	37/315
Tal	Taylor's Chance	200	2 Mar 1680	24/228;29/266
Dor	Taylor's Desire	400	5 Aug 1680	24/251;28/526
Tears, Hugh—See under Elinor Bale.				
Tegg, Edward:				
Cec	Pembroke	160	10 Oct 1695	40/483
Cec	Tegg's Delight	100	10 Nov 1695	40/484
Tench, John of Liverpool, England, mariner:				
Dor	John's Delight	200	30 Aug 1682	29/147
Tench, John:				
Dor	Tench's Range	800	16 May 1687	25/303;33/420
Tench, Thomas of Anne Arundel Co:				
Bal	Brown's Discovery	500	5 Jun 1702	35/377
Tennison, John of Charles Co:				
Cec	Hazard	32	1 Oct 1700	34/212
Terratt, Nicholas:				
AA	Mat---- Plains	300	10 Nov 1697	39/7
AA	Wrighten	715	10 Nov 1697	39/6
Terson, Andrew:				
Cec	Terson's Neck	300	[16 Sep 1681]	24/133;28/258
Thacker, Thomas:				
Dor	Broken Hayes	25	10 Nov 1695	37/264
Theobalds, John, planter:				
Tal	Theobalds' Addition	20	10 Oct 1687	25/326;33/618
Thomas, Alexander, planter:				
Som	Good Success	100	28 Nov 1685	25/277
Som	Happy Enjoyment	144	29 Apr 1684	25/362
Som	North Wales	400	24 Nov 1685	25/286;30/327
Thomas, David of Charles Co.—See under Smith, William.				
Thomas, Gabriel:				
Tal	Conoway	470	13 May 1687	25/339;33/651
Thomas, Hugh:				
Cha	Fortune	100	[2 Nov 1680]	24/198;28/437
Thomas, John, planter:				
Bal	Chevy Chase	400	10 Aug 1695	40/440
Bal	Good Luck	200	11 Aug 1684	25/141;32/308
Bal	Jurdistone	299	28 Feb 1689	25/439;34/160,167
Bal	Major's Choice	140	10 Nov 1695	40/441
Bal	Thomas's Adventure	165	2 Sep 1688	25/443;34/161
Bal	Thomas's Range	150	1 Jun 1685	32/307
Thomas, Joseph:				
Dor	Joseph's Venture	50	1 May 1701	34/358

County	Name of Tract	Acreage	Date	Reference(s)
Thomas, Lambrooke:				
Som	Mill Lot	100	10 Nov 1695	34/058;40/202
Thomas, Samuel:				
AA	Samuel's Purchase	200	16 Jan 1700	34/236;38/132
Thomas, Solomon:				
Tal	Chance	40	27 Mar 1687	25/315;33/651
Thomas, Susanna:				
Transported by her husband William Thomas of Charles Co. (q.v.) before September 1680.				28/121
Thomas, Tristram:				
Tal	Tristram's Addition	1,300	20 May 1681	24/338
Thomas, William:				
Cha	Manniseclear	250	23 Sep 1680	28/121;29/83
Cha	Thomas's Choice	368	19 Dec 1687	25/323;33/699
Thomas, William of Dorchester Co:				
Tal	Spring Gardens	123	26 May 1682	24/458
Dor	Spring Gardens Addition	123	1 Oct 1683	29/357
Dor	Thomas's Addition	47	2 Mar 1687	25/293;33/567
Thompson, Anthony:				
Dor	Chance	50	22 Jly 1687	25/408;32/702
Dor	Green Bank	25	12 Jun 1696	37/473
Dor	Thompson's Desire	50	27 Jly 1681	24/370;31/392
Dor	Thompson's Range	100	10 Aug 1683	31/390
Dor	Westphalia	136	21 Jly 1681	24/369;31/389
Dor	White Oak Range	50	28 Jly 1687	25/408;32/703
Dor	Whitehaven	50	15 Feb 1683	24/536;30/152
Thompson, Arthur:				
StM	Hampstead	200	26 Jan 1683	24/522
StM	Highgate	150	12 May 1681	24/363;29/310
StM	St. Osward	200	7 May 1683	25/100
Thompson, Christopher of Calvert Co:				
Cha	Whiteoak Range	300	31 Mar 1685	25/165;32/140
Thomson, Christopher of Virginia:				
Som	Thomson's Purchase	500	10 Nov 1695	37/86
Thompson, George of St. Mary's Co., gent:				
Cha		550	16 Jun 1684	25/101
StM		350	[19 Nov 1680]	24/205
Cha	Thompson's Yeamer	250	19 May 1684	30/117
Bal	Attleborough	600	2 Mar 1685	25/161;29/527
StM	Chelsey	100	25 Apr 1682	25/63;31/482
Bal	Cooknow	600	31 Jly 1686	25/215;33/198
StM	Eyre	328	30 Nov 1680	24/206;28/114
StM	Farnham	80	28 Feb 1685	25/161;33/1
Cha	Hab Nab at a Venture	250	16 Jun 1684	25/101;30/118
Cha	Ingerstone	230	18 Apr 1682	24/406;29/330

County	*Name of Tract*	*Acreage*	*Date*	*Reference(s)*
Bal	St. George	400	13 Jan 1685	25/158;30/134
StM	Square Adventure	100	10 Apr 1682	24/406;29/329
Bal	Thompson's Lot	600	26 Oct 1685	25/180;33/41
StM	Trophy	100	28 Feb 1685	25/162;33/2
StM	Wellingborough	70	2 May 1684	25/180;33/41
Thompson, George:				
Dor	Hampstead	600	24 Oct 1682	24/522;31/51
Thompson, James:				
Cha	Thompson Town	73	22 Mar 1688	25/377;32/552
Thompson, James of Calvert Co., gent:				
Cal	Tottnam	150	[27 Sep 1680]	24/132;28/122
Cha	Yarrow	500	24 Sep 1685	25/268;33/301
Thompson, Joseph:				
Dor		400	28 Oct 1684	25/156
Dor	Thompson's Addition	235	24 Mar 1686	25/206
Som	Thompson's Lot	100	1 Apr 1673	24/234;28/455
Dor	Thompson's Meadow	200	2 Apr 1685	25/294
Thompson, Robert:				
StM	Hard Fortune	100	5 Oct 1695	40/25
Thompson, Walter:				
Cha	Neck	500	16 Feb 1686	25/214;32/372
Thompson, William of Calvert Co:				
Cha	Scotland	300	30 Mar 1685	25/164;32/148
Thompson, William, planter:				
Cha	Little Worth	189	13 Mar 1689	25/433;34/9
Cha	Thompson's Delight	120	24 Jun 1688	25/402;32/617
Cha	Thompson's Range	230	10 Jly 1683	25/115
Cha	Thompson's Chance	230	10 Jly 1683	24/523
Thornborough [Thornbury], Rowland:				
Bal	Goose Harbour	41	11 Jun 1688	25/442;31/201
Bal	Selsea	900	10 Jly 1695	40/518
Thorne, Parley:				
Transported before Aug 1680 by William Jones of Bristol, England.				28/31
Thornell, Robert:				
Dor	Robin Hood's Well	50	10 Mar 1682	24/398;31/346
Thornton, Richard:				
Cec	Cheame	250	[1679]	24/133
Thorpe, Thomas:				
Transported by John Abington of Calvert Co. before August 1680.				28/34
Thurston, Thomas, planter:				
Bal	Agreement	500	20 Jan 1687	25/302;33/473
Bal	Come by Chance	200	10 Nov 1686	32/441

escheated estate of Thomas Byram, merchant, who was killed by Indians 13 years ago leaving a widow and two daughters, all now deceased, & no other heirs.

County	Name of Tract	Acreage	Date	Reference(s)
Bal	Elberton	1,000	15 Aug 1683	25/86;33/131
Bal	Littleton	632	14 May 1684	25/34
Bal	Strawberry Hill	200	14 May 1684	25/34;30/51
Tick, William:				
Dor	Tickson	50	-- Dec 1679	24/181;28/311
Tideings, Richard:				
AA	Hazlenut Ridge	166	29 Jly 1680	28/14
Bal	New Year's Purchase	500	25 Feb 1684	25/34;31/521
Tigman, John:				
Cha	Paindon	137	10 Nov 1695	37/260
Tilden, Charles:				
Knt	Bishford	200	26 Jun 1686	25/226;33/221
Tilghman, Mary of Talbot Co., widow:				
Tal	[unnamed]	500	20 May 1683	24/539
Tal	Recovery	100	29 Oct 1679	24/224;28/440
Tilghman, Richard:				
Tal	Tilghman's Range	98	10 Nov 1695	34/92;40/214
Tilghman, William:				
Tal	Partnership	1,000	20 Mar 1680	24/231;29/187
Tal	Tilghman's Pasture	300	14 Nov 1681	24/383
Till, Edward:				
Cha	Half Steed	95	16 Mar 1689	25/432;34/10
Tillman, Gideon:				
Som	Tillman's Adventure	50	15 Jly 1684	25/135;32/266
Timothy, William:				
Cha	Putney	80	[4 May 1680]	24/177;28/170
Timson, John of Charles Co:				
StM	St. John's	115	10 Dec 1694	37/238
Tinland?, Stephen:				
Bal	Stephen's -----	?	[1697]	39/37
Tinsley, Thomas:				
Cal	Tinsley's Lot	46	3 Nov 1694	27/266
Toaes, Daniel of Kent Co., merchant:				
Tal	Lower Fords	200	6 May 1687	25/313;33/586
Knt	Partnership	3,000	31 Jan 1685	25/97
Todd, James:				
Bal	Plains	187	2 Jly 1688	25/442
Bal	Todd's Range	510	17 Feb 1698	30/367
To(a)dveine, Nicholas:				
Som	Gernsey	150	28 May 1681	24/330;28/540
Som	Jersey	100	14 May 1689	27/50
Toll, Roger:				
StM	Toll's Last Shift	100	1 Apr 1682	24/404;29/346

County	Name of Tract	Acreage	Date	Reference(s)
Tolly, Richard—See under Hill, Richard.				
Tolly, Thomas:				
AA	Tolly's Point	140	9 Nov 1683	25/69
Tomkins, William:				
Som	Bourly	300	12 Jly 1683	29/476
Som	Tomkins' Meadow	53	15 Dec 1683	25/127;30/220
Toogood, Josias of Anne Arundel Co:				
PG	Bristol	140	1 Nov 1701	34/326
Townsend, Jeremiah:				
Som	Desire	100	[1697]	39/42
Townsend, John:				
Som	Townsends Discovery	100	25 Nov 1679	24/59
Travers, William, gent. (merchant):				
Dor	Stafford	103	16 Apr 1682	24/423
Dor	Travers' Addition	50	19 Mar 1680	24/169;29/131
Dor	Travers' Parcel of Points	13	6 Mar 1680	24/169;29/132
Trayle, Mr. William:				
Som	Chance	200	27 Apr 1689	27/62
Tregoe, William, mariner:				
Dor	Refuge	50	19 Apr 1683	24/541;30/85
Trevett, George:				
Som	Hogsdon	300	1 Jly 1696	38/76
Trevor, Matthew Jr:				
Dor	Bachelor's Ridge	78	10 May 1695	40/588
Tripp, Capt. Henry:				
Dor	Apparley	200	1 Jly 1683	25/109,121;32/158
Dor	Dale's Addition	100	19 Apr 1683	24/542;30/109
Dor	Dale's Right	100	19 Apr 1683	24/534;33/210
Dor	Exchange	50	4 Apr 1683	24/508;33/212
Dor	Tripelo's Farm Addition	40	17 Aug 1681	24/355;31/371
Dor	Tripp's Neglect	200	[5 Apr 1683]	24/542;30/106
Troth, William, planter:				
Tal	Acton Addition	57	10 Nov 1695	37/304
Tal	Hackney Marsh	50	10 Nov 1695	37/305
Tal	Moorefield's Addition	200	10 Nov 1682	24/546;31/184
Tal	Shoreditch	25	22 May 1683	24/528;32/53
Tal	Troth's Fortune	400	5 Jan 1680	24/82
True, John:				
Knt	Addition	72	8 Aug 1684	25/343
Trueman, Nathaniel:				
Cal	Truman's Lodge	200	before 1679	24/97
devised by his will to Thomas Trueman.				
Trueman, Maj. Thomas:				
Devisee by will of Nathaniel Truman (q.v.).				

County	*Name of Tract*	*Acreage*	*Date*	*Reference(s)*
Cal	Blackwell	200	21 Jun 1680	28/3
Cal	Inclosure	110	24 Jun 1680	28/3
Cal	Little Worth	279	18 Apr 1684	25/47;31/495
Cal	Long Leak	225	18 Jun 1680	28/1
Cal	Newton	70	25 Jun 1680	28/4
Cal	Nottingham	300	26 Sep 1683	25/19
Bal	Truman's Acquaintance	500	15 May 1683	25/2;31/498
Cal	Trueman's Choice	645	-- -- 1679	24/155,25/47;28/164
Cal	Seigby	164	20 Jun 1680	28/2
Cal	Spenton	100	22 Jun 1680	28/5
Cal	Wedge	75	24 Jun 1680	28/6
Cal	Wolf's Den	50	21 Jun 1680	28/5
Truett [Truitt], George, planter:				
Som	Truitt's Harbour	300	18 Sep 1684	25/262;38/99
Som	Truett's Purchase	140	1 May 1689	27/6
Truett, George Jr. of Virginia:				
Som	Folorn Hope	250	20 Feb 1699	30/403
Truett, John:				
Som	Truett's Lot	30	10 Nov 1695	34/60;40/204
Som	Wolf's Den	100	[1697]	39/41
Trulock, Henry of Calvert Co:				
Cec	Forrester's Delight	400	19 Jun 1683	31/247
Trull?, Thomas:				
Tal	T-----'s Lot	300	1 Oct 1698	39/49
Trusum, Edward of Calvert Co:				
Cec	Forrester's Delight	400	19 Jun 1683	31/247
Tucker, Thomas:				
Cal	Broad Point	150	10 May 1681	24/298;29/41
Tull, Richard:				
Som	Colman's Adventure	500	26 Jun 1687	25/401;33/682
Tull, Thomas:				
Som	Winter Range	200	2 Jly 1688	25/388;32/643
Tully, Stephen:				
Tal	Content	200	10 Aug 1681	24/375;31/107
Tal	Lord's Gift	300	2 Mar 1680	24/228;31/205
Tal	Providence	600	24 May 1681	24/365
Tal	Sandwich	150	24 May 1682	24/457;31/132
Tal	Stepney	200	6 Dec 1682	24/492;32/63
Tal	Tulley's Addition	300	2 Mar 1680	24/228;31/168
Tal	Tulley's Reserve	300	2 Mar 1680	24/228;31/279
Tully, Stephen Jr:				
Som	Steventon	85	10 Nov 1695	34/72;40/189
Turbutt, Michael:				
Assignor of lands in Talbot Co. in May 1681.				24/337

County	Name of Tract	Acreage	Date	Reference(s)
Turbut, Richard of Talbot Co:				
Cec	Sedgfield	500	15 Apr 1683	25/49;31/524
Turle, William:				
Tal	Emery Fortune	190	10 Mar 1696	40/456
Turner, Henry:				
Dor	Harridge	100	14 Jan 1680	24/267
Turner, James:				
Cha	Maiden's Point	50	5 Jly 1687	25/371;33/686
Turner, Richard:				
Tal	Beaver Dam Neck	141	10 Mar 1697	38/5
Turner, Samuel:				
Som	Turner's Choice	150	1 Jun 1700	34/270
Turner, Thomas:				
Cec	Audley End	190	17 Sep 1694	27/358
Turner, William:				
Cal	Turner's Chance	50	1 Mar 1698	38/46
Turpin, William:				
Som	Tottonais	250	28 May 1681	24/313;29/32
Turvill [Turvile], William, planter:				
Som	Key	100	26 Mar 1680	24/257
Som	Northampton	250	17 Dec 1683	25/139;32/378
Som	Royal Oak	450	28 May 1681	24/314;29/36
Tweegg, John:				
Cec	Redriffe	100	1 Sep 1701	34/318
Tweeley, Robert:				
Som	Woodstock	200	[3 Jun 1679]	24/243;28/277
Tyler, Robert:				
PG	Tyler's Chance	?	[1698]	39/56
Cal	Tyler's Choice	210	10 Mar 1696	37/149
PG	Tyler's Discovery	264	[1698]	39/55
AA	Tyler's Lot	100	1 Jly 1680	28/14
Underwood, Mr. Anthony of St. Mary's Co:				
Som	Cox's Advice	200	16 May 1683	25/47;30/139
StM	St. Peter's	10	8 Mar 1687	25/255
Cha	Underwood	300	15 Feb 1686	25/214;33/184
StM	Underwood's Choice	200	28 Apr 1684	25/98;33/31
Underwood, Peter:				
Dor	Underwood's	9	9 Jun 1679	24/96
Underwood, Samuel:				
AA	Addition	22	29 Sep 1682	24/465;31/170
AA	Mutual Consent	50	20 Jun 1683	25/96;32/181
Utie, George:				
Bal	Utie's Addition	45	19 May 1687	25/309;33/518

County	Name of Tract	Acreage	Date	Reference(s)
Vallon, Peter:				
Transported by Lawrence Knowles of Charles Co. before September 1680				28/127
Vanderleyden, Mathias, gent:				
Cec	Lowest Neck	120	3 May 1687	25/351;33/728
Vaughan, Rowland:				
Dor	Vaughan's Rest	50	15 Sep 1684	25/206;32/473
Vaughan, Thomas of Talbot Co., gent:				
Tal	Eaton's Addition	300	11 Aug 1681	24/375
Tal	Inclosure	300	24 Oct 1681	24/381
Dor	Range	100	20 Aug 1682	24/490
Tal	Vaughan's Discovery	400	24 Oct 1681	24/381
Vaughan, Thomas:				
Cec	Stocton	500	13 Sep 1682	24/517;29/160
Vaughan, William, planter:				
Tal	Moorfields	94	10 May 1687	25/314;33/594
Tal	Moorfields Addition	30	15 Oct 1687	25/324;33/624
Tal	Pooly's Discovery	168	20 Oct 1687	25/369;33/635
Veasey, Nathaniel:				
Som	Bachelor's Adventure	200	29 Jun 1679	24/235;28/273
Som	Key	100	26 Mar 1680	24/257
Viccars, Thomas, planter:				
Dor	Harwish	100	20 Apr 1683	24/536;33/151
Vickery, John:				
Dor	Bristol	200	10 Mar 1696	37/358
Vigerous, John:				
Som	Good Success	300	8 Apr 1686	25/282
Viner, John:				
Transported himself before Sep 1680.				28/66
Vines, William:				
AA	Vines' Fancy	60	20 Mar 1698	38/18
Waddle, John:				
StM	Bissing	100	6 Mar 1682	24/513
Wade, John:				
Knt	Bloomsbury	30	14 Sep 1688	25/437;34/37
Wadle, Thomas:				
Assignor of lands in Dorchester Co. in 1680.				24/250
Wahop, Thomas of St. Mary's Co:				
Cha	Wahop Dale	300	21 Sep 1685	25/267;33/255
Waite, William:				
Som	Tanners' Hall	150	30 May 1683	25/67
Wakefield, Thos, planter:				
Cha	Ratts Dale	80	15 Mar 1683	24/505;33/23

County	*Name of Tract*	*Acreage*	*Date*	*Reference(s)*
Wakelyn, Richard:				
Cha	Green Chase	200	18 Apr 1680	24/258;29/82
Wale, Edward:				
Som	Genesar	2,200	10 Jan 1680	24/101
Som	Mount Pleasant	450	3 Dec 1679	24/126
Walker, Daniel:				
Tal	Daniel's Addition	100	2 Jly 1687	25/341;33/632
Tal	Walker's Tooth	147	10 Nov 1695	40/209
Tal	Woodland Neck	100	16 Jan 1682	24/390;31/335
Walker, John:				
Dor	Walker's Addition	25	30 Sep 1684	25/204
Dor	Walker's Garden	36	30 Sep 1684	25/204;32/448
Walker, John, planter:				
Tal	Walker's Square	300	19 Mar 1686	25/246;30/315
Walker, Richard:				
StM	Berry	65	4 Nov 1682	24/481;31/56
Walker, Capt. Thomas:				
Assignor of lands in Somerset Co. in August 1680.				24/287
Walker, Thomas, son of Capt. Thomas Walker deceased who devised his property by his will:				
Som	Addition	100	24 Feb 1682	24/336;28/503
Walker, Thomas who married Sarah, daughter of Henry Osbourne of Calvert Co., deceased:				
Dor	Alexander's Place	650	5 Oct 1680	28/59
Walker, Thomas & Susan, children of Capt. Thomas Walker deceased:				
Som	Coscoway	1,100	29 Apr 1681	24/334;28/508
Som	Father's Care	200	30 Jly 1683	25/73;32/288
Som	Middle Neck	400	29 Apr 1681	24/334;28/507
Som	Whitfield	700	23 Feb 1682	24/334;28/504
Som	Woodfield	350	29 Apr 1681	24/334;28/506
Walker, William:				
Dor	Walker's Chance	200	5 Sep 1684	25/152
Wall, Thomas:				
Dor	Broken Wharf	50	19 May 1682	24/436;29/372;30/111
Dor	Thames Street	100	10 Mar 1682	24/399;31/364
Dor	Wallborough	50	26 Jun 1683	25/41,120;32/162
Wallace, James:				
Som	Wallace's Adventure	200	5 Aug 1695	37/66
Wallace, Mathew:				
Som	Kirkminster	200	29 May 1689	27/65
Wallace, Richard:				
Som	Father & Son's Desire	85	1 Jun 1700	34/221
Wallace, William:				
Som	Golden Quarter	100	1 Jun 1695	37/225
Som	Great Neck	100	17 Apr 1695	37/48

County	Name of Tract	Acreage	Date	Reference(s)
Waller, William, son of John Waller deceased:				
Som	Friend's Advice	45	1 Jun 1700	34/284
Som	Waller's Adventure	300	10 Aug 1696	38/93
Wally, John:				
Bal	Jerusalem	318	25 May 1687	25/310;33/577
Walstone, Thomas:				
Som	Promised Land	100	2 Jun 1688	25/424;32/712
Walter, Richard:				
Som	Friends' Kindness	46	1 Jun 1696	37/42
Walter, Thomas:				
Som	Chance	120	10 Mar 1696	37/84
Som	Marlborough	150	26 Dec 1681	24/449;29/452
Som	Rainsbury	200	10 Nov 1679	24/246
Walton, John, planter:				
Som	Walton's Addition	200	22 Nov 1686	25/283
Walton, Samuel of Anne Arundel Co:				
PG	Jencoe	70	20 Jly 1696	37/484
Walton, William:				
Som	Key	100	26 Mar 1680	24/257
Som	Neighbours	1,400	26 Nov 1679	24/40
W(h)aples, Peter:				
Som	Colchester	169	26 Mar 1688	25/359,402;32/648
Som	Colgester	150	10 Nov 1695	37/284
Som	Come by Chance	100	14 Feb 1682	24/392
Som	Venture	300	12 Jun 1683	25/71;30/184
Warburton, Cassandra:				
Transported by Christopher Rousby of Calvert Co.				24/22
Ward, Cornelius:				
Som	Chestnut Ridge	100	29 Sep 1683	29/445
Som	White Oak Swamp	150	28 May 1681	24/328;29/31; 33/203
Ward, Cornelius Sr.:				
Som	Long Acre	525	4 Jly 1702	35/386
Ward, Capt. Henry:				
Cec	Cobham	1,000	7 Jan 1683	24/506,25/5
Cec	Levels	500	5 May 1683	24/554
Cec	Long Acre	900	19 Oct 1682	24/506
Ward, John:				
Cec	Ward's Knowledge	140	3 Nov 1694	27/139
Ward, Murphy:				
Cal	Little Groves	91	10 Jan 1696	37/154
PG	Londonderry	149	1 Oct 1696	39/52
Cal	Stoke	100	17 Sep 1688	25/428;34/31
Cal	Ward's Pasture	200	5 Mar 1682	24/395;31/33
Cal	Ward's Pasture	60	10 Jan 1696	37/175

County	*Name of Tract*	*Acreage*	*Date*	*Reference(s)*
Ward, Thomas:				
Assignor of lands in Cecil Co. in 1680.				24/66
Ward, William:				
Cec	Neighbour's Grudge	175	14 Dec 1681	24/388;31/270
identical with Powles Corner (*see below*).				
Cec	North Level	300	10 Oct 1681	24/347;32/496
Cec	Lowest Thicket	500	[1679]	24/131;32/499
Cec	Powles Corner	175	14 Dec 1681	24/449
Cha	Ward's Chance	60	10 Jun 1682	24/470;31/192
Wardner, George, gent:				
Cec	Hopeful Unity	150	12 May 1682	24/454;29/517
Cec	Wardner's Adventure	200	9 May 1682	24/454;31/278
Warfield, John:				
AA	Warfield's Range	1,080	26 Mar 1696	40/354
Warfield, Richard, gent:				
AA	Addition	50	11 Aug 1682	24/462;29/411
AA	Brandy	300	29 Sep 1681	24/352;29/496
AA	Warfield's Plain	300	30 Mar 1681	24/295;28/412
AA	Warfield's Range	1,080	26 Mar 1696	40/354
Waring, Basil:				
Cal	Waring's Chance	56	10 Aug 1682	24/415;31/38
Warkins, Francis:				
Bal	Shrewsbury	65	29 Feb 1688	25/349
Warman, Henry:				
Dor	Tidenton	85	10 Apr 1695	37/278
Warner, George:				
Cec	Warner's Addition	112	11 Aug 1694	27/174
Cec	Warner's Level	276	1 Jly 1687	25/332;32/526
Cec	Warner's Marsh	124	4 Jly 1687	25/332;32/510
Warner, John:				
Tal	Poor Man's Portion	80	30 Jly 1688	25/417;32/694
Warner, Samuel:				
Cal		125	[19 May 1680]	24/174
Cal	Joune House	125	6 Jly 1681	28/175
Warner, William:				
Dor	Warner's Chance	50	5 Nov 1695	40/446
Tal	Warner's Discovery	200	24 Jly 1689	27/193;34/79
Warren, Capt. Humphrey:				
Cha	Warren's Discovery	280	31 Jly 1683	25/240;30/273
Cha	Tanyard	79	28 Nov 1688	25/434;34/6
Warren, Notley of Charles Co:				
StM	Rippon	350	15 Aug 1683	25/6
Warrilow, William:				
Tal	Warrilow's Exchange	326	10 Nov 1695	40/119

County	*Name of Tract*	*Acreage*	*Date*	*Reference(s)*
Wassle, Samuel, millwright:				
Tal	Milland	130	19 Feb 1687	25/338
Waterman, Nicholas:				
AA	Lockwood's Gift	100	10 Aug 1685	33/100
Waters, Alexander:				
Knt	Dundee	100	26 Jly 1680	25/14
Tal	Maiden's Choice	65	10 Apr 1698	38/63
Knt	Piney Neck	50	1 Aug 1682	25/16
Waters, Charles & John:				
Som	Partners' Desire	325	10 Nov 1697	39/16
Waters, John of Charles Co:				
StM	Bristol	100	27 Sep 1680	28/125
Waters, John:				
StM	James's Gift	100	7 Mar 1683	24/488;29/388
Waterton, Capt. John:				
Bal	Waterton's Angle	31	21 Jun 1681	28/179
Bal	Watertown	50	4 Nov 1679	24/152;28/15
Watkins, Francis, gent:				
Bal	Barnsbury	65	12 Jun 1688	33/670
Bal	Better Hopes	74	6 Feb 1686	25/288;33/519
Bal	Sister's Hope	200	13 Sep 1695	40/501
Watkins, John, planter:				
AA	Watkins' Inheritance	300	1 Sep 1681	28/218
AA	Watkins' Purchase	554	1 Sep 1681	28/220
Watkins, Thomas & Lydia--See under Baldwin, John.				
Watkinson, Cornelius:				
Cal	Addition	78	24 Feb 1680	24/81
Watson, Edward, Deputy Surveyor for Calvert Co.				
Watson, John of St. Mary's Co:				
Cha	Newbottle	300	27 Sep 1685	25/267;30/309
Watson, Peter of Somerset Co: Transported himself, Jane his wife and his children Peter, John & Mary before August 1681.				
Som	Peterson	250	18 May 1680	24/248;28/233
Watson, William of Dorchester Co., planter:				
Dor	[unnamed]	317	20 Feb 1687	25/304
Dor	Chance	64	14 Apr 1696	37/15
Dor	Contention	50	24 May 1681	24/294;28/493
Dor	Marsh Creek	317	1 Oct 1687	33/432
Dor	Plains	300	14 Jun 1682	24/539;30/103
Tal	Watson's	150	[1679]	24/131;28/128
Dor	Watson's Lot	100	27 Sep 1680	28/117

County	*Name of Tract*	*Acreage*	*Date*	*Reference(s)*
Watson, William of Anne Arundel Co:				
Bal	Watson's Chance	176	8 Jly 1681	28/146
Watson, William:				
StM	Freestone Point	324	5 Mar 1688	25/350;33/700
StM	Partnership	260	5 Oct 1695	40/63
Waughob, Archibald:				
Transported by Job Chandler, gent, bef. 1651.				29/149
Wayman, Edmund:				
AA	Town Mill	100	1 Oct 1698	39/43
Wayman, Leonard:				
AA	Owen Wood Thicket	200	26 Jun 1688	25/407;32/629
AA	Tangiers	10	28 Feb 1695	27/317
We(a)therly, James:				
Som	Addition	450	15 May 1688	25/419;32/649
Som	Bedford	500	29 Apr 1680	24/239;28/364
Som	Chance	300	10 Nov 1695	37/417
Som	Discovery	160	18 May 1688	25/418;32/649
Som	Crane Ridge	550	12 Jun 1683	25/62
Som	Friends' Discovery	300	18 May 1688	25/420
Som	Marish Hooke	100	15 Dec 1679	24/275;28/538
Som	Marrish Point	200	12 Jun 1683	25/62;31/535
Som	Once Again	100	14 Dec 1679	24/277;29/67
Som	Pasteridge	50	14 Dec 1679	24/276;29/63
Som	Peching's Ridge	250	10 Aug 1683	29/471
Som	Prevention	90	18 May 1688	25/419
Som	Quankeson's Neck	500	1 Dec 1688	27/189
Som	Sankey's Island	100	15 Dec 1679	24/275,37/530
Som	Slipe	50	14 Dec 1679	24/276;28/537
Som	Wetherley's Adventure	300	[24 Oct 1679]	24/238
Som	Weatherly's Chance	250	16 Dec 1679	24/259,307; 28/370,402
Som	Weatherly's Contrivance	300	28 May 1681	24/323;29/64
Som	Weatherly's Convenience	200	1 Jun 1700	34/280
Som	Weatherly's Reserve	300	16 Dec 1679	24/259;28/372
Som	Weatherly's Ridge	200	15 Dec 1679	24/275;29/58
Som	Wilson's Discovery	500	1 Dec 1688	27/199
Som	Wilson's Mistake	200	10 Nov 1695	37/416
Webb, Edmond:				
Tal	Bolton	100	4 Dec 1682	24/492;32/67
Tal	Bolton's Addition	50	18 Feb 1685	25/173;33/155
Webb, John of Somerset Co:				
Transported himself, Calibray his wife & 2 others.				30/149
Som	Coleraine	200	2 Feb 1683	24/530
Webb, John, innholder:				
Som	Houndsditch	500	20 Nov 1685	25/234;33/336
Webb, Richard, planter:				
Som	Motelack	200	17 Dec 1683	25/132;30/177

County	Name of Tract	Acreage	Date	Reference(s)
Webster, Edward:				
Transported by Mark Cordea before Sep 1680.				28/51
Webster, John:				
Bal	Webster's Enlargement	106	10 Oct 1698	35/411,474
Wedge, John:				
Knt	Mount Pleasant:	300	5 Sep 1679	24/106
Knt	Wedge's Recovery	100	27 Sep 1680	28/120
Wedy, Mary:				
Transported by John Abington of Calvert Co. before August 1680.				28/34
Weeden, William & Ann, orphan children of James Weeden of Somerset Co., gent deceased:				
Som	Back Land	800	15 Jly 1684	25/137;32/299
Som	Gift	200	15 Jly 1695	25/58;40/38
Weekes [Wicks], John:				
Cec	Probus	150	19 Oct 1681	24/348;29/367
Weeks, William:				
Transported by William Stone Esq. after 1650.				29/149
Welborne, Thomas of Accomack Co., Virginia:				
Som	Black Ridge	300	13 Sep 1684	25/176;32/349
Welding, Henry:				
Bal	Henry's Park	184	12 Nov 1686	25/287
Wellard, Daniel:				
Dor	Yorke	200	[10 Jun 1677]	24/139;29/106
Wells, Daniel of Anne Arundel Co:				
Bal	Bachelor's Delight	298	1 Jun 1700	30/343;38/154
Wells, Joseph:				
Bal	Wells' Angles	178	1 Oct 1698	35/358
Cal	Greenwood	488	8 Jan 1684	25/21
Wells, Swithin:				
Assignor of lands in Cecil Co. in Oct 1680.				25/10
Wells, Zerobabell:				
Tal	Wells' Outlet	50	28 Mar 1682	24/403;31/339
Welsh, Daniel:				
Bal	Welsh's Adventure	102	29 Jun 1688	25/439
Welsh, John of Anne Arundel Co:				
Bal	Three Sisters	1,000	13 Aug 1680	28/25
Wese, Anthony, orphan son & heir of Christopher Wese deceased:				
Tal	Gore	45	10 Aug 1686	25/297;33/418
Wese, Christopher, orphan son of Christopher Wese deceased:				
Tal	Naseby	100	6 May 1687	25/340;33/662
West, Thomas:				
Cal	Turkey Thicket	22	27 Oct 1685	25/185
Som	West's Recovery	500	30 Jly 1696	37/481

County	*Name of Tract*	*Acreage*	*Date*	*Reference(s)*
Westbury, William:				
Bal	Chestnut Neck	150	8 Jly 1681	28/142
Westlock, Magdaline:				
Som	Venture	200	19 Dec 1679	24/153
Wetherby, Thomas:				
Tal	Sleeford	200	4 Jun 1685	25/181
Wetherill, Samuel:				
Cec	Wetherill's Hope	100	6 May 1687	25/333;32/550
Whaples—See Waples.				
Whealing, Philip of St. Mary's Co:				
Cha		500	15 Nov 1683	25/35
Wheatley, Andrew:				
StM	Nintoquint	116	13 Mar 1684	25/171;33/87
StM	Wheatley's Hills	28	13 Mar 1684	25/190;32/394
Tal	Wheatly's Field	200	3 Aug 1682	24/476;31/337
Wheatley, John:				
Dor	Bachelor's Comfort	190	27 Apr 1682	24/408;31/59
Dor	Wheatley's Chance	22	27 Oct 1681	24/382;31/134
Dor	Wheately's Meadows	110	27 Apr 1682	24/409;29/336
StM	Maiden's Lot	100	10 Aug 1685	32/371
granted to his wife Winifred Horne in 1681.				
StM	Wheatley's Chance	272	8 Dec 1680	24/196;28/353
StM	Wheatley's Content	297	24 Nov 1681	24/359;31/61
Wheatley, Sampson:				
Som	Greenfield	125	8 May 1695	37/121
Wheeler, Ann, widow of Richard Nash:				
Cec	Wheeler's Purchase	100	1 Oct 1680	25/10
Cec	Wheeler's Warren	100	18 Nov 1680	24/547
Wheeler, Edward:				
Som	Marlborough	150	5 Oct 1695	40/39
Wheeler, Henry:				
Dor	Henry's Neck	50	4 Jly 1684	25/151
Wheeler, Ignatius of Charles Co:				
Cha	Aix	422	[12 Sep 1687]	25/372
Cha	Indian Field	299	20 Mar 1688	25/375;32/579
Cha	New Design	281	1 Mar 1698	38/71
Cha	Piscatoway Forest	693	27 Mar 1687	25/382
PG	Red Bud	113	1 Mar 1699	38/60
Cha	Wheeler's Folly	116	20 Mar 1689	25/432;34/7
Wheeler, Maj. John:				
Cha	Apple Hill	552	21 Mar 1688	25/371
Cha	Major's Choice	187	28 Jun 1687	25/321;33/696
Cha	Middleton's Lot	96	9 May 1688	25/374;32/582
Wheeler, John:				
AA	Wheeler's Lot	200	23 Jan 1682	24/391;31/98

County	*Name of Tract*	*Acreage*	*Date*	*Reference(s)*
Wheeler, John son of James Wheeler of Charles Co:				
Cha	Wheeler's Adventure	76	16 Oct 1684	25/241;33/300
Wheeler, Robert, orphan son of Robert Wheeler:				
Tal	Adventure	70	9 Aug 1686	25/297;33/548
Wheeler, Samuel:				
Cec	Browning's Neglect	482	6 Oct 1685	25/254;33/348
Wheeler, Thomas:				
Cha	Wheeler's Delight	112	18 Mar 1688	25/320;33/687
Whicherly, James:				
Som	Whicherly's Adventure	300	1 Sep 1681	28/268
Whicherly, Thomas:				
Cha	Tower Hill	166	26 Sep 1688	25/401;32/616
White, Ambrose:				
Som	Smith's Choice	200	3 Dec 1680	24/12
White, John, gent:				
Som	Amadorpin	300	1, Dec 1679	24/44
Som	Buckingham	1,500	10 Mar 1682	28/518
Som	Father & Son's Desire	85	1 Jun 1700	34/221
Som	Fishing Harbour	400	1 Dec 1679	24/5
Som	Hope	100	2 May 1682	24/485;29/442
Som	Newport Pagnell	700	10 Mar 1682	28/517
Som	Oxford	100	2 May 1682	24/486;29/433
Som	Richins' Addition	100	3 May 1682	24/486
Som	Unity	650	9 Oct 1683	25/24;29/521
PG	Nursland	88	10 Nov 1697	38/20
White, Robert:				
Tal	Rock Neck Addition	50	15 Aug 1681	24/375;31/292
White, Thomas of Northumberland Co., Virginia, millwright:				
Dor	Plains	300	10 Sep 1684	32/43
Whitehead, Francis:				
Bal	Billingsgate	79	10 May 1695	40/541
Whittacre, John:				
AA	Whittacre's Chance	150	26 Mar 1696	40/357
AA	Whittacre's Purchase	79	10 Apr 1696	40/342
Whittall, John:				
Tal	Whittall	100	11 Jun 1679	24/214;29/246
Whittecoe, Samuel:				
Transported by Thomas Clipsham before Sep 1680.				28/44
Whittiars, John:				
AA	Whittiars' Purchase	79	10 Apr 1696	34/125
Whittington, Andrew, innholder:				
Som	[unnamed]	100	13Nov1673 (s*)	24/514
Som	Friend's Choice	300	8 Jan 1687	25/317
Som	Monmouth	50	15 Nov 1685	25/264;33/359

County	Name of Tract	Acreage	Date	Reference(s)
Som	Woodland	150	28 May 1681	24/328;29/192;33/201
Som	Woover	100	8 Oct 1681	24/515
Som	Webley	250	24 Dec 1679	24/152
Whittington, John of Chester River, planter:				
Tal	Chestnut Neck	150	16 Jan 1682	24/390;31/328
Tal	Fishborne	130	7 Feb 1680	24/271
Tal	Fishbourne's Neglect	130	[27 Sep 1680]	24/132;28/124
Tal	Forest of Sherwood	200	31 May 1696	37/439
Tal	Whittington's Addition	35	22 May 1683	24/526;32/47
Tal	Whittington's Lot	200	15 Jan 1685	24/386,25/191;31/72
Whittington, Capt. William of Virginia:				
Cha	Nangemy Indian Town	600	18 Nov 1685	25/197
Whittington, William of Accomack Co., Virginia, son & heir of Capt. William Whittington:				
[unnamed]		1,200		29/149
Som	Meadfield	400	19 Apr 1686	25/232
Whittington, Capt. William of Somerset Co:				
Som	Fair Meadow	438	31 Aug 1688	25/385;32/639
Som	Springfield	486	31 Aug 1688	25/385;34/40
Som	Summerfield	400	9 Jun 1695	37/229
Whitton, Richard:				
Cec	Whitton Forest	150	3 Jly 1683	31/254
Whitty, Richard of Somerset Co., planter:				
Assignor of lands in Dorchester Co. in Apr 1682.				24/484
Som	Whittey's Lot	50	28 Nov 1685	25/283
Whooton, John:				
Som	Discovery	225	10 Nov 1695	40/292
Wicks—See Weekes.				
Wight, John:				
Cal	Hobson's Choice	220	27 Dec 1688	25/426;34/32
Wilcocks, Henry:				
Tal	Mount Hope's Addition	100	18 Jun 1681	24/337;31/65
Wilkinson, John, planter:				
Tal	Wilkinson's Addition	100	16 Feb 1683	24/489;31/309;33/392
Wilkinson, Thomas:				
His time of service completed by 1679.				24/119
Wilki(n)son, William:				
Bal	Wilkison's Folly	89	2 Jly 1688	25/438;34/29110
Bal	Wilkinson's Spring	50	3 Mar 1682	24/499;30/35
Williams, Benjamin of Anne Arundel Co:				
PG	Bare Neck	151	1 Nov 1701	34/360
AA	Williams' Addition	26	27 Mar 1688	25/346;33/734
AA	Williams' Angle	15	16 Feb 1686	25/249;33/597
Bal	Williams' Contrivance	327	-- Feb 1700	30/355;38/154

County	Name of Tract	Acreage	Date	Reference(s)
Williams, Charles:				
Som	Roberts' Lot	100	16 Apr 1681	24/262;28/391
Williams alias Williamson, David of Somerset Co. who died without heirs by 1680—See under Covington, John.				
Williams, Edward, planter:				
Som	Betty's Rest	100	4 May 1686	25/284;33/373
Williams, Ennion:				
Tal	Ennion's Lot	151	10 Nov 1695	37/376
Tal	Ennion's Range	220	10 Nov 1695	39/9
Williams, Francis:				
Som	Key	100	26 Mar 1680	24/257
Williams, Henry:				
Knt	Amsterdam	50	13 Jun 1681	24/304;31/181
Williams, John:				
Cha	Williams' Folly	265	22 Mar 1689	25/433;34/8
Williams, Joseph:				
Cal	Catch	50	9 May 1681	24/359;31/28
Cal	Wooten	100	3 Apr 1680	24/77
Williams, Michael:				
Som	Williams' Adventure	100	10 Nov 1696	38/27
Williams, Nathaniel:				
Transported before August 1680 by William Jones of Bristol, England.				28/31
Williams, Thomas:				
StM	Good Fortune	99	10 Nov 1695	40/139
Willis, Thomas:				
Som	Amity	150	10 Aug 1683	29/430
Som	Bashan	200	30 Nov 1681	24/382
Willish, John:				
Cec	Wayhill Down	100	4 Jun 1686	25/229
Wil(l)mer, Simon, Deputy Surveyor for Cecil Co:				
	[unnamed]	500	20 May 1683	24/539
Knt	Buckingham	500	31 Jly 1680	24/546;32/159
Knt	Chigwell	200	10 Nov 1695	40/186
Knt	Kemp's Beginning	320	22 Sep 1687	25/351
Knt	Piney Grove	260	25 Aug 1687	25/350
Knt	Rich Level & Addn.	400	23 Mar 1699	34/204
Knt	Wilmer's Farm	500	13 Aug 1680	28/21
Tal	Wilmer's Range	1,000	21 Nov 1681	24/385;31/113
Will(y)mott, Henry:				
Dor	Willmott's Adventure	50	28 Apr 1686	25/293;33/471
Will(y)mot, Mr. John:				
Cal	Hay Marsh	18	21 Feb 1686	25/213;32/358
Cal	Piney Point	50	15 May 1681	24/300;29/184
Cal	Spott	4	17 May 1687	25/329;32/517

County	Name of Tract	Acreage	Date	Reference(s)
Willmott, John:				
Bal	Willmott's Fancy	140	2 Jly 1688	25/438
Willens, Richard:				
Dor	Rodley	260	5 Oct 1684	25/301;33/460
Willoughby, Elizabeth:				
Transported by John Erickson of Kent Co.			28/434	
Willoughby, William:				
Dor	Raxall	50	17 Jun 1680	28/22
Dor	William & Hannah's Choice	100	14 Feb 1682	24/420;30/93; 31/399
Dor	Willoby's Neglect	50	3 Aug 1686	25/292;33/488
Wilne, Robert:				
Assignor of lands in Dorchester Co. in 1679.				24/179
Wilson, Ephraim:				
Som	Brothers' Agreement	500	27 Nov 1685	25/237;33/271
Wilson, George, planter:				
Som	Hog Ridge	100	5 Jly 1680	24/248;28/394
Wilson, James, planter:				
Tal	Wilson's Beginning	100	4 Jun 1685	25/185;32/304
Tal	Wilson's Beginning	250	10 Nov 1695	37/310
Wilson, John:				
Transported by John Abington of Calvert Co. bef. Aug 1680.				28/34
Wilson, John of Anne Arundel Co., gent:				
Bal	Wilson's Range	100	18 Nov 1686	25/290;33/383
Wilson, Nicholas:				
Transported by John Abington of Calvert Co. before August 1680.				28/34
Wilson, Richard:				
Som	Far Kill Hummock	30	12 Oct 1681	24/529;32/131
Wilson, Thomas:				
Som	Derby	350	28 May 1681	24/314;28/531
Som	Radburn's	140	10 Nov 1695	40/294
Som	Willson's Lot	200	10 Nov 1695	34/74;40/192
Wilson, William:				
Tal	Wilson's Adventure	54	1 May 1698	38/80
Winchester, Isaac of Kent Co:				
Knt	Isaac's Addition	80	2 Nov 1680	24/256;29/108
Knt	Isaac's Chance	100	11 Jun 1681	24/343;31/489
Tal	Sarah's Portion	300	1 Sep 1681	24/377;29/394
Tal	Winchester's Folly	230	26 Apr 1689	27/176;34/108
Windall, Thomas:				
AA	Garratt's Town	59	6 Jly 1684	25/169
Winder, Lieut. John:				
Som	Debtford	110	30 Aug 1680	24/277;29/35
Som	Pemberton's Goodwill	700	27 May 1680	24/443;29/425

County	Name of Tract	Acreage	Date	Reference(s)
Winder, John—See under Lane, Walter.				
Windle, Thomas:				
Transported by William Thomas of Charles Co. before September 1680.				28/121
Window, Thomas:				
Transported himself, William Window & Elizabeth Window before August 1681:				28/305
Windsor, John:				
Som	Cox's Performance	1,000	10 Nov 1696	38/17
Wine [Wyne], Francis:				
Cha	Burton	90	23 Sep 1680	28/116
Cha	Skidmore's Adventure	37	28 Sep 1680	28/127
Cha	Susquehannah	37	27 Sep 1680	28/123
Wyne, John, son of Elizabeth Wyne:				
Cha	Addition	112	20 Jly 1682	24/474
land formerly laid out for Francis Wyne.				
Wingod, Thomas, planter:				
Dor	Colchester	340	28 Oct 1682	24/537;32/416
Dor	Helens Bumstead	700	30 Dec 1679	24/195;28/312
Dor	Waxford	150	[1679]	24/131;28/118
Winslow, Elizabeth:				
Transported by Samuel Gibson by 1675.				24/4
Winslow [Winsloe], William:				
Som	Paxen Hills	100	22 Sep 1682	25/88;33/218
Som	Windsor Castle	150	28 Sep 1681	24/378;29/436
Winters, William:				
Tal	Wintersell	200	20 Oct 1684	25/260
Wintersell, William:				
Tal	Devices	440	10 Oct 1683	25/29,113;32/110
Wiseman, John:				
StM	Wiseman's Chance	100	6 Apr 1682	24/405;31/25
Withgott, Joseph:				
Tal	Joseph's Lot	100	10 Aug 1683	31/120
Wood, John:				
Som	Wood's Land	150	10 Nov 1695	34/68;40/191
Wood, Thomas:				
AA	Woodcock's Neck	30	7 Aug 1681	24/351;31/195
Woodard, John & Thomas:				
Transported by John Abington of Calvert Co. before August 1680.				28/34
Woodcroft, Richard:				
Som	Fair Low Worth	217	25 Oct 1684	25/360
Som	Smithfield	153	2 Oct 1687	25/389;34/38
Som	Woodscroft	100	10 Nov 1695	37/506

County	Name of Tract	Acreage	Date	Reference(s)
Woodford, Roger:				
Assignor of lands in Somerset Co. in Sep 1688.				27/114
Woodgate, William:				
Dor	Beckett's	50	31 May 1696	37/464
Woodnet, Lawrence:				
Dor	Paradise	50	9 May 1680	24/185;28/356
Woodward, John:				
Dor	Aye's Addition	20	16 Aug 1684	25/205;32/411
Dor	Betty's Delight	500	29 Jun 1685	25/203
Som	Woodhall	200	30 Aug 1679	24/262;29/70
Dor	Woodward's Content	20	3 Jly 1684	25/152;33/239
Woolford, Roger, gent:				
Som	Chance	300	24 Oct 1681	24/348;28/362
Som	Happy Addition	200	17 Mar 1687	25/326;40/41
Som	Harmsworth	300	20 Apr 1682	24/515;33/86
Som	Woolford's Venture	50	10 Nov 1696	38/42
Woolman, Richard, planter:				
StM		50	10 Jan 1696	37/526
Tal	Woolman's Hermitage	164	2 May 1696	40/566
Woolson, Rachel:				
Completed her time of service in 1680.				24/20
Woolson, Thomas:				
Assignor of lands in Somerset Co. in 1680.				24/20
Wootters, John:				
Tal	Buckbye	400	24 Jun 1679	24/216
Tal	Coventry	250	29 Jly 1681	24/371
Tal	Dunsmore Heath	200	4 Jun 1682	24/469
Tal	Sybland	200	29 Jly 1681	24/371
Workman, Anthony:				
Completed his time of service before Sep 1680.				28/128
Knt	Timber Ridge	250	1 --- 1680	24/281;28/432
Workman, Anthony:				
Knt	Workman's Hazard	150	27 Jly 1680	24/305;28/433
including land for transporting himself & his wife Elizabeth.				
Worth, John:				
Knt	Worth's Folly	1,036	19 Aug 1687	25/334
Wouldhave, William, planter:				
Som	Cumberland	100	24 Sep 1687	25/353;33/672
Som	Medley	100	28 Sep 1687	25/353;33/711
Som	Newberry	230	16 Dec 1686	25/336;34/39
Som	Silver Tree	100	30 Aug 1681	24/247;28/274
land granted for transporting himself & his wife Ann.				
Wraughton, William:				
Dor	Prevention	50	12 Dec 1681	24/388;31/385

County	*Name of Tract*	*Acreage*	*Date*	*Reference(s)*
Wrench, William:				
Tal	Brickland's Addition	100	21 Jun 1685	25/228;32/345
Tal	Wrench's Discovery	386	10 Nov 1695	34/91;40/223
Wright, Edward, planter:				
Som	Aldgate	150	12 Nov 1688	27/45
Som	Barren Quarter	250	1 Jun 1702	35/419
Som	Goshen	300	[6 Oct 1680]	24/190;28/244
Som	Mile End	300	22 May 1688	25/422;32/652
Som	Whitechapel	500	20 Nov 1685	25/234;33/283
Wright, Nathaniel:				
Tal	Adventure	100	6 Aug 1682	24/490
Tal	Guilford	300	17 Jun 1689	27/177
Tal	Wright's Choice	300	7 Feb 1683	24/544
Knt	Newbrough	1,000	10 Nov 1695	39/40
Wright, Samuel:				
Tal	Wright's Chance	124	10 Nov 1695	34/107;40/128
Wright, Solomon:				
Tal	Adventure	100	6 Aug 1682	24/490
Tal	Guilford	300	9 Dec 1684	25/168;33/149
Tal	Worplesdon	300	3 Feb 1686	25/296;33/430
Knt	Newbrough	1,000	10 Nov 1695	39/40
Wright, William, planter:				
Som	Elson	50	14 Feb 1682	29/021
Som	Penny Wise	45	5 Jun 1688	25/393;32/716
Som	Venture	50	25 Jly 1679	24/275;28/527
Som	Wolves' Quarter	100	5 Jun 1688	25/393;32/635
Som	Wright's Choice	100	25 Jly 1679	24/274;29/68
Som	Wright's Venture	105	5 Jun 1688	25/394;32/717
Wriothesley, Henry:				
Bal	Ann's Delight	200	24 Apr 1701	34/306
Bal	South Hampton	500	1 May 1701	34/310
Wyatt, James:				
Knt	Wyatt's Addition	44	5 Jly 1701	34/311
Knt	Wyatt's Chance	200	14 Apr 1686	25/201;32/302
Wyatt; Thomas—See under Howden, Judith.				
Wylmer—See Willmer.				
Wyne—See Wine.				
Wyth, James:				
Som	Bachelor's Contrivance	150	15 Jun 1683	25/62;30/5
Som	Bachelor's Delight	250	15 Jun 1683	25/60;32/132
Som	Bachelor's Invention	250	15 Jun 1683	25/61
Ya(u)lding, William:				
Som	Hounsloe	100	10 Oct 1695	37/128
Som	Whitechapel Green	50	16 Feb 1683	25/32

County	Name of Tract	Acreage	Date	Reference(s)
Yate(s), George, Deputy Surveyor for Anne Arundel Co:				
Bal	Addition	48	8 Jly 1684	25/94
Bal	Cheveny	360	17 Jly 1683	25/4;31/431
AA	Come by Chance	214	10 Aug 1684	31/432
AA	Health	236	9 Jly 1684	25/98
Bal	Levels Addition	118	15 Dec 1686	25/289;33/377
Cal	Lower Gronery	440	12 Jly 1682	24/414
Cal	Padworth Farm	600	1 Jly 1680	24/175;28/143
AA	Range	211	2 Jly 1684	25/101
Bal	Yates' Forbearance	770	20 Jun 1683	25/3,5;31/429
Bal	Yates' Fork	140	17 Jly 1683	25/3
Yeildhall, William:				
AA	Narrow Neck	41	6 Sep 1682	24/463;31/420
Yeo, John, gent:				
Bal	Hazard	100	24 Jun 1681	24/500
Bal	Mount Yeo	400	18 Jun 1683	25/3
Bal	New Park	150	25 Sep 1683	25/84;33/124
Bal	Spring Garden	200	18 Apr 1685	25/183;32/305
Yerbury, Thomas, cooper:				
Cec	Mulberry Dock	204	12 Dec 1685	25/291
Cec	Strawberry Bank	89	13 Jun 1684	25/343
See also under Nicholls, Thomas.				
Yewle, Thomas:				
Tal	Lincoln	200	7 Jan 1680	24/227;29/119
York, William, planter:				
Bal	Edward's Lot	300	9 Jly 1686	25/290;33/538
Young, Elizabeth:				
Cha	Dover	300	20 Dec 1679	24/130
Young, George:				
Transported by Samuel Smith of Virginia in 1680.				24/33
Cal	Friendship	300	9 Jan 1681	24/273;28/496
Cal	Young's Attempt	262	25 Jly 1694	27/4
Cal	Young's Desire	100	10 Jun 1680	24/193;28/213
Cal	Young's Fortune	100	6 Sep 1681	28/217
Young, Lawrence, planter:				
Som	Ireland's Eye	300	1 Oct 1688	27/21
Som	New Ireland	500	25 Nov 1685	25/236;33/263
Young, Samuel:				
AA	Brushy Neck	113	20 Dec 1699	38/161
Young, Samuel of Anne Arundel Co., Esq:				
AA	Francis' Freedom	1,000	22 May 1696	40/413
formerly lands of Thomas Francis deceased whose widow and administratrix Mary married Samuel Young.				
AA	Good Mother's Care	213	8 Oct 1699	30/349
Bal	Good Neighbourhood	699	10 Dec 1699	30/340;38/156

County	Name of Tract	Acreage	Date	Reference(s)
Young, Theodorus:				
AA	Truswell	30	14 May 1683	25/7;31/438
See also under Rawlins, Aron.				
Young, William, planter:				
Tal	Addition	200	6 Jan 1680	24/227
Cha	Blackash	146	4 Aug 1686	25/238;33/362
Tal	Standford	200	4 Sep 1679	24/222;28/451
Tal	Young's Adventure	175	4 Nov 1682	24/491
Tal	Young's Chance	100	7 Dec 1682	24/494
Tal	Young's Fortune	240	11 Oct 1683	25/30

INDEX OF TRACTS

An asterisk beside an entry indicates that the name appears more than once on a page.

INDEX OF TRACTS

INDEX OF TRACTS

INDEX OF TRACTS

Printed in the USA
CPSIA information can be obtained
at www.ICGtesting.com
LVHW020724291023
762460LV00024B/258

9 780806 314778